Machine Learning Foundations and Applications

A Practical Guide to Supervised, Unsupervised, and Reinforcement Learning.

Jarrel E.

First Edition: 2025
Author: Jarrel E.
Publisher: Independently Published
Printed in the United States of America

Preface

The journey to understanding machine learning is as much about mastering theory as it is about translating that theory into practical application. This book, *Machine Learning Foundations and Applications: A Practical Guide to Supervised, Unsupervised, and Reinforcement Learning*, was written to bridge that gap—offering a clear, structured, and applied perspective on core concepts that power modern intelligent systems.

Machine learning continues to revolutionize industries ranging from healthcare and finance to retail, manufacturing, and autonomous systems. However, the path to building a solid foundation in this field often becomes complicated by overly abstract explanations or fragmented tutorials that fail to connect theoretical models to real-world problems. As a result, many learners—students, professionals, and self-taught engineers alike—struggle to form a complete mental model of how machine learning algorithms are developed, evaluated, and deployed in practice.

This book was developed in response to that need. It is designed to serve as a reliable guide for readers who seek not only to learn about supervised, unsupervised, and reinforcement learning but also to understand the principles behind algorithmic decision-making, generalization, regularization, optimization, and modern neural architectures. Whether you are pursuing academic study, building career-ready data science skills, or designing systems powered by artificial intelligence, this guide was written with your goals in mind.

The structure of the book follows a pedagogical arc that begins with foundational supervised learning algorithms—including linear regression, logistic regression, and support vector machines—then advances to deep learning principles and neural network training using gradient-based methods. We explore critical aspects of generalization, model selection, and regularization strategies to prepare readers for scalable applications. The chapters on unsupervised learning delve into clustering, dimensionality reduction, and latent variable models, followed by modern developments in self-supervised learning and foundational models. Finally, the section on reinforcement learning covers Markov Decision Processes, policy optimization techniques, and control algorithms, drawing clear connections to real-time decision systems.

Acknowledgements

This book is the product of persistent effort, deep reflection, and an ongoing pursuit of clarity in a complex field. It would not have come to life without the support, inspiration, and collaboration of several individuals and communities whose contributions were instrumental at various stages of its development.

First and foremost, I would like to express my deepest gratitude to the academic pioneers, research scientists, and engineers whose foundational work laid the groundwork for modern machine learning. The field has advanced through the collective effort of many minds—those who introduced the first principles of statistical learning, those who refined algorithmic efficiency, and those who continue to push the boundaries of what is computationally possible.

I extend my appreciation to the global open-source community. Projects such as Python, NumPy, Scikit-learn, TensorFlow, PyTorch, and Jupyter have made experimentation and application accessible to learners and developers across the world. The tools and libraries made freely available by these communities have empowered countless practitioners, including myself, to explore ideas, test models, and bring innovation into production.

To the educators, mentors, and authors who inspired me through lectures, research papers, and technical books—thank you. Your commitment to knowledge sharing encouraged me to build this book as a practical and structured learning experience for others who are starting out or deepening their understanding of machine learning.

I am also thankful for the critical readers, early reviewers, and technical peers who offered feedback on drafts, challenged assumptions, and helped shape this book into a more rigorous and reader-friendly guide. Your insights strengthened the clarity, accuracy, and accessibility of the material presented.

To my family and close friends, thank you for your patience and encouragement throughout the writing process. Your support made the long hours of research, writing, editing, and revision possible.

Finally, I would like to acknowledge the countless learners—students, developers, and professionals—who are navigating their own path through the field of artificial intelligence. It is for you that this book was written. Your curiosity and determination inspire continued growth in this domain and drive the evolution of responsible, applied machine learning.

Contents

Part I

Supervised learning

Let's start by talking about a few examples of supervised learning problems. Suppose we have a dataset giving the living areas and prices of 47 houses from Portland, Oregon:

Living area (feet^2)	Price (1000\$s)
2104	400
1600	330
2400	369
1416	232
3000	540
⋮	⋮

We can plot this data:

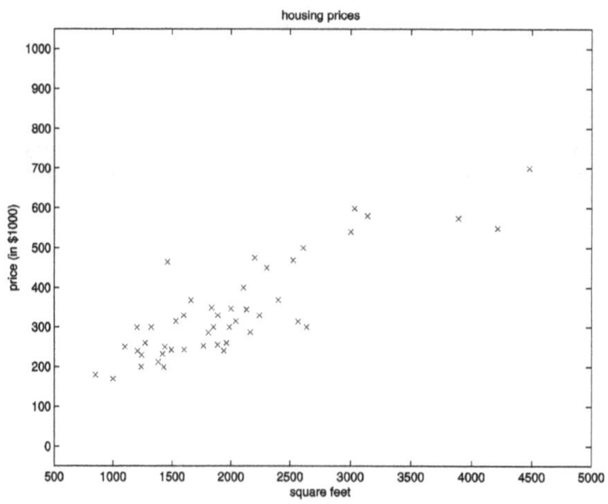

Given data like this, how can we learn to predict the prices of other houses in Portland, as a function of the size of their living areas?

To establish notation for future use, we'll use $x^{(i)}$ to denote the "input" variables (living area in this example), also called input **features**, and $y^{(i)}$ to denote the "output" or **target** variable that we are trying to predict (price). A pair $(x^{(i)}, y^{(i)})$ is called a **training example**, and the dataset that we'll be using to learn—a list of n training examples $\{(x^{(i)}, y^{(i)}); i = 1, \ldots, n\}$—is called a **training set**. Note that the superscript "(i)" in the notation is simply an index into the training set, and has nothing to do with exponentiation. We will also use $\mathcal{X}$ denote the space of input values, and $\mathcal{Y}$ the space of output values. In this example, $\mathcal{X} = \mathcal{Y} = \mathbb{R}$.

To describe the supervised learning problem slightly more formally, our goal is, given a training set, to learn a function $h : \mathcal{X} \mapsto \mathcal{Y}$ so that $h(x)$ is a "good" predictor for the corresponding value of y. For historical reasons, this function h is called a **hypothesis**. Seen pictorially, the process is therefore like this:

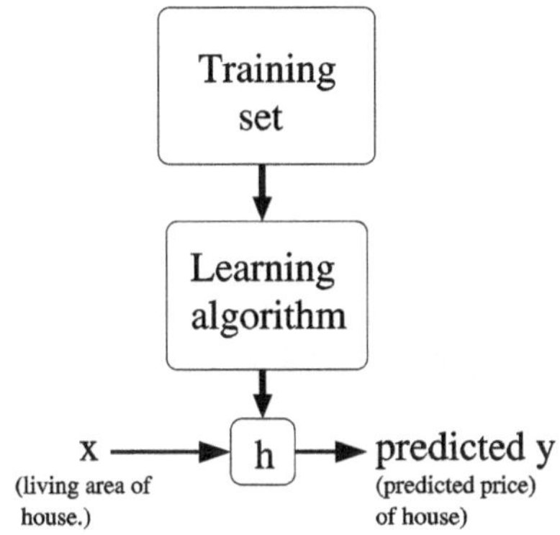

When the target variable that we're trying to predict is continuous, such as in our housing example, we call the learning problem a **regression** problem. When y can take on only a small number of discrete values (such as if, given the living area, we wanted to predict if a dwelling is a house or an apartment, say), we call it a **classification** problem.

Chapter 1

Linear regression

To make our housing example more interesting, let's consider a slightly richer dataset in which we also know the number of bedrooms in each house:

Living area (feet^2)	#bedrooms	Price (1000$s)
2104	3	400
1600	3	330
2400	3	369
1416	2	232
3000	4	540
⋮	⋮	⋮

Here, the x's are two-dimensional vectors in $\mathbb{R}^2$. For instance, $x_1^{(i)}$ is the living area of the i-th house in the training set, and $x_2^{(i)}$ is its number of bedrooms. (In general, when designing a learning problem, it will be up to you to decide what features to choose, so if you are out in Portland gathering housing data, you might also decide to include other features such as whether each house has a fireplace, the number of bathrooms, and so on. We'll say more about feature selection later, but for now let's take the features as given.)

To perform supervised learning, we must decide how we're going to represent functions/hypotheses h in a computer. As an initial choice, let's say we decide to approximate y as a linear function of x:

$$h_\theta(x) = \theta_0 + \theta_1 x_1 + \theta_2 x_2$$

Here, the θ_i's are the **parameters** (also called **weights**) parameterizing the space of linear functions mapping from $\mathcal{X}$ to $\mathcal{Y}$. When there is no risk of confusion, we will drop the θ subscript in $h_\theta(x)$, and write it more simply as $h(x)$. To simplify our notation, we also introduce the convention of letting $x_0 = 1$ (this is the **intercept term**), so that

$$h(x) = \sum_{i=0}^{d} \theta_i x_i = \theta^T x,$$

where on the right-hand side above we are viewing θ and x both as vectors, and here d is the number of input variables (not counting x_0).

Now, given a training set, how do we pick, or learn, the parameters θ? One reasonable method seems to be to make $h(x)$ close to y, at least for the training examples we have. To formalize this, we will define a function that measures, for each value of the θ's, how close the $h(x^{(i)})$'s are to the corresponding $y^{(i)}$'s. We define the **cost function**:

$$J(\theta) = \frac{1}{2} \sum_{i=1}^{n} (h_\theta(x^{(i)}) - y^{(i)})^2.$$

If you've seen linear regression before, you may recognize this as the familiar least-squares cost function that gives rise to the **ordinary least squares** regression model. Whether or not you have seen it previously, let's keep going, and we'll eventually show this to be a special case of a much broader family of algorithms.

1.1 LMS algorithm

We want to choose θ so as to minimize $J(\theta)$. To do so, let's use a search algorithm that starts with some "initial guess" for θ, and that repeatedly changes θ to make $J(\theta)$ smaller, until hopefully we converge to a value of θ that minimizes $J(\theta)$. Specifically, let's consider the **gradient descent** algorithm, which starts with some initial θ, and repeatedly performs the update:

$$\theta_j := \theta_j - \alpha \frac{\partial}{\partial \theta_j} J(\theta).$$

(This update is simultaneously performed for all values of $j = 0, \ldots, d$.) Here, α is called the **learning rate**. This is a very natural algorithm that repeatedly takes a step in the direction of steepest decrease of J.

In order to implement this algorithm, we have to work out what is the partial derivative term on the right hand side. Let's first work it out for the case of if we have only one training example (x, y), so that we can neglect the sum in the definition of J. We have:

$$\begin{aligned}
\frac{\partial}{\partial \theta_j} J(\theta) &= \frac{\partial}{\partial \theta_j} \frac{1}{2} \left(h_\theta(x) - y\right)^2 \\
&= 2 \cdot \frac{1}{2} \left(h_\theta(x) - y\right) \cdot \frac{\partial}{\partial \theta_j} \left(h_\theta(x) - y\right) \\
&= \left(h_\theta(x) - y\right) \cdot \frac{\partial}{\partial \theta_j} \left(\sum_{i=0}^{d} \theta_i x_i - y \right) \\
&= \left(h_\theta(x) - y\right) x_j
\end{aligned}$$

For a single training example, this gives the update rule:[1]

$$\theta_j := \theta_j + \alpha \left(y^{(i)} - h_\theta(x^{(i)})\right) x_j^{(i)}.$$

The rule is called the **LMS** update rule (LMS stands for "least mean squares"), and is also known as the **Widrow-Hoff** learning rule. This rule has several properties that seem natural and intuitive. For instance, the magnitude of the update is proportional to the **error** term $(y^{(i)} - h_\theta(x^{(i)}))$; thus, for instance, if we are encountering a training example on which our prediction nearly matches the actual value of $y^{(i)}$, then we find that there is little need to change the parameters; in contrast, a larger change to the parameters will be made if our prediction $h_\theta(x^{(i)})$ has a large error (i.e., if it is very far from $y^{(i)}$).

We'd derived the LMS rule for when there was only a single training example. There are two ways to modify this method for a training set of more than one example. The first is replace it with the following algorithm:

Repeat until convergence {

$$\theta_j := \theta_j + \alpha \sum_{i=1}^{n} \left(y^{(i)} - h_\theta(x^{(i)})\right) x_j^{(i)}, \text{(for every } j) \tag{1.1}$$

}

[1]We use the notation "$a := b$" to denote an operation (in a computer program) in which we *set* the value of a variable a to be equal to the value of b. In other words, this operation overwrites a with the value of b. In contrast, we will write "$a = b$" when we are asserting a statement of fact, that the value of a is equal to the value of b.

By grouping the updates of the coordinates into an update of the vector θ, we can rewrite update (1.1) in a slightly more succinct way:

$$\theta := \theta + \alpha \sum_{i=1}^{n} \left(y^{(i)} - h_\theta(x^{(i)})\right) x^{(i)}$$

The reader can easily verify that the quantity in the summation in the update rule above is just $\partial J(\theta)/\partial\theta_j$ (for the original definition of J). So, this is simply gradient descent on the original cost function J. This method looks at every example in the entire training set on every step, and is called **batch gradient descent**. Note that, while gradient descent can be susceptible to local minima in general, the optimization problem we have posed here for linear regression has only one global, and no other local, optima; thus gradient descent always converges (assuming the learning rate α is not too large) to the global minimum. Indeed, J is a convex quadratic function. Here is an example of gradient descent as it is run to minimize a quadratic function.

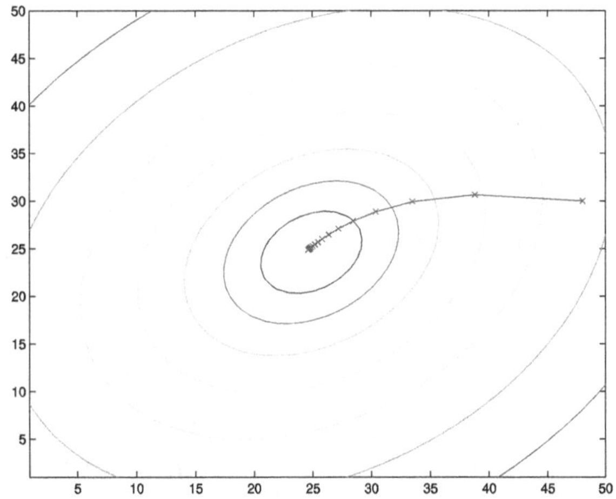

The ellipses shown above are the contours of a quadratic function. Also shown is the trajectory taken by gradient descent, which was initialized at (48,30). The x's in the figure (joined by straight lines) mark the successive values of θ that gradient descent went through.

When we run batch gradient descent to fit θ on our previous dataset, to learn to predict housing price as a function of living area, we obtain $\theta_0 = 71.27$, $\theta_1 = 0.1345$. If we plot $h_\theta(x)$ as a function of x (area), along with the training data, we obtain the following figure:

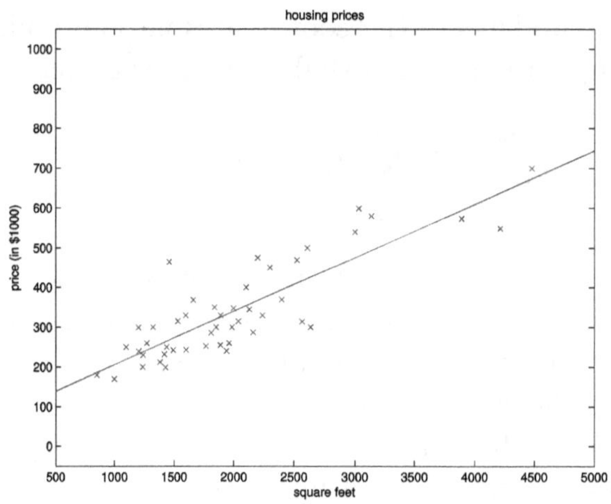

If the number of bedrooms were included as one of the input features as well, we get $\theta_0 = 89.60, \theta_1 = 0.1392$, $\theta_2 = -8.738$.

The above results were obtained with batch gradient descent. There is an alternative to batch gradient descent that also works very well. Consider the following algorithm:

Loop {

for $i = 1$ to n, {

$$\theta_j := \theta_j + \alpha \left(y^{(i)} - h_\theta(x^{(i)})\right) x_j^{(i)}, \quad \text{(for every } j\text{)} \tag{1.2}$$

}

}

By grouping the updates of the coordinates into an update of the vector θ, we can rewrite update (1.2) in a slightly more succinct way:

$$\theta := \theta + \alpha \left(y^{(i)} - h_\theta(x^{(i)})\right) x^{(i)}$$

In this algorithm, we repeatedly run through the training set, and each time we encounter a training example, we update the parameters according to the gradient of the error with respect to that single training example only. This algorithm is called **stochastic gradient descent** (also **incremental gradient descent**). Whereas batch gradient descent has to scan through the entire training set before taking a single step—a costly operation if n is large—stochastic gradient descent can start making progress right away, and continues to make progress with each example it looks at. Often, stochastic gradient descent gets θ "close" to the minimum much faster than batch gradient descent. (Note however that it may never "converge" to the minimum, and the parameters θ will keep oscillating around the minimum of $J(\theta)$; but in practice most of the values near the minimum will be reasonably good approximations to the true minimum.[2]) For these reasons, particularly when the training set is large, stochastic gradient descent is often preferred over batch gradient descent.

1.2 The normal equations

Gradient descent gives one way of minimizing J. Let's discuss a second way of doing so, this time performing the minimization explicitly and without resorting to an iterative algorithm. In this method, we will minimize J by explicitly taking its derivatives with respect to the θ_j's, and setting them to zero. To enable us to do this without having to write reams of algebra and pages full of matrices of derivatives, let's introduce some notation for doing calculus with matrices.

1.2.1 Matrix derivatives

For a function $f : \mathbb{R}^{n \times d} \mapsto \mathbb{R}$ mapping from n-by-d matrices to the real numbers, we define the derivative of f with respect to A to be:

$$\nabla_A f(A) = \begin{bmatrix} \frac{\partial f}{\partial A_{11}} & \cdots & \frac{\partial f}{\partial A_{1d}} \\ \vdots & \ddots & \vdots \\ \frac{\partial f}{\partial A_{n1}} & \cdots & \frac{\partial f}{\partial A_{nd}} \end{bmatrix}$$

Thus, the gradient $\nabla_A f(A)$ is itself an n-by-d matrix, whose (i,j)-element is $\partial f / \partial A_{ij}$. For example, suppose $A = \begin{bmatrix} A_{11} & A_{12} \\ A_{21} & A_{22} \end{bmatrix}$ is a 2-by-2 matrix, and the function $f : \mathbb{R}^{2 \times 2} \mapsto \mathbb{R}$ is given by

$$f(A) = \frac{3}{2}A_{11} + 5A_{12}^2 + A_{21}A_{22}.$$

[2]By slowly letting the learning rate α decrease to zero as the algorithm runs, it is also possible to ensure that the parameters will converge to the global minimum rather than merely oscillate around the minimum.

Here, A_{ij} denotes the (i, j) entry of the matrix A. We then have

$$\nabla_A f(A) = \begin{bmatrix} \frac{3}{2} & 10A_{12} \\ A_{22} & A_{21} \end{bmatrix}.$$

1.2.2 Least squares revisited

Armed with the tools of matrix derivatives, let us now proceed to find in closed-form the value of θ that minimizes $J(\theta)$. We begin by re-writing J in matrix-vectorial notation.

Given a training set, define the **design matrix** X to be the n-by-d matrix (actually n-by-$d+1$, if we include the intercept term) that contains the training examples' input values in its rows:

$$X = \begin{bmatrix} — (x^{(1)})^T — \\ — (x^{(2)})^T — \\ \vdots \\ — (x^{(n)})^T — \end{bmatrix}.$$

Also, let $\vec{y}$ be the n-dimensional vector containing all the target values from the training set:

$$\vec{y} = \begin{bmatrix} y^{(1)} \\ y^{(2)} \\ \vdots \\ y^{(n)} \end{bmatrix}.$$

Now, since $h_\theta(x^{(i)}) = (x^{(i)})^T\theta$, we can easily verify that

$$\begin{aligned} X\theta - \vec{y} &= \begin{bmatrix} (x^{(1)})^T\theta \\ \vdots \\ (x^{(n)})^T\theta \end{bmatrix} - \begin{bmatrix} y^{(1)} \\ \vdots \\ y^{(n)} \end{bmatrix} \\ &= \begin{bmatrix} h_\theta(x^{(1)}) - y^{(1)} \\ \vdots \\ h_\theta(x^{(n)}) - y^{(n)} \end{bmatrix}. \end{aligned}$$

Thus, using the fact that for a vector z, we have that $z^Tz = \sum_i z_i^2$:

$$\begin{aligned} \frac{1}{2}(X\theta - \vec{y})^T(X\theta - \vec{y}) &= \frac{1}{2}\sum_{i=1}^{n}(h_\theta(x^{(i)}) - y^{(i)})^2 \\ &= J(\theta) \end{aligned}$$

Finally, to minimize J, let's find its derivatives with respect to θ. Hence,

$$\begin{aligned}
\nabla_\theta J(\theta) &= \nabla_\theta \frac{1}{2}(X\theta - \vec{y})^T(X\theta - \vec{y}) \\
&= \frac{1}{2}\nabla_\theta \left((X\theta)^T X\theta - (X\theta)^T\vec{y} - \vec{y}^T(X\theta) + \vec{y}^T\vec{y}\right) \\
&= \frac{1}{2}\nabla_\theta \left(\theta^T(X^TX)\theta - \vec{y}^T(X\theta) - \vec{y}^T(X\theta)\right) \\
&= \frac{1}{2}\nabla_\theta \left(\theta^T(X^TX)\theta - 2(X^T\vec{y})^T\theta\right) \\
&= \frac{1}{2}\left(2X^TX\theta - 2X^T\vec{y}\right) \\
&= X^TX\theta - X^T\vec{y}
\end{aligned}$$

In the third step, we used the fact that $a^Tb = b^Ta$, and in the fifth step used the facts $\nabla_x b^Tx = b$ and $\nabla_x x^TAx = 2Ax$ for symmetric matrix A (for more details, see Section 4.3 of "Linear Algebra Review and Reference"). To minimize J, we set its derivatives to zero, and obtain the **normal equations**:

$$X^TX\theta = X^T\vec{y}$$

Thus, the value of θ that minimizes $J(\theta)$ is given in closed form by the equation

$$\theta = (X^TX)^{-1}X^T\vec{y}.$$ [3]

1.3 Probabilistic interpretation

When faced with a regression problem, why might linear regression, and specifically why might the least-squares cost function J, be a reasonable choice? In this section, we will give a set of probabilistic assumptions, under which least-squares regression is derived as a very natural algorithm.

Let us assume that the target variables and the inputs are related via the equation

$$y^{(i)} = \theta^Tx^{(i)} + \epsilon^{(i)},$$

[3] Note that in the above step, we are implicitly assuming that X^TX is an invertible matrix. This can be checked before calculating the inverse. If either the number of linearly independent examples is fewer than the number of features, or if the features are not linearly independent, then X^TX will not be invertible. Even in such cases, it is possible to "fix" the situation with additional techniques, which we skip here for the sake of simplicty.

where $\epsilon^{(i)}$ is an error term that captures either unmodeled effects (such as if there are some features very pertinent to predicting housing price, but that we'd left out of the regression), or random noise. Let us further assume that the $\epsilon^{(i)}$ are distributed IID (independently and identically distributed) according to a Gaussian distribution (also called a Normal distribution) with mean zero and some variance σ^2. We can write this assumption as "$\epsilon^{(i)} \sim \mathcal{N}(0, \sigma^2)$." I.e., the density of $\epsilon^{(i)}$ is given by

$$p(\epsilon^{(i)}) = \frac{1}{\sqrt{2\pi}\sigma} \exp\left(-\frac{(\epsilon^{(i)})^2}{2\sigma^2}\right).$$

This implies that

$$p(y^{(i)}|x^{(i)};\theta) = \frac{1}{\sqrt{2\pi}\sigma} \exp\left(-\frac{(y^{(i)} - \theta^T x^{(i)})^2}{2\sigma^2}\right).$$

The notation "$p(y^{(i)}|x^{(i)};\theta)$" indicates that this is the distribution of $y^{(i)}$ given $x^{(i)}$ and parameterized by θ. Note that we should not condition on θ ("$p(y^{(i)}|x^{(i)},\theta)$"), since θ is not a random variable. We can also write the distribution of $y^{(i)}$ as $y^{(i)} \mid x^{(i)};\theta \sim \mathcal{N}(\theta^T x^{(i)}, \sigma^2)$.

Given X (the design matrix, which contains all the $x^{(i)}$'s) and θ, what is the distribution of the $y^{(i)}$'s? The probability of the data is given by $p(\vec{y}|X;\theta)$. This quantity is typically viewed a function of $\vec{y}$ (and perhaps X), for a fixed value of θ. When we wish to explicitly view this as a function of θ, we will instead call it the **likelihood** function:

$$L(\theta) = L(\theta; X, \vec{y}) = p(\vec{y}|X;\theta).$$

Note that by the independence assumption on the $\epsilon^{(i)}$'s (and hence also the $y^{(i)}$'s given the $x^{(i)}$'s), this can also be written

$$\begin{aligned} L(\theta) &= \prod_{i=1}^{n} p(y^{(i)} \mid x^{(i)};\theta) \\ &= \prod_{i=1}^{n} \frac{1}{\sqrt{2\pi}\sigma} \exp\left(-\frac{(y^{(i)} - \theta^T x^{(i)})^2}{2\sigma^2}\right). \end{aligned}$$

Now, given this probabilistic model relating the $y^{(i)}$'s and the $x^{(i)}$'s, what is a reasonable way of choosing our best guess of the parameters θ? The principal of **maximum likelihood** says that we should choose θ so as to make the data as high probability as possible. I.e., we should choose θ to maximize $L(\theta)$.

Instead of maximizing $L(\theta)$, we can also maximize any strictly increasing function of $L(\theta)$. In particular, the derivations will be a bit simpler if we instead maximize the **log likelihood** $\ell(\theta)$:

$$\begin{aligned}
\ell(\theta) &= \log L(\theta) \\
&= \log \prod_{i=1}^{n} \frac{1}{\sqrt{2\pi}\sigma} \exp\left(-\frac{(y^{(i)} - \theta^T x^{(i)})^2}{2\sigma^2}\right) \\
&= \sum_{i=1}^{n} \log \frac{1}{\sqrt{2\pi}\sigma} \exp\left(-\frac{(y^{(i)} - \theta^T x^{(i)})^2}{2\sigma^2}\right) \\
&= n \log \frac{1}{\sqrt{2\pi}\sigma} - \frac{1}{\sigma^2} \cdot \frac{1}{2} \sum_{i=1}^{n} (y^{(i)} - \theta^T x^{(i)})^2.
\end{aligned}$$

Hence, maximizing $\ell(\theta)$ gives the same answer as minimizing

$$\frac{1}{2} \sum_{i=1}^{n} (y^{(i)} - \theta^T x^{(i)})^2,$$

which we recognize to be $J(\theta)$, our original least-squares cost function.

To summarize: Under the previous probabilistic assumptions on the data, least-squares regression corresponds to finding the maximum likelihood estimate of θ. This is thus one set of assumptions under which least-squares regression can be justified as a very natural method that's just doing maximum likelihood estimation. (Note however that the probabilistic assumptions are by no means *necessary* for least-squares to be a perfectly good and rational procedure, and there may—and indeed there are—other natural assumptions that can also be used to justify it.)

Note also that, in our previous discussion, our final choice of θ did not depend on what was σ^2, and indeed we'd have arrived at the same result even if σ^2 were unknown. We will use this fact again later, when we talk about the exponential family and generalized linear models.

1.4 Locally weighted linear regression (optional reading)

Consider the problem of predicting y from $x \in \mathbb{R}$. The leftmost figure below shows the result of fitting a $y = \theta_0 + \theta_1 x$ to a dataset. We see that the data doesn't really lie on straight line, and so the fit is not very good.

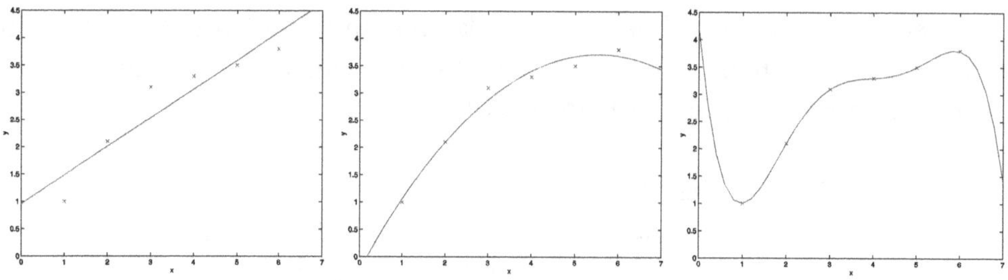

Instead, if we had added an extra feature x^2, and fit $y = \theta_0 + \theta_1 x + \theta_2 x^2$, then we obtain a slightly better fit to the data. (See middle figure) Naively, it might seem that the more features we add, the better. However, there is also a danger in adding too many features: The rightmost figure is the result of fitting a 5-th order polynomial $y = \sum_{j=0}^{5} \theta_j x^j$. We see that even though the fitted curve passes through the data perfectly, we would not expect this to be a very good predictor of, say, housing prices (y) for different living areas (x). Without formally defining what these terms mean, we'll say the figure on the left shows an instance of **underfitting**—in which the data clearly shows structure not captured by the model—and the figure on the right is an example of **overfitting**. (Later in this class, when we talk about learning theory we'll formalize some of these notions, and also define more carefully just what it means for a hypothesis to be good or bad.)

As discussed previously, and as shown in the example above, the choice of features is important to ensuring good performance of a learning algorithm. (When we talk about model selection, we'll also see algorithms for automatically choosing a good set of features.) In this section, let us briefly talk about the locally weighted linear regression (LWR) algorithm which, assuming there is sufficient training data, makes the choice of features less critical. This treatment will be brief, since you'll get a chance to explore some of the properties of the LWR algorithm yourself in the homework.

In the original linear regression algorithm, to make a prediction at a query point x (i.e., to evaluate $h(x)$), we would:

1. Fit θ to minimize $\sum_i (y^{(i)} - \theta^T x^{(i)})^2$.

2. Output $\theta^T x$.

In contrast, the locally weighted linear regression algorithm does the following:

1. Fit θ to minimize $\sum_i w^{(i)} (y^{(i)} - \theta^T x^{(i)})^2$.

2. Output $\theta^T x$.

Here, the $w^{(i)}$'s are non-negative valued **weights**. Intuitively, if $w^{(i)}$ is large for a particular value of i, then in picking θ, we'll try hard to make $(y^{(i)} - \theta^T x^{(i)})^2$ small. If $w^{(i)}$ is small, then the $(y^{(i)} - \theta^T x^{(i)})^2$ error term will be pretty much ignored in the fit.

A fairly standard choice for the weights is[4]

$$w^{(i)} = \exp\left(-\frac{(x^{(i)} - x)^2}{2\tau^2}\right)$$

Note that the weights depend on the particular point x at which we're trying to evaluate x. Moreover, if $|x^{(i)} - x|$ is small, then $w^{(i)}$ is close to 1; and if $|x^{(i)} - x|$ is large, then $w^{(i)}$ is small. Hence, θ is chosen giving a much higher "weight" to the (errors on) training examples close to the query point x. (Note also that while the formula for the weights takes a form that is cosmetically similar to the density of a Gaussian distribution, the $w^{(i)}$'s do not directly have anything to do with Gaussians, and in particular the $w^{(i)}$ are not random variables, normally distributed or otherwise.) The parameter τ controls how quickly the weight of a training example falls off with distance of its $x^{(i)}$ from the query point x; τ is called the **bandwidth** parameter, and is also something that you'll get to experiment with in your homework.

Locally weighted linear regression is the first example we're seeing of a **non-parametric** algorithm. The (unweighted) linear regression algorithm that we saw earlier is known as a **parametric** learning algorithm, because it has a fixed, finite number of parameters (the θ_i's), which are fit to the data. Once we've fit the θ_i's and stored them away, we no longer need to keep the training data around to make future predictions. In contrast, to make predictions using locally weighted linear regression, we need to keep the entire training set around. The term "non-parametric" (roughly) refers to the fact that the amount of stuff we need to keep in order to represent the hypothesis h grows linearly with the size of the training set.

---

[4]If x is vector-valued, this is generalized to be $w^{(i)} = \exp(-(x^{(i)} - x)^T (x^{(i)} - x)/(2\tau^2))$, or $w^{(i)} = \exp(-(x^{(i)} - x)^T \Sigma^{-1} (x^{(i)} - x)/(2\tau^2))$, for an appropriate choice of τ or Σ.

Chapter 2

Classification and logistic regression

Let's now talk about the classification problem. This is just like the regression problem, except that the values y we now want to predict take on only a small number of discrete values. For now, we will focus on the **binary classification** problem in which y can take on only two values, 0 and 1. (Most of what we say here will also generalize to the multiple-class case.) For instance, if we are trying to build a spam classifier for email, then $x^{(i)}$ may be some features of a piece of email, and y may be 1 if it is a piece of spam mail, and 0 otherwise. 0 is also called the **negative class**, and 1 the **positive class**, and they are sometimes also denoted by the symbols "-" and "+." Given $x^{(i)}$, the corresponding $y^{(i)}$ is also called the **label** for the training example.

2.1 Logistic regression

We could approach the classification problem ignoring the fact that y is discrete-valued, and use our old linear regression algorithm to try to predict y given x. However, it is easy to construct examples where this method performs very poorly. Intuitively, it also doesn't make sense for $h_\theta(x)$ to take values larger than 1 or smaller than 0 when we know that $y \in \{0, 1\}$.

To fix this, let's change the form for our hypotheses $h_\theta(x)$. We will choose

$$h_\theta(x) = g(\theta^T x) = \frac{1}{1 + e^{-\theta^T x}},$$

where

$$g(z) = \frac{1}{1 + e^{-z}}$$

is called the **logistic function** or the **sigmoid function**. Here is a plot showing $g(z)$:

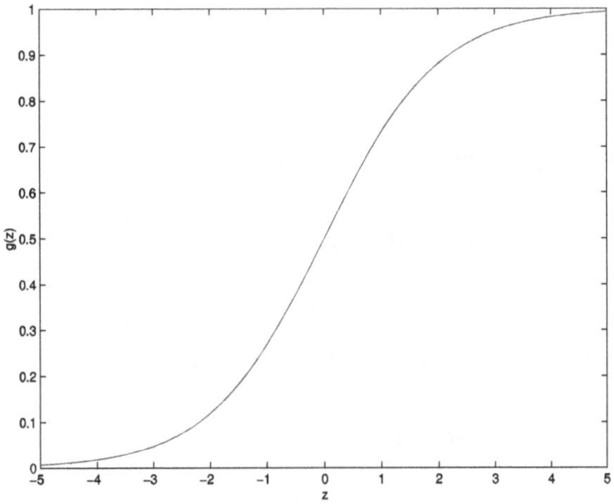

Notice that $g(z)$ tends towards 1 as $z \to \infty$, and $g(z)$ tends towards 0 as $z \to -\infty$. Moreover, g(z), and hence also $h(x)$, is always bounded between 0 and 1. As before, we are keeping the convention of letting $x_0 = 1$, so that $\theta^T x = \theta_0 + \sum_{j=1}^{d} \theta_j x_j$.

For now, let's take the choice of g as given. Other functions that smoothly increase from 0 to 1 can also be used, but for a couple of reasons that we'll see later (when we talk about GLMs, and when we talk about generative learning algorithms), the choice of the logistic function is a fairly natural one. Before moving on, here's a useful property of the derivative of the sigmoid function, which we write as g':

$$\begin{aligned} g'(z) &= \frac{d}{dz} \frac{1}{1+e^{-z}} \\ &= \frac{1}{(1+e^{-z})^2} \left(e^{-z}\right) \\ &= \frac{1}{(1+e^{-z})} \cdot \left(1 - \frac{1}{(1+e^{-z})}\right) \\ &= g(z)(1-g(z)). \end{aligned}$$

So, given the logistic regression model, how do we fit θ for it? Following how we saw least squares regression could be derived as the maximum likelihood estimator under a set of assumptions, let's endow our classification model with a set of probabilistic assumptions, and then fit the parameters via maximum likelihood.

Let us assume that

$$\begin{aligned} P(y = 1 \mid x; \theta) &= h_\theta(x) \\ P(y = 0 \mid x; \theta) &= 1 - h_\theta(x) \end{aligned}$$

Note that this can be written more compactly as

$$p(y \mid x; \theta) = (h_\theta(x))^y \, (1 - h_\theta(x))^{1-y}$$

Assuming that the n training examples were generated independently, we can then write down the likelihood of the parameters as

$$\begin{aligned} L(\theta) &= p(\vec{y} \mid X; \theta) \\ &= \prod_{i=1}^{n} p(y^{(i)} \mid x^{(i)}; \theta) \\ &= \prod_{i=1}^{n} \left(h_\theta(x^{(i)})\right)^{y^{(i)}} \left(1 - h_\theta(x^{(i)})\right)^{1-y^{(i)}} \end{aligned}$$

As before, it will be easier to maximize the log likelihood:

$$\ell(\theta) = \log L(\theta) = \sum_{i=1}^{n} y^{(i)} \log h(x^{(i)}) + (1 - y^{(i)}) \log(1 - h(x^{(i)})) \tag{2.1}$$

How do we maximize the likelihood? Similar to our derivation in the case of linear regression, we can use gradient ascent. Written in vectorial notation, our updates will therefore be given by $\theta := \theta + \alpha \nabla_\theta \ell(\theta)$. (Note the positive rather than negative sign in the update formula, since we're maximizing, rather than minimizing, a function now.) Let's start by working with just one training example (x, y), and take derivatives to derive the stochastic gradient ascent rule:

$$\begin{aligned} \frac{\partial}{\partial \theta_j} \ell(\theta) &= \left(y \frac{1}{g(\theta^T x)} - (1 - y) \frac{1}{1 - g(\theta^T x)} \right) \frac{\partial}{\partial \theta_j} g(\theta^T x) \\ &= \left(y \frac{1}{g(\theta^T x)} - (1 - y) \frac{1}{1 - g(\theta^T x)} \right) g(\theta^T x)(1 - g(\theta^T x)) \frac{\partial}{\partial \theta_j} \theta^T x \\ &= \left(y(1 - g(\theta^T x)) - (1 - y) g(\theta^T x) \right) x_j \\ &= (y - h_\theta(x)) \, x_j \end{aligned} \tag{2.2}$$

Above, we used the fact that $g'(z) = g(z)(1 - g(z))$. This therefore gives us the stochastic gradient ascent rule

$$\theta_j := \theta_j + \alpha \left(y^{(i)} - h_\theta(x^{(i)})\right) x_j^{(i)}$$

If we compare this to the LMS update rule, we see that it looks identical; but this is *not* the same algorithm, because $h_\theta(x^{(i)})$ is now defined as a non-linear function of $\theta^T x^{(i)}$. Nonetheless, it's a little surprising that we end up with the same update rule for a rather different algorithm and learning problem. Is this coincidence, or is there a deeper reason behind this? We'll answer this when we get to GLM models.

Remark 2.1.1: An alternative notational viewpoint of the same loss function is also useful, especially for Section 7.1 where we study nonlinear models. Let $\ell_{\text{logistic}} : \mathbb{R} \times \{0, 1\} \to \mathbb{R}_{\geq 0}$ be the *logistic loss* defined as

$$\ell_{\text{logistic}}(t, y) \triangleq y \log(1 + \exp(-t)) + (1 - y) \log(1 + \exp(t)) . \tag{2.3}$$

One can verify by plugging in $h_\theta(x) = 1/(1 + e^{-\theta^\top x})$ that the *negative* log-likelihood (the negation of $\ell(\theta)$ in equation (2.1)) can be re-written as

$$-\ell(\theta) = \ell_{\text{logistic}}(\theta^\top x, y). \tag{2.4}$$

Oftentimes $\theta^\top x$ or t is called the *logit*. Basic calculus gives us that

$$\begin{aligned} \frac{\partial \ell_{\text{logistic}}(t, y)}{\partial t} &= y \frac{-\exp(-t)}{1 + \exp(-t)} + (1 - y) \frac{1}{1 + \exp(-t)} && (2.5) \\ &= 1/(1 + \exp(-t)) - y. && (2.6) \end{aligned}$$

Then, using the chain rule, we have that

$$\begin{aligned} \frac{\partial}{\partial \theta_j} \ell(\theta) &= -\frac{\partial \ell_{\text{logistic}}(t, y)}{\partial t} \cdot \frac{\partial t}{\partial \theta_j} && (2.7) \\ &= (y - 1/(1 + \exp(-t))) \cdot x_j = (y - h_\theta(x)) x_j , && (2.8) \end{aligned}$$

which is consistent with the derivation in equation (2.2). We will see this viewpoint can be extended nonlinear models in Section 7.1.

2.2 Digression: the perceptron learning algorithm

We now digress to talk briefly about an algorithm that's of some historical interest, and that we will also return to later when we talk about learning theory. Consider modifying the logistic regression method to "force" it to output values that are either 0 or 1 or exactly. To do so, it seems natural to change the definition of g to be the threshold function:

$$g(z) = \begin{cases} 1 & \text{if } z \geq 0 \\ 0 & \text{if } z < 0 \end{cases}$$

If we then let $h_\theta(x) = g(\theta^T x)$ as before but using this modified definition of g, and if we use the update rule

$$\theta_j := \theta_j + \alpha \left(y^{(i)} - h_\theta(x^{(i)}) \right) x_j^{(i)}.$$

then we have the **perceptron learning algorithn**.

In the 1960s, this "perceptron" was argued to be a rough model for how individual neurons in the brain work. Given how simple the algorithm is, it will also provide a starting point for our analysis when we talk about learning theory later in this class. Note however that even though the perceptron may be cosmetically similar to the other algorithms we talked about, it is actually a very different type of algorithm than logistic regression and least squares linear regression; in particular, it is difficult to endow the perceptron's predictions with meaningful probabilistic interpretations, or derive the perceptron as a maximum likelihood estimation algorithm.

2.3 Multi-class classification

Consider a classification problem in which the response variable y can take on any one of k values, so $y \in \{1, 2, \ldots, k\}$. For example, rather than classifying emails into the two classes spam or not-spam—which would have been a binary classification problem—we might want to classify them into three classes, such as spam, personal mails, and work-related mails. The label / response variable is still discrete, but can now take on more than two values. We will thus model it as distributed according to a multinomial distribution.

In this case, $p(y \mid x; \theta)$ is a distribution over k possible discrete outcomes and is thus a multinomial distribution. Recall that a multinomial distribution involves k numbers $\phi_1, \ldots, \phi_k$ specifying the probability of each of the outcomes. Note that these numbers must satisfy $\sum_{i=1}^k \phi_i = 1$. We will design a parameterized model that outputs $\phi_1, \ldots, \phi_k$ satisfying this constraint given the input x.

We introduce k groups of parameters $\theta_1, \ldots, \theta_k$, each of them being a vector in $\mathbb{R}^d$. Intuitively, we would like to use $\theta_1^\top x, \ldots, \theta_k^\top x$ to represent

$\phi_1, \ldots, \phi_k$, the probabilities $P(y = 1 \mid x; \theta), \ldots, P(y = k \mid x; \theta)$. However, there are two issues with such a direct approach. First, $\theta_j^\top x$ is not necessarily within $[0, 1]$. Second, the summation of $\theta_j^\top x$'s is not necessarily 1. Thus, instead, we will use the softmax function to turn $(\theta_1^\top x, \cdots, \theta_k^\top x)$ into a probability vector with nonnegative entries that sum up to 1.

Define the softmax function softmax : $\mathbb{R}^k \to \mathbb{R}^k$ as

$$\text{softmax}(t_1, \ldots, t_k) = \begin{bmatrix} \frac{\exp(t_1)}{\sum_{j=1}^k \exp(t_j)} \\ \vdots \\ \frac{\exp(t_k)}{\sum_{j=1}^k \exp(t_j)} \end{bmatrix}. \tag{2.9}$$

The inputs to the softmax function, the vector t here, are often called *logits*. Note that by definition, the output of the softmax function is always a probability vector whose entries are nonnegative and sum up to 1.

Let $(t_1, \ldots, t_k) = (\theta_1^\top x, \cdots, \theta_k^\top x)$. We apply the softmax function to $(t_1, \ldots, t_k)$, and use the output as the probabilities $P(y = 1 \mid x; \theta), \ldots, P(y = k \mid x; \theta)$. We obtain the following probabilistic model:

$$\begin{bmatrix} P(y = 1 \mid x; \theta) \\ \vdots \\ P(y = k \mid x; \theta) \end{bmatrix} = \text{softmax}(t_1, \cdots, t_k) = \begin{bmatrix} \frac{\exp(\theta_1^\top x)}{\sum_{j=1}^k \exp(\theta_j^\top x)} \\ \vdots \\ \frac{\exp(\theta_k^\top x)}{\sum_{j=1}^k \exp(\theta_j^\top x)} \end{bmatrix}. \tag{2.10}$$

For notational convenience, we will let $\phi_i = \frac{\exp(t_i)}{\sum_{j=1}^k \exp(t_j)}$. More succinctly, the equation above can be written as:

$$P(y = i \mid x; \theta) = \phi_i = \frac{\exp(t_i)}{\sum_{j=1}^k \exp(t_j)} = \frac{\exp(\theta_i^\top x)}{\sum_{j=1}^k \exp(\theta_j^\top x)}. \tag{2.11}$$

Next, we compute the negative log-likelihood of a single example (x, y).

$$-\log p(y \mid x, \theta) = -\log\left(\frac{\exp(t_y)}{\sum_{j=1}^k \exp(t_j)}\right) = -\log\left(\frac{\exp(\theta_y^\top x)}{\sum_{j=1}^k \exp(\theta_j^\top x)}\right) \tag{2.12}$$

Thus, the loss function, the negative log-likelihood of the training data, is given as

$$\ell(\theta) = \sum_{i=1}^n -\log\left(\frac{\exp(\theta_{y^{(i)}}^\top x^{(i)})}{\sum_{j=1}^k \exp(\theta_j^\top x^{(i)})}\right). \tag{2.13}$$

It's convenient to define the cross-entropy loss $\ell_{\text{ce}} : \mathbb{R}^k \times \{1, \ldots, k\} \to \mathbb{R}_{\geq 0}$, which modularizes in the complex equation above:[1]

$$\ell_{\text{ce}}((t_1, \ldots, t_k), y) = -\log\left(\frac{\exp(t_y)}{\sum_{j=1}^k \exp(t_j)}\right). \tag{2.14}$$

With this notation, we can simply rewrite equation (2.13) as

$$\ell(\theta) = \sum_{i=1}^n \ell_{\text{ce}}((\theta_1^\top x^{(i)}, \ldots, \theta_k^\top x^{(i)}), y^{(i)}). \tag{2.15}$$

Moreover, conveniently, the cross-entropy loss also has a simple gradient. Let $t = (t_1, \ldots, t_k)$, and recall $\phi_i = \frac{\exp(t_i)}{\sum_{j=1}^k \exp(t_j)}$. By basic calculus, we can derive

$$\frac{\partial \ell_{\text{ce}}(t, y)}{\partial t_i} = \phi_i - 1\{y = i\}, \tag{2.16}$$

where $1\{\cdot\}$ is the indicator function, that is, $1\{y = i\} = 1$ if $y = i$, and $1\{y = i\} = 0$ if $y \neq i$. Alternatively, in vectorized notations, we have the following form which will be useful for Chapter 7:

$$\frac{\partial \ell_{\text{ce}}(t, y)}{\partial t} = \phi - e_y, \tag{2.17}$$

where $e_s \in \mathbb{R}^k$ is the s-th natural basis vector (where the s-th entry is 1 and all other entries are zeros.) Using Chain rule, we have that

$$\frac{\partial \ell_{\text{ce}}((\theta_1^\top x, \ldots, \theta_k^\top x), y)}{\partial \theta_i} = \frac{\partial \ell(t, y)}{\partial t_i} \cdot \frac{\partial t_i}{\partial \theta_i} = (\phi_i - 1\{y = i\}) \cdot x. \tag{2.18}$$

Therefore, the gradient of the loss with respect to the part of parameter θ_i is

$$\frac{\partial \ell(\theta)}{\partial \theta_i} = \sum_{j=1}^n (\phi_i^{(j)} - 1\{y^{(j)} = i\}) \cdot x^{(j)}, \tag{2.19}$$

where $\phi_i^{(j)} = \frac{\exp(\theta_i^\top x^{(j)})}{\sum_{s=1}^k \exp(\theta_s^\top x^{(j)})}$ is the probability that the model predicts item i for example $x^{(j)}$. With the gradients above, one can implement (stochastic) gradient descent to minimize the loss function $\ell(\theta)$.

[1]There are some ambiguity in the naming here. Some people call the cross-entropy loss the function that maps the probability vector (the ϕ in our language) and label y to the final real number, and call our version of cross-entropy loss softmax-cross-entropy loss. We choose our current naming convention because it's consistent with the naming of most modern deep learning library such as PyTorch and Jax.

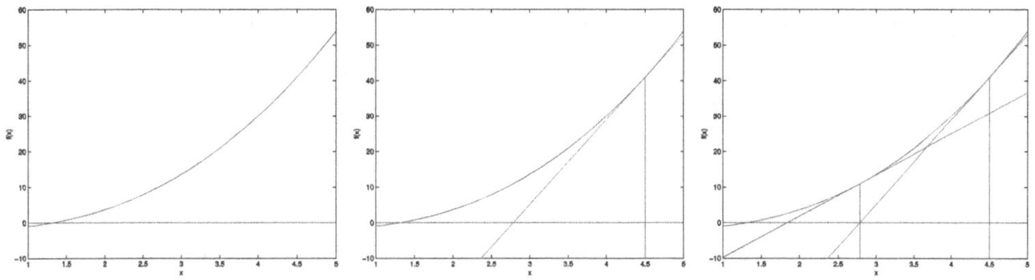

2.4 Another algorithm for maximizing $\ell(\theta)$

Returning to logistic regression with $g(z)$ being the sigmoid function, let's now talk about a different algorithm for maximizing $\ell(\theta)$.

To get us started, let's consider Newton's method for finding a zero of a function. Specifically, suppose we have some function $f : \mathbb{R} \mapsto \mathbb{R}$, and we wish to find a value of θ so that $f(\theta) = 0$. Here, $\theta \in \mathbb{R}$ is a real number. Newton's method performs the following update:

$$\theta := \theta - \frac{f(\theta)}{f'(\theta)}.$$

This method has a natural interpretation in which we can think of it as approximating the function f via a linear function that is tangent to f at the current guess θ, solving for where that linear function equals to zero, and letting the next guess for θ be where that linear function is zero.

Here's a picture of the Newton's method in action:

In the leftmost figure, we see the function f plotted along with the line $y = 0$. We're trying to find θ so that $f(\theta) = 0$; the value of θ that achieves this is about 1.3. Suppose we initialized the algorithm with $\theta = 4.5$. Newton's method then fits a straight line tangent to f at $\theta = 4.5$, and solves for the where that line evaluates to 0. (Middle figure.) This give us the next guess for θ, which is about 2.8. The rightmost figure shows the result of running one more iteration, which the updates θ to about 1.8. After a few more iterations, we rapidly approach $\theta = 1.3$.

Newton's method gives a way of getting to $f(\theta) = 0$. What if we want to use it to maximize some function ℓ? The maxima of ℓ correspond to points where its first derivative $\ell'(\theta)$ is zero. So, by letting $f(\theta) = \ell'(\theta)$, we can use the same algorithm to maximize ℓ, and we obtain update rule:

$$\theta := \theta - \frac{\ell'(\theta)}{\ell''(\theta)}.$$

(Something to think about: How would this change if we wanted to use Newton's method to minimize rather than maximize a function?)

Lastly, in our logistic regression setting, θ is vector-valued, so we need to generalize Newton's method to this setting. The generalization of Newton's method to this multidimensional setting (also called the Newton-Raphson method) is given by

$$\theta := \theta - H^{-1}\nabla_\theta \ell(\theta).$$

Here, $\nabla_\theta \ell(\theta)$ is, as usual, the vector of partial derivatives of $\ell(\theta)$ with respect to the θ_i's; and H is an d-by-d matrix (actually, $d{+}1{-}by{-}$d+1, assuming that we include the intercept term) called the **Hessian**, whose entries are given by

$$H_{ij} = \frac{\partial^2 \ell(\theta)}{\partial \theta_i \partial \theta_j}.$$

Newton's method typically enjoys faster convergence than (batch) gradient descent, and requires many fewer iterations to get very close to the minimum. One iteration of Newton's can, however, be more expensive than one iteration of gradient descent, since it requires finding and inverting an d-by-d Hessian; but so long as d is not too large, it is usually much faster overall. When Newton's method is applied to maximize the logistic regression log likelihood function $\ell(\theta)$, the resulting method is also called **Fisher scoring.**

Chapter 3

Generalized linear models

So far, we've seen a regression example, and a classification example. In the regression example, we had $y|x;\theta \sim \mathcal{N}(\mu, \sigma^2)$, and in the classification one, $y|x;\theta \sim \text{Bernoulli}(\phi)$, for some appropriate definitions of μ and ϕ as functions of x and θ. In this section, we will show that both of these methods are special cases of a broader family of models, called Generalized Linear Models (GLMs).[1] We will also show how other models in the GLM family can be derived and applied to other classification and regression problems.

3.1 The exponential family

To work our way up to GLMs, we will begin by defining exponential family distributions. We say that a class of distributions is in the exponential family if it can be written in the form

$$p(y;\eta) = b(y)\exp(\eta^T T(y) - a(\eta)) \tag{3.1}$$

Here, η is called the **natural parameter** (also called the **canonical parameter**) of the distribution; $T(y)$ is the **sufficient statistic** (for the distributions we consider, it will often be the case that $T(y) = y$); and $a(\eta)$ is the **log partition function**. The quantity $e^{-a(\eta)}$ essentially plays the role of a normalization constant, that makes sure the distribution $p(y;\eta)$ sums/integrates over y to 1.

A fixed choice of T, a and b defines a *family* (or set) of distributions that is parameterized by η; as we vary η, we then get different distributions within this family.

[1]The presentation of the material in this section takes inspiration from Michael I. Jordan, *Learning in graphical models* (unpublished book draft), and also McCullagh and Nelder, *Generalized Linear Models (2nd ed.)*.

We now show that the Bernoulli and the Gaussian distributions are examples of exponential family distributions. The Bernoulli distribution with mean ϕ, written Bernoulli(ϕ), specifies a distribution over $y \in \{0, 1\}$, so that $p(y = 1; \phi) = \phi$; $p(y = 0; \phi) = 1 - \phi$. As we vary ϕ, we obtain Bernoulli distributions with different means. We now show that this class of Bernoulli distributions, ones obtained by varying ϕ, is in the exponential family; i.e., that there is a choice of T, a and b so that Equation (3.1) becomes exactly the class of Bernoulli distributions.

We write the Bernoulli distribution as:

$$\begin{aligned} p(y; \phi) &= \phi^y (1 - \phi)^{1-y} \\ &= \exp(y \log \phi + (1 - y) \log(1 - \phi)) \\ &= \exp\left(\left(\log \left(\frac{\phi}{1 - \phi} \right) \right) y + \log(1 - \phi) \right). \end{aligned}$$

Thus, the natural parameter is given by $\eta = \log(\phi/(1 - \phi))$. Interestingly, if we invert this definition for η by solving for ϕ in terms of η, we obtain $\phi = 1/(1 + e^{-\eta})$. This is the familiar sigmoid function! This will come up again when we derive logistic regression as a GLM. To complete the formulation of the Bernoulli distribution as an exponential family distribution, we also have

$$\begin{aligned} T(y) &= y \\ a(\eta) &= -\log(1 - \phi) \\ &= \log(1 + e^{\eta}) \\ b(y) &= 1 \end{aligned}$$

This shows that the Bernoulli distribution can be written in the form of Equation (3.1), using an appropriate choice of T, a and b.

Let's now move on to consider the Gaussian distribution. Recall that, when deriving linear regression, the value of σ^2 had no effect on our final choice of θ and $h_\theta(x)$. Thus, we can choose an arbitrary value for σ^2 without changing anything. To simplify the derivation below, let's set $\sigma^2 = 1$.[2] We

[2]If we leave σ^2 as a variable, the Gaussian distribution can also be shown to be in the exponential family, where $\eta \in \mathbb{R}^2$ is now a 2-dimension vector that depends on both μ and σ. For the purposes of GLMs, however, the σ^2 parameter can also be treated by considering a more general definition of the exponential family: $p(y; \eta, \tau) = b(a, \tau) \exp((\eta^T T(y) - a(\eta))/c(\tau))$. Here, τ is called the **dispersion parameter**, and for the Gaussian, $c(\tau) = \sigma^2$; but given our simplification above, we won't need the more general definition for the examples we will consider here.

then have:

$$\begin{aligned} p(y;\mu) &= \frac{1}{\sqrt{2\pi}}\exp\left(-\frac{1}{2}(y-\mu)^2\right) \\ &= \frac{1}{\sqrt{2\pi}}\exp\left(-\frac{1}{2}y^2\right)\cdot\exp\left(\mu y-\frac{1}{2}\mu^2\right) \end{aligned}$$

Thus, we see that the Gaussian is in the exponential family, with

$$\begin{aligned} \eta &= \mu \\ T(y) &= y \\ a(\eta) &= \mu^2/2 \\ &= \eta^2/2 \\ b(y) &= (1/\sqrt{2\pi})\exp(-y^2/2). \end{aligned}$$

There're many other distributions that are members of the exponential family: The multinomial (which we'll see later), the Poisson (for modelling count-data; also see the problem set); the gamma and the exponential (for modelling continuous, non-negative random variables, such as time-intervals); the beta and the Dirichlet (for distributions over probabilities); and many more. In the next section, we will describe a general "recipe" for constructing models in which y (given x and θ) comes from any of these distributions.

3.2 Constructing GLMs

Suppose you would like to build a model to estimate the number y of customers arriving in your store (or number of page-views on your website) in any given hour, based on certain features x such as store promotions, recent advertising, weather, day-of-week, etc. We know that the Poisson distribution usually gives a good model for numbers of visitors. Knowing this, how can we come up with a model for our problem? Fortunately, the Poisson is an exponential family distribution, so we can apply a Generalized Linear Model (GLM). In this section, we will we will describe a method for constructing GLM models for problems such as these.

More generally, consider a classification or regression problem where we would like to predict the value of some random variable y as a function of x. To derive a GLM for this problem, we will make the following three assumptions about the conditional distribution of y given x and about our model:

1. $y \mid x; \theta \sim \text{ExponentialFamily}(\eta)$. I.e., given x and θ, the distribution of y follows some exponential family distribution, with parameter η.

2. Given x, our goal is to predict the expected value of $T(y)$ given x. In most of our examples, we will have $T(y) = y$, so this means we would like the prediction $h(x)$ output by our learned hypothesis h to satisfy $h(x) = \mathrm{E}[y|x]$. (Note that this assumption is satisfied in the choices for $h_\theta(x)$ for both logistic regression and linear regression. For instance, in logistic regression, we had $h_\theta(x) = p(y = 1|x; \theta) = 0 \cdot p(y = 0|x; \theta) + 1 \cdot p(y = 1|x; \theta) = \mathrm{E}[y|x; \theta]$.)

3. The natural parameter η and the inputs x are related linearly: $\eta = \theta^T x$. (Or, if η is vector-valued, then $\eta_i = \theta_i^T x$.)

The third of these assumptions might seem the least well justified of the above, and it might be better thought of as a "design choice" in our recipe for designing GLMs, rather than as an assumption per se. These three assumptions/design choices will allow us to derive a very elegant class of learning algorithms, namely GLMs, that have many desirable properties such as ease of learning. Furthermore, the resulting models are often very effective for modelling different types of distributions over y; for example, we will shortly show that both logistic regression and ordinary least squares can both be derived as GLMs.

3.2.1 Ordinary least squares

To show that ordinary least squares is a special case of the GLM family of models, consider the setting where the target variable y (also called the **response variable** in GLM terminology) is continuous, and we model the conditional distribution of y given x as a Gaussian $\mathcal{N}(\mu, \sigma^2)$. (Here, μ may depend x.) So, we let the *ExponentialFamily*(η) distribution above be the Gaussian distribution. As we saw previously, in the formulation of the Gaussian as an exponential family distribution, we had $\mu = \eta$. So, we have

$$\begin{aligned} h_\theta(x) &= E[y|x; \theta] \\ &= \mu \\ &= \eta \\ &= \theta^T x. \end{aligned}$$

The first equality follows from Assumption 2, above; the second equality follows from the fact that $y|x; \theta \sim \mathcal{N}(\mu, \sigma^2)$, and so its expected value is given by μ; the third equality follows from Assumption 1 (and our earlier derivation showing that $\mu = \eta$ in the formulation of the Gaussian as an exponential family distribution); and the last equality follows from Assumption 3.

3.2.2 Logistic regression

We now consider logistic regression. Here we are interested in binary classification, so $y \in \{0, 1\}$. Given that y is binary-valued, it therefore seems natural to choose the Bernoulli family of distributions to model the conditional distribution of y given x. In our formulation of the Bernoulli distribution as an exponential family distribution, we had $\phi = 1/(1 + e^{-\eta})$. Furthermore, note that if $y|x;\theta \sim \text{Bernoulli}(\phi)$, then $\text{E}[y|x;\theta] = \phi$. So, following a similar derivation as the one for ordinary least squares, we get:

$$
\begin{aligned}
h_\theta(x) &= E[y|x;\theta] \\
&= \phi \\
&= 1/(1 + e^{-\eta}) \\
&= 1/(1 + e^{-\theta^T x})
\end{aligned}
$$

So, this gives us hypothesis functions of the form $h_\theta(x) = 1/(1 + e^{-\theta^T x})$. If you are previously wondering how we came up with the form of the logistic function $1/(1 + e^{-z})$, this gives one answer: Once we assume that y conditioned on x is Bernoulli, it arises as a consequence of the definition of GLMs and exponential family distributions.

To introduce a little more terminology, the function g giving the distribution's mean as a function of the natural parameter ($g(\eta) = \text{E}[T(y);\eta]$) is called the **canonical response function**. Its inverse, g^{-1}, is called the **canonical link function**. Thus, the canonical response function for the Gaussian family is just the identify function; and the canonical response function for the Bernoulli is the logistic function.[3]

[3]Many texts use g to denote the link function, and g^{-1} to denote the response function; but the notation we're using here, inherited from the early machine learning literature, will be more consistent with the notation used in the rest of the class.

Chapter 4

Generative learning algorithms

So far, we've mainly been talking about learning algorithms that model $p(y|x;\theta)$, the conditional distribution of y given x. For instance, logistic regression modeled $p(y|x;\theta)$ as $h_\theta(x) = g(\theta^T x)$ where g is the sigmoid function. In these notes, we'll talk about a different type of learning algorithm.

Consider a classification problem in which we want to learn to distinguish between elephants ($y = 1$) and dogs ($y = 0$), based on some features of an animal. Given a training set, an algorithm like logistic regression or the perceptron algorithm (basically) tries to find a straight line—that is, a decision boundary—that separates the elephants and dogs. Then, to classify a new animal as either an elephant or a dog, it checks on which side of the decision boundary it falls, and makes its prediction accordingly.

Here's a different approach. First, looking at elephants, we can build a model of what elephants look like. Then, looking at dogs, we can build a separate model of what dogs look like. Finally, to classify a new animal, we can match the new animal against the elephant model, and match it against the dog model, to see whether the new animal looks more like the elephants or more like the dogs we had seen in the training set.

Algorithms that try to learn $p(y|x)$ directly (such as logistic regression), or algorithms that try to learn mappings directly from the space of inputs $\mathcal{X}$ to the labels $\{0, 1\}$, (such as the perceptron algorithm) are called **discriminative** learning algorithms. Here, we'll talk about algorithms that instead try to model $p(x|y)$ (and $p(y)$). These algorithms are called **generative** learning algorithms. For instance, if y indicates whether an example is a dog (0) or an elephant (1), then $p(x|y = 0)$ models the distribution of dogs' features, and $p(x|y = 1)$ models the distribution of elephants' features.

After modeling $p(y)$ (called the **class priors**) and $p(x|y)$, our algorithm can then use Bayes rule to derive the posterior distribution on y given x:

$$p(y|x) = \frac{p(x|y)p(y)}{p(x)}.$$

Here, the denominator is given by $p(x) = p(x|y = 1)p(y = 1) + p(x|y = 0)p(y = 0)$ (you should be able to verify that this is true from the standard properties of probabilities), and thus can also be expressed in terms of the quantities $p(x|y)$ and $p(y)$ that we've learned. Actually, if were calculating $p(y|x)$ in order to make a prediction, then we don't actually need to calculate the denominator, since

$$\begin{aligned} \arg\max_y p(y|x) &= \arg\max_y \frac{p(x|y)p(y)}{p(x)} \\ &= \arg\max_y p(x|y)p(y). \end{aligned}$$

4.1 Gaussian discriminant analysis

The first generative learning algorithm that we'll look at is Gaussian discriminant analysis (GDA). In this model, we'll assume that $p(x|y)$ is distributed according to a multivariate normal distribution. Let's talk briefly about the properties of multivariate normal distributions before moving on to the GDA model itself.

4.1.1 The multivariate normal distribution

The multivariate normal distribution in d-dimensions, also called the multivariate Gaussian distribution, is parameterized by a **mean vector** $\mu \in \mathbb{R}^d$ and a **covariance matrix** $\Sigma \in \mathbb{R}^{d \times d}$, where $\Sigma \geq 0$ is symmetric and positive semi-definite. Also written "$\mathcal{N}(\mu, \Sigma)$", its density is given by:

$$p(x; \mu, \Sigma) = \frac{1}{(2\pi)^{d/2}|\Sigma|^{1/2}} \exp\left(-\frac{1}{2}(x - \mu)^T \Sigma^{-1}(x - \mu)\right).$$

In the equation above, "$|\Sigma|$" denotes the determinant of the matrix Σ.

For a random variable X distributed $\mathcal{N}(\mu, \Sigma)$, the mean is (unsurprisingly) given by μ:

$$\mathrm{E}[X] = \int_x x\, p(x; \mu, \Sigma) dx = \mu$$

The **covariance** of a vector-valued random variable Z is defined as $\mathrm{Cov}(Z) = \mathrm{E}[(Z - \mathrm{E}[Z])(Z - \mathrm{E}[Z])^T]$. This generalizes the notion of the variance of a real-valued random variable. The covariance can also be defined as $\text{Cov}(Z) = \text{E}[ZZ^T] - (\text{E}[Z])(\text{E}[Z])^T$. (You should be able to prove to yourself that these two definitions are equivalent.) If $X \sim \mathcal{N}(\mu, \Sigma)$, then

$$\text{Cov}(X) = \Sigma.$$

Here are some examples of what the density of a Gaussian distribution looks like:

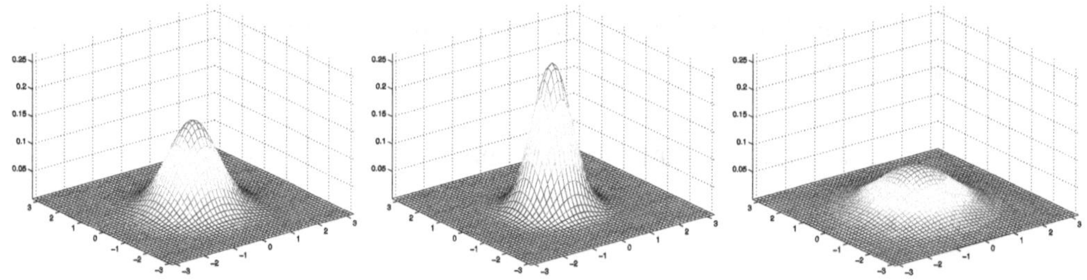

The left-most figure shows a Gaussian with mean zero (that is, the 2x1 zero-vector) and covariance matrix $\Sigma = I$ (the 2x2 identity matrix). A Gaussian with zero mean and identity covariance is also called the **standard normal distribution**. The middle figure shows the density of a Gaussian with zero mean and $\Sigma = 0.6I$; and in the rightmost figure shows one with , $\Sigma = 2I$. We see that as Σ becomes larger, the Gaussian becomes more "spread-out," and as it becomes smaller, the distribution becomes more "compressed."

Let's look at some more examples.

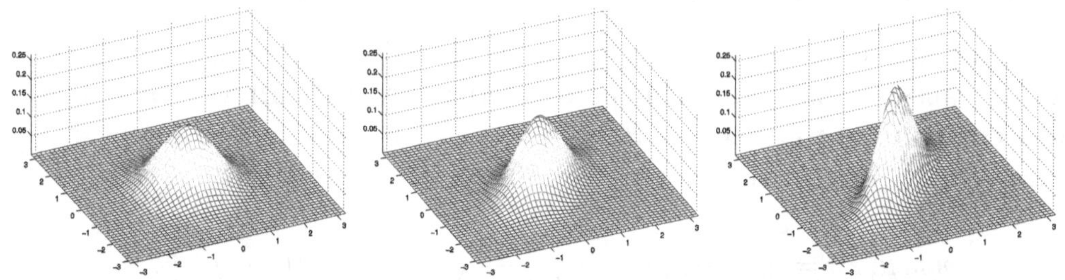

The figures above show Gaussians with mean 0, and with covariance matrices respectively

$$\Sigma = \begin{bmatrix} 1 & 0 \\ 0 & 1 \end{bmatrix}; \quad \Sigma = \begin{bmatrix} 1 & 0.5 \\ 0.5 & 1 \end{bmatrix}; \quad \Sigma = \begin{bmatrix} 1 & 0.8 \\ 0.8 & 1 \end{bmatrix}.$$

The leftmost figure shows the familiar standard normal distribution, and we see that as we increase the off-diagonal entry in Σ, the density becomes more "compressed" towards the 45° line (given by $x_1 = x_2$). We can see this more clearly when we look at the contours of the same three densities:

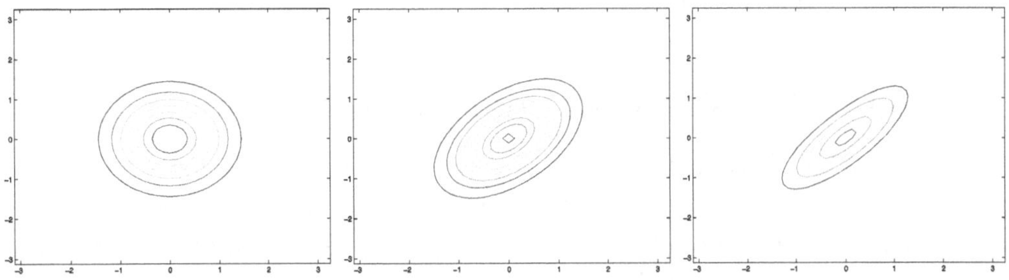

Here's one last set of examples generated by varying Σ:

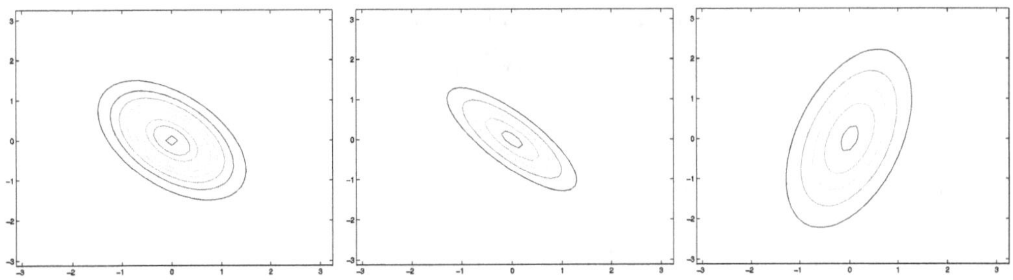

The plots above used, respectively,

$$\Sigma = \begin{bmatrix} 1 & \text{-0.5} \\ \text{-0.5} & 1 \end{bmatrix}; \; \Sigma = \begin{bmatrix} 1 & \text{-0.8} \\ \text{-0.8} & 1 \end{bmatrix}; \; \Sigma = \begin{bmatrix} 3 & 0.8 \\ 0.8 & 1 \end{bmatrix}.$$

From the leftmost and middle figures, we see that by decreasing the off-diagonal elements of the covariance matrix, the density now becomes "compressed" again, but in the opposite direction. Lastly, as we vary the parameters, more generally the contours will form ellipses (the rightmost figure showing an example).

As our last set of examples, fixing $\Sigma = I$, by varying μ, we can also move the mean of the density around.

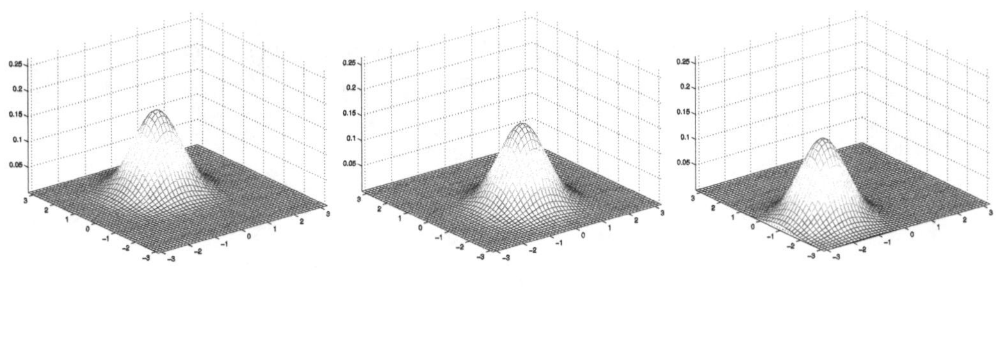

The figures above were generated using $\Sigma = I$, and respectively

$$\mu = \begin{bmatrix} 1 \\ 0 \end{bmatrix}; \quad \mu = \begin{bmatrix} \text{-0.5} \\ 0 \end{bmatrix}; \quad \mu = \begin{bmatrix} \text{-1} \\ \text{-1.5} \end{bmatrix}.$$

4.1.2 The Gaussian discriminant analysis model

When we have a classification problem in which the input features x are continuous-valued random variables, we can then use the Gaussian Discriminant Analysis (GDA) model, which models $p(x|y)$ using a multivariate normal distribution. The model is:

$$\begin{aligned} y &\sim \text{Bernoulli}(\phi) \\ x|y=0 &\sim \mathcal{N}(\mu_0, \Sigma) \\ x|y=1 &\sim \mathcal{N}(\mu_1, \Sigma) \end{aligned}$$

Writing out the distributions, this is:

$$\begin{aligned} p(y) &= \phi^y (1-\phi)^{1-y} \\ p(x|y=0) &= \frac{1}{(2\pi)^{d/2}|\Sigma|^{1/2}} \exp\left(-\frac{1}{2}(x-\mu_0)^T\Sigma^{-1}(x-\mu_0)\right) \\ p(x|y=1) &= \frac{1}{(2\pi)^{d/2}|\Sigma|^{1/2}} \exp\left(-\frac{1}{2}(x-\mu_1)^T\Sigma^{-1}(x-\mu_1)\right) \end{aligned}$$

Here, the parameters of our model are ϕ, Σ, μ_0 and μ_1. (Note that while there're two different mean vectors μ_0 and μ_1, this model is usually applied using only one covariance matrix Σ.) The log-likelihood of the data is given by

$$\begin{aligned} \ell(\phi, \mu_0, \mu_1, \Sigma) &= \log \prod_{i=1}^{n} p(x^{(i)}, y^{(i)}; \phi, \mu_0, \mu_1, \Sigma) \\ &= \log \prod_{i=1}^{n} p(x^{(i)}|y^{(i)}; \mu_0, \mu_1, \Sigma) p(y^{(i)}; \phi). \end{aligned}$$

By maximizing ℓ with respect to the parameters, we find the maximum likelihood estimate of the parameters (see problem set 1) to be:

$$\begin{aligned}
\phi &= \frac{1}{n}\sum_{i=1}^{n} 1\{y^{(i)} = 1\} \\
\mu_0 &= \frac{\sum_{i=1}^{n} 1\{y^{(i)} = 0\}x^{(i)}}{\sum_{i=1}^{n} 1\{y^{(i)} = 0\}} \\
\mu_1 &= \frac{\sum_{i=1}^{n} 1\{y^{(i)} = 1\}x^{(i)}}{\sum_{i=1}^{n} 1\{y^{(i)} = 1\}} \\
\Sigma &= \frac{1}{n}\sum_{i=1}^{n}(x^{(i)} - \mu_{y^{(i)}})(x^{(i)} - \mu_{y^{(i)}})^T.
\end{aligned}$$

Pictorially, what the algorithm is doing can be seen in as follows:

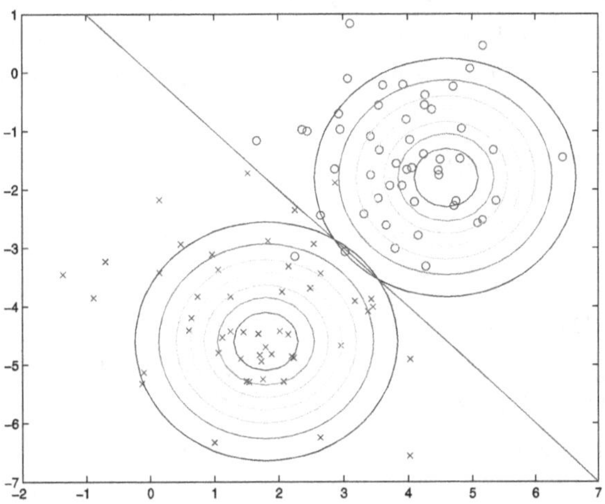

Shown in the figure are the training set, as well as the contours of the two Gaussian distributions that have been fit to the data in each of the two classes. Note that the two Gaussians have contours that are the same shape and orientation, since they share a covariance matrix Σ, but they have different means μ_0 and μ_1. Also shown in the figure is the straight line giving the decision boundary at which $p(y = 1|x) = 0.5$. On one side of the boundary, we'll predict $y = 1$ to be the most likely outcome, and on the other side, we'll predict $y = 0$.

4.1.3 Discussion: GDA and logistic regression

The GDA model has an interesting relationship to logistic regression. If we view the quantity $p(y = 1|x; \phi, \mu_0, \mu_1, \Sigma)$ as a function of x, we'll find that it can be expressed in the form

$$p(y = 1|x; \phi, \Sigma, \mu_0, \mu_1) = \frac{1}{1 + \exp(-\theta^T x)},$$

where θ is some appropriate function of $\phi, \Sigma, \mu_0, \mu_1$.[1] This is exactly the form that logistic regression—a discriminative algorithm—used to model $p(y = 1|x)$.

When would we prefer one model over another? GDA and logistic regression will, in general, give different decision boundaries when trained on the same dataset. Which is better?

We just argued that if $p(x|y)$ is multivariate gaussian (with shared Σ), then $p(y|x)$ necessarily follows a logistic function. The converse, however, is not true; i.e., $p(y|x)$ being a logistic function does not imply $p(x|y)$ is multivariate gaussian. This shows that GDA makes *stronger* modeling assumptions about the data than does logistic regression. It turns out that when these modeling assumptions are correct, then GDA will find better fits to the data, and is a better model. Specifically, when $p(x|y)$ is indeed gaussian (with shared Σ), then GDA is **asymptotically efficient**. Informally, this means that in the limit of very large training sets (large n), there is no algorithm that is strictly better than GDA (in terms of, say, how accurately they estimate $p(y|x)$). In particular, it can be shown that in this setting, GDA will be a better algorithm than logistic regression; and more generally, even for small training set sizes, we would generally expect GDA to better.

In contrast, by making significantly weaker assumptions, logistic regression is also more *robust* and less sensitive to incorrect modeling assumptions. There are many different sets of assumptions that would lead to $p(y|x)$ taking the form of a logistic function. For example, if $x|y = 0 \sim \text{Poisson}(\lambda_0)$, and $x|y = 1 \sim \text{Poisson}(\lambda_1)$; then $p(y|x)$ will be logistic. Logistic regression will also work well on Poisson data like this. But if we were to use GDA on such data—and fit Gaussian distributions to such non-Gaussian data—then the results will be less predictable, and GDA may (or may not) do well.

To summarize: GDA makes stronger modeling assumptions, and is more data efficient (i.e., requires less training data to learn "well") when the modeling assumptions are correct or at least approximately correct. Logistic

[1]This uses the convention of redefining the $x^{(i)}$'s on the right-hand-side to be $(d+1)$-dimensional vectors by adding the extra coordinate $x_0^{(i)} = 1$; see problem set 1.

regression makes weaker assumptions, and is significantly more robust to deviations from modeling assumptions. Specifically, when the data is indeed non-Gaussian, then in the limit of large datasets, logistic regression will almost always do better than GDA. For this reason, in practice logistic regression is used more often than GDA. (Some related considerations about discriminative vs. generative models also apply for the Naive Bayes algorithm that we discuss next, but the Naive Bayes algorithm is still considered a very good, and is certainly also a very popular, classification algorithm.)

4.2 Naive bayes (Option Reading)

In GDA, the feature vectors x were continuous, real-valued vectors. Let's now talk about a different learning algorithm in which the x_j's are discrete-valued.

For our motivating example, consider building an email spam filter using machine learning. Here, we wish to classify messages according to whether they are unsolicited commercial (spam) email, or non-spam email. After learning to do this, we can then have our mail reader automatically filter out the spam messages and perhaps place them in a separate mail folder. Classifying emails is one example of a broader set of problems called **text classification**.

Let's say we have a training set (a set of emails labeled as spam or non-spam). We'll begin our construction of our spam filter by specifying the features x_j used to represent an email.

We will represent an email via a feature vector whose length is equal to the number of words in the dictionary. Specifically, if an email contains the j-th word of the dictionary, then we will set $x_j = 1$; otherwise, we let $x_j = 0$. For instance, the vector

$$x = \begin{bmatrix} 1 \\ 0 \\ 0 \\ \vdots \\ 1 \\ \vdots \\ 0 \end{bmatrix} \begin{matrix} \text{a} \\ \text{aardvark} \\ \text{aardwolf} \\ \vdots \\ \text{buy} \\ \vdots \\ \text{zygmurgy} \end{matrix}$$

is used to represent an email that contains the words "a" and "buy," but not "aardvark," "aardwolf" or "zygmurgy."[2] The set of words encoded into the feature vector is called the **vocabulary**, so the dimension of x is equal to the size of the vocabulary.

Having chosen our feature vector, we now want to build a generative model. So, we have to model $p(x|y)$. But if we have, say, a vocabulary of 50000 words, then $x \in \{0,1\}^{50000}$ (x is a 50000-dimensional vector of 0's and 1's), and if we were to model x explicitly with a multinomial distribution over the 2^{50000} possible outcomes, then we'd end up with a $(2^{50000}-1)$-dimensional parameter vector. This is clearly too many parameters.

To model $p(x|y)$, we will therefore make a very strong assumption. We will assume that the x_i's are conditionally independent given y. This assumption is called the **Naive Bayes (NB) assumption**, and the resulting algorithm is called the **Naive Bayes classifier**. For instance, if $y = 1$ means spam email; "buy" is word 2087 and "price" is word 39831; then we are assuming that if I tell you $y = 1$ (that a particular piece of email is spam), then knowledge of x_{2087} (knowledge of whether "buy" appears in the message) will have no effect on your beliefs about the value of x_{39831} (whether "price" appears). More formally, this can be written $p(x_{2087}|y) = p(x_{2087}|y, x_{39831})$. (Note that this is *not* the same as saying that x_{2087} and x_{39831} are independent, which would have been written "$p(x_{2087}) = p(x_{2087}|x_{39831})$"; rather, we are only assuming that x_{2087} and x_{39831} are conditionally independent *given* y.)

We now have:

$$
\begin{aligned}
& p(x_1, \ldots, x_{50000}|y) \\
&\quad = p(x_1|y)p(x_2|y, x_1)p(x_3|y, x_1, x_2) \cdots p(x_{50000}|y, x_1, \ldots, x_{49999}) \\
&\quad = p(x_1|y)p(x_2|y)p(x_3|y) \cdots p(x_{50000}|y) \\
&\quad = \prod_{j=1}^{d} p(x_j|y)
\end{aligned}
$$

The first equality simply follows from the usual properties of probabilities, and the second equality used the NB assumption. We note that even though

[2] Actually, rather than looking through an English dictionary for the list of all English words, in practice it is more common to look through our training set and encode in our feature vector only the words that occur at least once there. Apart from reducing the number of words modeled and hence reducing our computational and space requirements, this also has the advantage of allowing us to model/include as a feature many words that may appear in your email (such as "cs229") but that you won't find in a dictionary. Sometimes (as in the homework), we also exclude the very high frequency words (which will be words like "the," "of," "and"; these high frequency, "content free" words are called **stop words**) since they occur in so many documents and do little to indicate whether an email is spam or non-spam.

the Naive Bayes assumption is an extremely strong assumptions, the resulting algorithm works well on many problems.

Our model is parameterized by $\phi_{j|y=1} = p(x_j = 1|y = 1)$, $\phi_{j|y=0} = p(x_j = 1|y = 0)$, and $\phi_y = p(y = 1)$. As usual, given a training set $\{(x^{(i)}, y^{(i)}); i = 1, \ldots, n\}$, we can write down the joint likelihood of the data:

$$\mathcal{L}(\phi_y, \phi_{j|y=0}, \phi_{j|y=1}) = \prod_{i=1}^{n} p(x^{(i)}, y^{(i)}).$$

Maximizing this with respect to $\phi_y, \phi_{j|y=0}$ and $\phi_{j|y=1}$ gives the maximum likelihood estimates:

$$\begin{aligned}
\phi_{j|y=1} &= \frac{\sum_{i=1}^{n} 1\{x_j^{(i)} = 1 \wedge y^{(i)} = 1\}}{\sum_{i=1}^{n} 1\{y^{(i)} = 1\}} \\
\phi_{j|y=0} &= \frac{\sum_{i=1}^{n} 1\{x_j^{(i)} = 1 \wedge y^{(i)} = 0\}}{\sum_{i=1}^{n} 1\{y^{(i)} = 0\}} \\
\phi_y &= \frac{\sum_{i=1}^{n} 1\{y^{(i)} = 1\}}{n}
\end{aligned}$$

In the equations above, the "$\wedge$" symbol means "and." The parameters have a very natural interpretation. For instance, $\phi_{j|y=1}$ is just the fraction of the spam $(y = 1)$ emails in which word j does appear.

Having fit all these parameters, to make a prediction on a new example with features x, we then simply calculate

$$\begin{aligned}
p(y = 1|x) &= \frac{p(x|y = 1)p(y = 1)}{p(x)} \\
&= \frac{\left(\prod_{j=1}^{d} p(x_j|y = 1)\right) p(y = 1)}{\left(\prod_{j=1}^{d} p(x_j|y = 1)\right) p(y = 1) + \left(\prod_{j=1}^{d} p(x_j|y = 0)\right) p(y = 0)},
\end{aligned}$$

and pick whichever class has the higher posterior probability.

Lastly, we note that while we have developed the Naive Bayes algorithm mainly for the case of problems where the features x_j are binary-valued, the generalization to where x_j can take values in $\{1, 2, \ldots, k_j\}$ is straightforward. Here, we would simply model $p(x_j|y)$ as multinomial rather than as Bernoulli. Indeed, even if some original input attribute (say, the living area of a house, as in our earlier example) were continuous valued, it is quite common to **discretize** it—that is, turn it into a small set of discrete values—and apply Naive Bayes. For instance, if we use some feature x_j to represent living area, we might discretize the continuous values as follows:

Living area (sq. feet)	< 400	400-800	800-1200	1200-1600	>1600
x_i	1	2	3	4	5

Thus, for a house with living area 890 square feet, we would set the value of the corresponding feature x_j to 3. We can then apply the Naive Bayes algorithm, and model $p(x_j|y)$ with a multinomial distribution, as described previously. When the original, continuous-valued attributes are not well-modeled by a multivariate normal distribution, discretizing the features and using Naive Bayes (instead of GDA) will often result in a better classifier.

4.2.1 Laplace smoothing

The Naive Bayes algorithm as we have described it will work fairly well for many problems, but there is a simple change that makes it work much better, especially for text classification. Let's briefly discuss a problem with the algorithm in its current form, and then talk about how we can fix it.

Consider spam/email classification, and let's suppose that, we are in the year of 20xx, after completing CS229 and having done excellent work on the project, you decide around May 20xx to submit work you did to the NeurIPS conference for publication.[3] Because you end up discussing the conference in your emails, you also start getting messages with the word "neurips" in it. But this is your first NeurIPS paper, and until this time, you had not previously seen any emails containing the word "neurips"; in particular "neurips" did not ever appear in your training set of spam/non-spam emails. Assuming that "neurips" was the 35000th word in the dictionary, your Naive Bayes spam filter therefore had picked its maximum likelihood estimates of the parameters $\phi_{35000|y}$ to be

$$\begin{aligned}
\phi_{35000|y=1} &= \frac{\sum_{i=1}^n 1\{x_{35000}^{(i)} = 1 \wedge y^{(i)} = 1\}}{\sum_{i=1}^n 1\{y^{(i)} = 1\}} = 0 \\
\phi_{35000|y=0} &= \frac{\sum_{i=1}^n 1\{x_{35000}^{(i)} = 1 \wedge y^{(i)} = 0\}}{\sum_{i=1}^n 1\{y^{(i)} = 0\}} = 0
\end{aligned}$$

I.e., because it has never seen "neurips" before in either spam or non-spam training examples, it thinks the probability of seeing it in either type of email is zero. Hence, when trying to decide if one of these messages containing

[3]NeurIPS is one of the top machine learning conferences. The deadline for submitting a paper is typically in May-June.

"neurips" is spam, it calculates the class posterior probabilities, and obtains

$$\begin{aligned} p(y=1|x) &= \frac{\prod_{j=1}^{d} p(x_j|y=1)p(y=1)}{\prod_{j=1}^{d} p(x_j|y=1)p(y=1) + \prod_{j=1}^{d} p(x_j|y=0)p(y=0)} \\ &= \frac{0}{0}. \end{aligned}$$

This is because each of the terms "$\prod_{j=1}^{d} p(x_j|y)$" includes a term $p(x_{35000}|y) = 0$ that is multiplied into it. Hence, our algorithm obtains 0/0, and doesn't know how to make a prediction.

Stating the problem more broadly, it is statistically a bad idea to estimate the probability of some event to be zero just because you haven't seen it before in your finite training set. Take the problem of estimating the mean of a multinomial random variable z taking values in $\{1, \ldots, k\}$. We can parameterize our multinomial with $\phi_j = p(z = j)$. Given a set of n independent observations $\{z^{(1)}, \ldots, z^{(n)}\}$, the maximum likelihood estimates are given by

$$\phi_j = \frac{\sum_{i=1}^{n} 1\{z^{(i)} = j\}}{n}.$$

As we saw previously, if we were to use these maximum likelihood estimates, then some of the ϕ_j's might end up as zero, which was a problem. To avoid this, we can use **Laplace smoothing**, which replaces the above estimate with

$$\phi_j = \frac{1 + \sum_{i=1}^{n} 1\{z^{(i)} = j\}}{k + n}.$$

Here, we've added 1 to the numerator, and k to the denominator. Note that $\sum_{j=1}^{k} \phi_j = 1$ still holds (check this yourself!), which is a desirable property since the ϕ_j's are estimates for probabilities that we know must sum to 1. Also, $\phi_j \neq 0$ for all values of j, solving our problem of probabilities being estimated as zero. Under certain (arguably quite strong) conditions, it can be shown that the Laplace smoothing actually gives the optimal estimator of the ϕ_j's.

Returning to our Naive Bayes classifier, with Laplace smoothing, we therefore obtain the following estimates of the parameters:

$$\begin{aligned} \phi_{j|y=1} &= \frac{1 + \sum_{i=1}^{n} 1\{x_j^{(i)} = 1 \wedge y^{(i)} = 1\}}{2 + \sum_{i=1}^{n} 1\{y^{(i)} = 1\}} \\ \phi_{j|y=0} &= \frac{1 + \sum_{i=1}^{n} 1\{x_j^{(i)} = 1 \wedge y^{(i)} = 0\}}{2 + \sum_{i=1}^{n} 1\{y^{(i)} = 0\}} \end{aligned}$$

(In practice, it usually doesn't matter much whether we apply Laplace smoothing to ϕ_y or not, since we will typically have a fair fraction each of spam and non-spam messages, so ϕ_y will be a reasonable estimate of $p(y = 1)$ and will be quite far from 0 anyway.)

4.2.2 Event models for text classification

To close off our discussion of generative learning algorithms, let's talk about one more model that is specifically for text classification. While Naive Bayes as we've presented it will work well for many classification problems, for text classification, there is a related model that does even better.

In the specific context of text classification, Naive Bayes as presented uses the what's called the **Bernoulli event model** (or sometimes **multi-variate Bernoulli event model**). In this model, we assumed that the way an email is generated is that first it is randomly determined (according to the class priors $p(y)$) whether a spammer or non-spammer will send you your next message. Then, the person sending the email runs through the dictionary, deciding whether to include each word j in that email independently and according to the probabilities $p(x_j = 1|y) = \phi_{j|y}$. Thus, the probability of a message was given by $p(y)\prod_{j=1}^{d} p(x_j|y)$.

Here's a different model, called the **Multinomial event model**. To describe this model, we will use a different notation and set of features for representing emails. We let x_j denote the identity of the j-th word in the email. Thus, x_j is now an integer taking values in $\{1, \ldots, |V|\}$, where $|V|$ is the size of our vocabulary (dictionary). An email of d words is now represented by a vector $(x_1, x_2, \ldots, x_d)$ of length d; note that d can vary for different documents. For instance, if an email starts with "A NeurIPS . . . ," then $x_1 = 1$ ("a" is the first word in the dictionary), and $x_2 = 35000$ (if "neurips" is the 35000th word in the dictionary).

In the multinomial event model, we assume that the way an email is generated is via a random process in which spam/non-spam is first determined (according to $p(y)$) as before. Then, the sender of the email writes the email by first generating x_1 from some multinomial distribution over words ($p(x_1|y)$). Next, the second word x_2 is chosen independently of x_1 but from the same multinomial distribution, and similarly for x_3, x_4, and so on, until all d words of the email have been generated. Thus, the overall probability of a message is given by $p(y)\prod_{j=1}^{d} p(x_j|y)$. Note that this formula looks like the one we had earlier for the probability of a message under the Bernoulli event model, but that the terms in the formula now mean very different things. In particular $x_j|y$ is now a multinomial, rather than a Bernoulli distribution.

The parameters for our new model are $\phi_y = p(y)$ as before, $\phi_{k|y=1} = p(x_j = k|y = 1)$ (for any j) and $\phi_{k|y=0} = p(x_j = k|y = 0)$. Note that we have assumed that $p(x_j|y)$ is the same for all values of j (i.e., that the distribution according to which a word is generated does not depend on its position j within the email).

If we are given a training set $\{(x^{(i)}, y^{(i)}); i = 1, \ldots, n\}$ where $x^{(i)} = (x_1^{(i)}, x_2^{(i)}, \ldots, x_{d_i}^{(i)})$ (here, d_i is the number of words in the i-training example), the likelihood of the data is given by

$$\begin{aligned}\mathcal{L}(\phi_y, \phi_{k|y=0}, \phi_{k|y=1}) &= \prod_{i=1}^{n} p(x^{(i)}, y^{(i)}) \\ &= \prod_{i=1}^{n} \left(\prod_{j=1}^{d_i} p(x_j^{(i)}|y; \phi_{k|y=0}, \phi_{k|y=1}) \right) p(y^{(i)}; \phi_y).\end{aligned}$$

Maximizing this yields the maximum likelihood estimates of the parameters:

$$\begin{aligned}\phi_{k|y=1} &= \frac{\sum_{i=1}^{n} \sum_{j=1}^{d_i} 1\{x_j^{(i)} = k \wedge y^{(i)} = 1\}}{\sum_{i=1}^{n} 1\{y^{(i)} = 1\} d_i} \\ \phi_{k|y=0} &= \frac{\sum_{i=1}^{n} \sum_{j=1}^{d_i} 1\{x_j^{(i)} = k \wedge y^{(i)} = 0\}}{\sum_{i=1}^{n} 1\{y^{(i)} = 0\} d_i} \\ \phi_y &= \frac{\sum_{i=1}^{n} 1\{y^{(i)} = 1\}}{n}.\end{aligned}$$

If we were to apply Laplace smoothing (which is needed in practice for good performance) when estimating $\phi_{k|y=0}$ and $\phi_{k|y=1}$, we add 1 to the numerators and $|V|$ to the denominators, and obtain:

$$\begin{aligned}\phi_{k|y=1} &= \frac{1 + \sum_{i=1}^{n} \sum_{j=1}^{d_i} 1\{x_j^{(i)} = k \wedge y^{(i)} = 1\}}{|V| + \sum_{i=1}^{n} 1\{y^{(i)} = 1\} d_i} \\ \phi_{k|y=0} &= \frac{1 + \sum_{i=1}^{n} \sum_{j=1}^{d_i} 1\{x_j^{(i)} = k \wedge y^{(i)} = 0\}}{|V| + \sum_{i=1}^{n} 1\{y^{(i)} = 0\} d_i}.\end{aligned}$$

While not necessarily the very best classification algorithm, the Naive Bayes classifier often works surprisingly well. It is often also a very good "first thing to try," given its simplicity and ease of implementation.

Chapter 5

Kernel methods

5.1 Feature maps

Recall that in our discussion about linear regression, we considered the problem of predicting the price of a house (denoted by y) from the living area of the house (denoted by x), and we fit a linear function of x to the training data. What if the price y can be more accurately represented as a *non-linear* function of x? In this case, we need a more expressive family of models than linear models.

We start by considering fitting cubic functions $y = \theta_3 x^3 + \theta_2 x^2 + \theta_1 x + \theta_0$. It turns out that we can view the cubic function as a linear function over the a different set of feature variables (defined below). Concretely, let the function $\phi : \mathbb{R} \to \mathbb{R}^4$ be defined as

$$\phi(x) = \begin{bmatrix} 1 \\ x \\ x^2 \\ x^3 \end{bmatrix} \in \mathbb{R}^4. \tag{5.1}$$

Let $\theta \in \mathbb{R}^4$ be the vector containing $\theta_0, \theta_1, \theta_2, \theta_3$ as entries. Then we can rewrite the cubic function in x as:

$$\theta_3 x^3 + \theta_2 x^2 + \theta_1 x + \theta_0 = \theta^T \phi(x)$$

Thus, a cubic function of the variable x can be viewed as a linear function over the variables $\phi(x)$. To distinguish between these two sets of variables, in the context of kernel methods, we will call the "original" input value the input **attributes** of a problem (in this case, x, the living area). When the original input is mapped to some new set of quantities $\phi(x)$, we will call those new quantities the **features** variables. (Unfortunately, different authors use different terms to describe these two things in different contexts.) We will call ϕ a **feature map**, which maps the attributes to the features.

5.2 LMS (least mean squares) with features

We will derive the gradient descent algorithm for fitting the model $\theta^T\phi(x)$. First recall that for ordinary least square problem where we were to fit $\theta^T x$, the batch gradient descent update is (see the first lecture note for its derivation):

$$\begin{aligned}
\theta &:= \theta + \alpha \sum_{i=1}^{n} \left(y^{(i)} - h_\theta(x^{(i)})\right) x^{(i)} \\
&:= \theta + \alpha \sum_{i=1}^{n} \left(y^{(i)} - \theta^T x^{(i)}\right) x^{(i)}. \qquad (5.2)
\end{aligned}$$

Let $\phi : \mathbb{R}^d \to \mathbb{R}^p$ be a feature map that maps attribute x (in $\mathbb{R}^d$) to the features $\phi(x)$ in $\mathbb{R}^p$. (In the motivating example in the previous subsection, we have $d = 1$ and $p = 4$.) Now our goal is to fit the function $\theta^T\phi(x)$, with θ being a vector in $\mathbb{R}^p$ instead of $\mathbb{R}^d$. We can replace all the occurrences of $x^{(i)}$ in the algorithm above by $\phi(x^{(i)})$ to obtain the new update:

$$\theta := \theta + \alpha \sum_{i=1}^{n} \left(y^{(i)} - \theta^T\phi(x^{(i)})\right) \phi(x^{(i)}) \qquad (5.3)$$

Similarly, the corresponding stochastic gradient descent update rule is

$$\theta := \theta + \alpha \left(y^{(i)} - \theta^T\phi(x^{(i)})\right) \phi(x^{(i)}) \qquad (5.4)$$

5.3 LMS with the kernel trick

The gradient descent update, or stochastic gradient update above becomes computationally expensive when the features $\phi(x)$ is high-dimensional. For example, consider the direct extension of the feature map in equation (5.1) to high-dimensional input x: suppose $x \in \mathbb{R}^d$, and let $\phi(x)$ be the vector that contains all the monomials of x with degree ≤ 3

$$\phi(x) = \begin{bmatrix} 1 \\ x_1 \\ x_2 \\ \vdots \\ x_1^2 \\ x_1x_2 \\ x_1x_3 \\ \vdots \\ x_2x_1 \\ \vdots \\ x_1^3 \\ x_1^2x_2 \\ \vdots \end{bmatrix}. \tag{5.5}$$

The dimension of the features $\phi(x)$ is on the order of d^3.[1] This is a prohibitively long vector for computational purpose — when $d = 1000$, each update requires at least computing and storing a $1000^3 = 10^9$ dimensional vector, which is 10^6 times slower than the update rule for for ordinary least squares updates (5.2).

It may appear at first that such d^3 runtime per update and memory usage are inevitable, because the vector θ itself is of dimension $p \approx d^3$, and we may need to update every entry of θ and store it. However, we will introduce the kernel trick with which we will not need to store θ explicitly, and the runtime can be significantly improved.

For simplicity, we assume the initialize the value $\theta = 0$, and we focus on the iterative update (5.3). The main observation is that at any time, θ can be represented as a linear combination of the vectors $\phi(x^{(1)}), \ldots, \phi(x^{(n)})$. Indeed, we can show this inductively as follows. At initialization, $\theta = 0 = \sum_{i=1}^n 0 \cdot \phi(x^{(i)})$. Assume at some point, θ can be represented as

$$\theta = \sum_{i=1}^n \beta_i \phi(x^{(i)}) \tag{5.6}$$

[1] Here, for simplicity, we include all the monomials with repetitions (so that, e.g., $x_1x_2x_3$ and $x_2x_3x_1$ both appear in $\phi(x)$). Therefore, there are totally $1 + d + d^2 + d^3$ entries in $\phi(x)$.

for some $\beta_1, \ldots, \beta_n \in \mathbb{R}$. Then we claim that in the next round, θ is still a linear combination of $\phi(x^{(1)}), \ldots, \phi(x^{(n)})$ because

$$\begin{aligned}
\theta &:= \theta + \alpha \sum_{i=1}^{n} \left(y^{(i)} - \theta^T \phi(x^{(i)})\right) \phi(x^{(i)}) \\
&= \sum_{i=1}^{n} \beta_i \phi(x^{(i)}) + \alpha \sum_{i=1}^{n} \left(y^{(i)} - \theta^T \phi(x^{(i)})\right) \phi(x^{(i)}) \\
&= \sum_{i=1}^{n} \underbrace{\left(\beta_i + \alpha \left(y^{(i)} - \theta^T \phi(x^{(i)})\right)\right)}_{\text{new } \beta_i} \phi(x^{(i)}) \qquad (5.7)
\end{aligned}$$

You may realize that our general strategy is to implicitly represent the p-dimensional vector θ by a set of coefficients $\beta_1, \ldots, \beta_n$. Towards doing this, we derive the update rule of the coefficients $\beta_1, \ldots, \beta_n$. Using the equation above, we see that the new β_i depends on the old one via

$$\beta_i := \beta_i + \alpha \left(y^{(i)} - \theta^T \phi(x^{(i)})\right) \tag{5.8}$$

Here we still have the old θ on the RHS of the equation. Replacing θ by $\theta = \sum_{j=1}^{n} \beta_j \phi(x^{(j)})$ gives

$$\forall i \in \{1, \ldots, n\}, \beta_i := \beta_i + \alpha \left(y^{(i)} - \sum_{j=1}^{n} \beta_j \phi(x^{(j)})^T \phi(x^{(i)})\right)$$

We often rewrite $\phi(x^{(j)})^T \phi(x^{(i)})$ as $\langle \phi(x^{(j)}), \phi(x^{(i)}) \rangle$ to emphasize that it's the inner product of the two feature vectors. Viewing β_i's as the new representation of θ, we have successfully translated the batch gradient descent algorithm into an algorithm that updates the value of β iteratively. It may appear that at every iteration, we still need to compute the values of $\langle \phi(x^{(j)}), \phi(x^{(i)}) \rangle$ for all pairs of i, j, each of which may take roughly $O(p)$ operation. However, two important properties come to rescue:

1. We can pre-compute the pairwise inner products $\langle \phi(x^{(j)}), \phi(x^{(i)}) \rangle$ for all pairs of i, j before the loop starts.

2. For the feature map ϕ defined in (5.5) (or many other interesting feature maps), computing $\langle \phi(x^{(j)}), \phi(x^{(i)}) \rangle$ can be efficient and does not

necessarily require computing $\phi(x^{(i)})$ explicitly. This is because:

$$\begin{aligned}
\langle\phi(x),\phi(z)\rangle &= 1+\sum_{i=1}^{d} x_i z_i + \sum_{i,j\in\{1,\ldots,d\}} x_i x_j z_i z_j + \sum_{i,j,k\in\{1,\ldots,d\}} x_i x_j x_k z_i z_j z_k \\
&= 1+\sum_{i=1}^{d} x_i z_i + \left(\sum_{i=1}^{d} x_i z_i\right)^2 + \left(\sum_{i=1}^{d} x_i z_i\right)^3 \\
&= 1+\langle x,z\rangle+\langle x,z\rangle^2+\langle x,z\rangle^3
\end{aligned} \tag{5.9}$$

Therefore, to compute $\langle\phi(x),\phi(z)\rangle$, we can first compute $\langle x,z\rangle$ with $O(d)$ time and then take another constant number of operations to compute $1+\langle x,z\rangle+\langle x,z\rangle^2+\langle x,z\rangle^3$.

As you will see, the inner products between the features $\langle\phi(x),\phi(z)\rangle$ are essential here. We define the **Kernel** corresponding to the feature map ϕ as a function that maps $\mathcal{X}\times\mathcal{X}\to\mathbb{R}$ satisfying: [2]

$$K(x,z)\triangleq\langle\phi(x),\phi(z)\rangle \tag{5.10}$$

To wrap up the discussion, we write the down the final algorithm as follows:

---

1. Compute all the values $K(x^{(i)},x^{(j)})\triangleq\langle\phi(x^{(i)}),\phi(x^{(j)})\rangle$ using equation (5.9) for all $i,j\in\{1,\ldots,n\}$. Set $\beta:=0$.

2. **Loop:**

$$\forall i\in\{1,\ldots,n\},\beta_i:=\beta_i+\alpha\left(y^{(i)}-\sum_{j=1}^{n}\beta_j K(x^{(i)},x^{(j)})\right) \tag{5.11}$$

Or in vector notation, letting K be the $n\times n$ matrix with $K_{ij}=K(x^{(i)},x^{(j)})$, we have

$$\beta:=\beta+\alpha(\vec{y}-K\beta)$$

With the algorithm above, we can update the representation β of the vector θ efficiently with $O(n)$ time per update. Finally, we need to show that

[2]Recall that $\mathcal{X}$ is the space of the input x. In our running example, $\mathcal{X}=\mathbb{R}^d$

the knowledge of the representation β suffices to compute the prediction $\theta^T\phi(x)$. Indeed, we have

$$\theta^T\phi(x) = \sum_{i=1}^{n} \beta_i \phi(x^{(i)})^T \phi(x) = \sum_{i=1}^{n} \beta_i K(x^{(i)}, x) \tag{5.12}$$

You may realize that fundamentally all we need to know about the feature map $\phi(\cdot)$ is encapsulated in the corresponding kernel function $K(\cdot,\cdot)$. We will expand on this in the next section.

5.4 Properties of kernels

In the last subsection, we started with an explicitly defined feature map ϕ, which induces the kernel function $K(x, z) \triangleq \langle\phi(x), \phi(z)\rangle$. Then we saw that the kernel function is so intrinsic so that as long as the kernel function is defined, the whole training algorithm can be written entirely in the language of the kernel without referring to the feature map ϕ, so can the prediction of a test example x (equation (5.12).)

Therefore, it would be tempted to define other kernel function $K(\cdot,\cdot)$ and run the algorithm (5.11). Note that the algorithm (5.11) does not need to explicitly access the feature map ϕ, and therefore we only need to ensure the existence of the feature map ϕ, but do not necessarily need to be able to explicitly write ϕ down.

What kinds of functions $K(\cdot,\cdot)$ can correspond to some feature map ϕ? In other words, can we tell if there is some feature mapping ϕ so that $K(x, z) = \phi(x)^T\phi(z)$ for all x, z?

If we can answer this question by giving a precise characterization of valid kernel functions, then we can completely change the interface of selecting feature maps ϕ to the interface of selecting kernel function K. Concretely, we can pick a function K, verify that it satisfies the characterization (so that there exists a feature map ϕ that K corresponds to), and then we can run update rule (5.11). The benefit here is that we don't have to be able to compute ϕ or write it down analytically, and we only need to know its existence. We will answer this question at the end of this subsection after we go through several concrete examples of kernels.

Suppose $x, z \in \mathbb{R}^d$, and let's first consider the function $K(\cdot,\cdot)$ defined as:

$$K(x, z) = (x^T z)^2.$$

We can also write this as

$$\begin{aligned} K(x,z) &= \left(\sum_{i=1}^{d} x_i z_i\right)\left(\sum_{j=1}^{d} x_j z_j\right) \\ &= \sum_{i=1}^{d}\sum_{j=1}^{d} x_i x_j z_i z_j \\ &= \sum_{i,j=1}^{d} (x_i x_j)(z_i z_j) \end{aligned}$$

Thus, we see that $K(x,z) = \langle\phi(x), \phi(z)\rangle$ is the kernel function that corresponds to the the feature mapping ϕ given (shown here for the case of $d = 3$) by

$$\phi(x) = \begin{bmatrix} x_1x_1 \\ x_1x_2 \\ x_1x_3 \\ x_2x_1 \\ x_2x_2 \\ x_2x_3 \\ x_3x_1 \\ x_3x_2 \\ x_3x_3 \end{bmatrix}.$$

Revisiting the computational efficiency perspective of kernel, note that whereas calculating the high-dimensional $\phi(x)$ requires $O(d^2)$ time, finding $K(x,z)$ takes only $O(d)$ time—linear in the dimension of the input attributes.

For another related example, also consider $K(\cdot,\cdot)$ defined by

$$\begin{aligned} K(x,z) &= (x^T z + c)^2 \\ &= \sum_{i,j=1}^{d} (x_i x_j)(z_i z_j) + \sum_{i=1}^{d} (\sqrt{2c}x_i)(\sqrt{2c}z_i) + c^2. \end{aligned}$$

(Check this yourself.) This function K is a kernel function that corresponds to the feature mapping (again shown for $d = 3$)

$$\phi(x) = \begin{bmatrix} x_1x_1 \\ x_1x_2 \\ x_1x_3 \\ x_2x_1 \\ x_2x_2 \\ x_2x_3 \\ x_3x_1 \\ x_3x_2 \\ x_3x_3 \\ \sqrt{2c}x_1 \\ \sqrt{2c}x_2 \\ \sqrt{2c}x_3 \\ c \end{bmatrix},$$

and the parameter c controls the relative weighting between the x_i (first order) and the x_ix_j (second order) terms.

More broadly, the kernel $K(x, z) = (x^Tz + c)^k$ corresponds to a feature mapping to an $\binom{d+k}{k}$ feature space, corresponding of all monomials of the form $x_{i_1}x_{i_2} \ldots x_{i_k}$ that are up to order k. However, despite working in this $O(d^k)$-dimensional space, computing $K(x, z)$ still takes only $O(d)$ time, and hence we never need to explicitly represent feature vectors in this very high dimensional feature space.

Kernels as similarity metrics. Now, let's talk about a slightly different view of kernels. Intuitively, (and there are things wrong with this intuition, but nevermind), if $\phi(x)$ and $\phi(z)$ are close together, then we might expect $K(x, z) = \phi(x)^T\phi(z)$ to be large. Conversely, if $\phi(x)$ and $\phi(z)$ are far apart—say nearly orthogonal to each other—then $K(x, z) = \phi(x)^T\phi(z)$ will be small. So, we can think of $K(x, z)$ as some measurement of how similar are $\phi(x)$ and $\phi(z)$, or of how similar are x and z.

Given this intuition, suppose that for some learning problem that you're working on, you've come up with some function $K(x, z)$ that you think might be a reasonable measure of how similar x and z are. For instance, perhaps you chose

$$K(x, z) = \exp\left(-\frac{||x - z||^2}{2\sigma^2}\right).$$

This is a reasonable measure of x and z's similarity, and is close to 1 when x and z are close, and near 0 when x and z are far apart. Does there exist a feature map ϕ such that the kernel K defined above satisfies $K(x,z) = \phi(x)^T\phi(z)$? In this particular example, the answer is yes. This kernel is called the **Gaussian kernel**, and corresponds to an infinite dimensional feature mapping ϕ. We will give a precise characterization about what properties a function K needs to satisfy so that it can be a valid kernel function that corresponds to some feature map ϕ.

Necessary conditions for valid kernels. Suppose for now that K is indeed a valid kernel corresponding to some feature mapping ϕ, and we will first see what properties it satisfies. Now, consider some finite set of n points (not necessarily the training set) $\{x^{(1)}, \dots, x^{(n)}\}$, and let a square, n-by-n matrix K be defined so that its (i,j)-entry is given by $K_{ij} = K(x^{(i)}, x^{(j)})$. This matrix is called the **kernel matrix**. Note that we've overloaded the notation and used K to denote both the kernel function $K(x,z)$ and the kernel matrix K, due to their obvious close relationship.

Now, if K is a valid kernel, then $K_{ij} = K(x^{(i)}, x^{(j)}) = \phi(x^{(i)})^T\phi(x^{(j)}) = \phi(x^{(j)})^T\phi(x^{(i)}) = K(x^{(j)}, x^{(i)}) = K_{ji}$, and hence K must be symmetric. Moreover, letting $\phi_k(x)$ denote the k-th coordinate of the vector $\phi(x)$, we find that for any vector z, we have

$$\begin{aligned}
z^T K z &= \sum_i \sum_j z_i K_{ij} z_j \\
&= \sum_i \sum_j z_i \phi(x^{(i)})^T \phi(x^{(j)}) z_j \\
&= \sum_i \sum_j z_i \sum_k \phi_k(x^{(i)}) \phi_k(x^{(j)}) z_j \\
&= \sum_k \sum_i \sum_j z_i \phi_k(x^{(i)}) \phi_k(x^{(j)}) z_j \\
&= \sum_k \left(\sum_i z_i \phi_k(x^{(i)}) \right)^2 \\
&\geq 0.
\end{aligned}$$

The second-to-last step uses the fact that $\sum_{i,j} a_i a_j = (\sum_i a_i)^2$ for $a_i = z_i\phi_k(x^{(i)})$. Since z was arbitrary, this shows that K is positive semi-definite ($K \geq 0$).

Hence, we've shown that if K is a valid kernel (i.e., if it corresponds to some feature mapping ϕ), then the corresponding kernel matrix $K \in \mathbb{R}^{n \times n}$ is symmetric positive semidefinite.

Sufficient conditions for valid kernels. More generally, the condition above turns out to be not only a necessary, but also a sufficient, condition for K to be a valid kernel (also called a Mercer kernel). The following result is due to Mercer.[3]

Theorem (Mercer). Let $K : \mathbb{R}^d \times \mathbb{R}^d \mapsto \mathbb{R}$ be given. Then for K to be a valid (Mercer) kernel, it is necessary and sufficient that for any $\{x^{(1)}, \dots, x^{(n)}\}$, $(n < \infty)$, the corresponding kernel matrix is symmetric positive semi-definite.

Given a function K, apart from trying to find a feature mapping ϕ that corresponds to it, this theorem therefore gives another way of testing if it is a valid kernel. You'll also have a chance to play with these ideas more in problem set 2.

In class, we also briefly talked about a couple of other examples of kernels. For instance, consider the digit recognition problem, in which given an image (16x16 pixels) of a handwritten digit (0-9), we have to figure out which digit it was. Using either a simple polynomial kernel $K(x, z) = (x^T z)^k$ or the Gaussian kernel, SVMs were able to obtain extremely good performance on this problem. This was particularly surprising since the input attributes x were just 256-dimensional vectors of the image pixel intensity values, and the system had no prior knowledge about vision, or even about which pixels are adjacent to which other ones. Another example that we briefly talked about in lecture was that if the objects x that we are trying to classify are strings (say, x is a list of amino acids, which strung together form a protein), then it seems hard to construct a reasonable, "small" set of features for most learning algorithms, especially if different strings have different lengths. However, consider letting $\phi(x)$ be a feature vector that counts the number of occurrences of each length-k substring in x. If we're considering strings of English letters, then there are 26^k such strings. Hence, $\phi(x)$ is a 26^k dimensional vector; even for moderate values of k, this is probably too big for us to efficiently work with. (e.g., $26^4 \approx 460000$.) However, using (dynamic programming-ish) string matching algorithms, it is possible to efficiently compute $K(x, z) = \phi(x)^T \phi(z)$, so that we can now implicitly work in this 26^k-dimensional feature space, but without ever explicitly computing feature vectors in this space.

[3]Many texts present Mercer's theorem in a slightly more complicated form involving L^2 functions, but when the input attributes take values in $\mathbb{R}^d$, the version given here is equivalent.

Application of kernel methods: We've seen the application of kernels to linear regression. In the next part, we will introduce the support vector machines to which kernels can be directly applied. dwell too much longer on it here. In fact, the idea of kernels has significantly broader applicability than linear regression and SVMs. Specifically, if you have any learning algorithm that you can write in terms of only inner products $\langle x, z\rangle$ between input attribute vectors, then by replacing this with $K(x, z)$ where K is a kernel, you can "magically" allow your algorithm to work efficiently in the high dimensional feature space corresponding to K. For instance, this kernel trick can be applied with the perceptron to derive a kernel perceptron algorithm. Many of the algorithms that we'll see later in this class will also be amenable to this method, which has come to be known as the "kernel trick."

Chapter 6

Support vector machines

This set of notes presents the Support Vector Machine (SVM) learning algorithm. SVMs are among the best (and many believe are indeed the best) "off-the-shelf" supervised learning algorithms. To tell the SVM story, we'll need to first talk about margins and the idea of separating data with a large "gap." Next, we'll talk about the optimal margin classifier, which will lead us into a digression on Lagrange duality. We'll also see kernels, which give a way to apply SVMs efficiently in very high dimensional (such as infinite-dimensional) feature spaces, and finally, we'll close off the story with the SMO algorithm, which gives an efficient implementation of SVMs.

6.1 Margins: intuition

We'll start our story on SVMs by talking about margins. This section will give the intuitions about margins and about the "confidence" of our predictions; these ideas will be made formal in Section 6.3.

Consider logistic regression, where the probability $p(y = 1|x; \theta)$ is modeled by $h_\theta(x) = g(\theta^T x)$. We then predict "1" on an input x if and only if $h_\theta(x) \geq 0.5$, or equivalently, if and only if $\theta^T x \geq 0$. Consider a positive training example ($y = 1$). The larger $\theta^T x$ is, the larger also is $h_\theta(x) = p(y = 1|x; \theta)$, and thus also the higher our degree of "confidence" that the label is 1. Thus, informally we can think of our prediction as being very confident that $y = 1$ if $\theta^T x \gg 0$. Similarly, we think of logistic regression as confidently predicting $y = 0$, if $\theta^T x \ll 0$. Given a training set, again informally it seems that we'd have found a good fit to the training data if we can find θ so that $\theta^T x^{(i)} \gg 0$ whenever $y^{(i)} = 1$, and $\theta^T x^{(i)} \ll 0$ whenever $y^{(i)} = 0$, since this would reflect a very confident (and correct) set of classifications for all the training examples. This seems to be a nice goal to aim for, and we'll soon formalize this idea using the notion of functional margins.

For a different type of intuition, consider the following figure, in which x's represent positive training examples, o's denote negative training examples, a decision boundary (this is the line given by the equation $\theta^T x = 0$, and is also called the **separating hyperplane**) is also shown, and three points have also been labeled A, B and C.

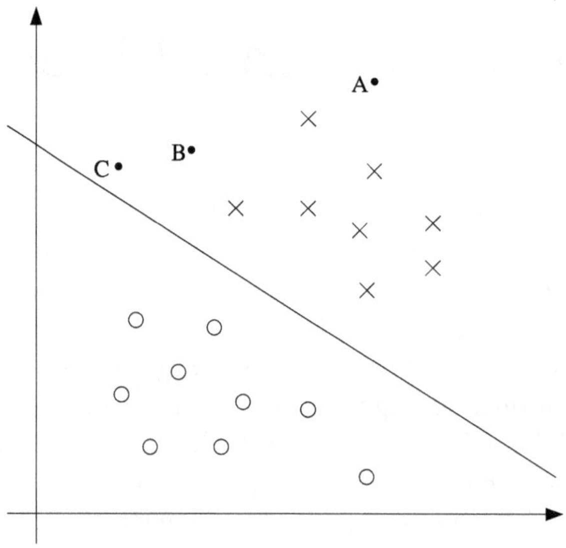

Notice that the point A is very far from the decision boundary. If we are asked to make a prediction for the value of y at A, it seems we should be quite confident that $y = 1$ there. Conversely, the point C is very close to the decision boundary, and while it's on the side of the decision boundary on which we would predict $y = 1$, it seems likely that just a small change to the decision boundary could easily have caused out prediction to be $y = 0$. Hence, we're much more confident about our prediction at A than at C. The point B lies in-between these two cases, and more broadly, we see that if a point is far from the separating hyperplane, then we may be significantly more confident in our predictions. Again, informally we think it would be nice if, given a training set, we manage to find a decision boundary that allows us to make all correct and confident (meaning far from the decision boundary) predictions on the training examples. We'll formalize this later using the notion of geometric margins.

6.2 Notation (option reading)

To make our discussion of SVMs easier, we'll first need to introduce a new notation for talking about classification. We will be considering a linear classifier for a binary classification problem with labels y and features x. From now, we'll use $y \in \{-1, 1\}$ (instead of $\{0, 1\}$) to denote the class labels. Also, rather than parameterizing our linear classifier with the vector θ, we will use parameters w, b, and write our classifier as

$$h_{w,b}(x) = g(w^T x + b).$$

Here, $g(z) = 1$ if $z \geq 0$, and $g(z) = -1$ otherwise. This "w, b" notation allows us to explicitly treat the intercept term b separately from the other parameters. (We also drop the convention we had previously of letting $x_0 = 1$ be an extra coordinate in the input feature vector.) Thus, b takes the role of what was previously θ_0, and w takes the role of $[\theta_1 \dots \theta_d]^T$.

Note also that, from our definition of g above, our classifier will directly predict either 1 or -1 (cf. the perceptron algorithm), without first going through the intermediate step of estimating $p(y = 1)$ (which is what logistic regression does).

6.3 Functional and geometric margins (option reading)

Let's formalize the notions of the functional and geometric margins. Given a training example $(x^{(i)}, y^{(i)})$, we define the **functional margin** of (w, b) with respect to the training example as

$$\hat{\gamma}^{(i)} = y^{(i)}(w^T x^{(i)} + b).$$

Note that if $y^{(i)} = 1$, then for the functional margin to be large (i.e., for our prediction to be confident and correct), we need $w^T x^{(i)} + b$ to be a large positive number. Conversely, if $y^{(i)} = -1$, then for the functional margin to be large, we need $w^T x^{(i)} + b$ to be a large negative number. Moreover, if $y^{(i)}(w^T x^{(i)} + b) > 0$, then our prediction on this example is correct. (Check this yourself.) Hence, a large functional margin represents a confident and a correct prediction.

For a linear classifier with the choice of g given above (taking values in $\{-1, 1\}$), there's one property of the functional margin that makes it not a very good measure of confidence, however. Given our choice of g, we note that if we replace w with $2w$ and b with $2b$, then since $g(w^Tx+b) = g(2w^Tx+2b)$, this would not change $h_{w,b}(x)$ at all. I.e., g, and hence also $h_{w,b}(x)$, depends only on the sign, but not on the magnitude, of w^Tx+b. However, replacing (w, b) with $(2w, 2b)$ also results in multiplying our functional margin by a factor of 2. Thus, it seems that by exploiting our freedom to scale w and b, we can make the functional margin arbitrarily large without really changing anything meaningful. Intuitively, it might therefore make sense to impose some sort of normalization condition such as that $||w||_2 = 1$; i.e., we might replace (w, b) with $(w/||w||_2, b/||w||_2)$, and instead consider the functional margin of $(w/||w||_2, b/||w||_2)$. We'll come back to this later.

Given a training set $S = \{(x^{(i)}, y^{(i)}); i = 1, \ldots, n\}$, we also define the function margin of (w, b) with respect to S as the smallest of the functional margins of the individual training examples. Denoted by $\hat{\gamma}$, this can therefore be written:

$$\hat{\gamma} = \min_{i=1,\ldots,n} \hat{\gamma}^{(i)}.$$

Next, let's talk about **geometric margins**. Consider the picture below:

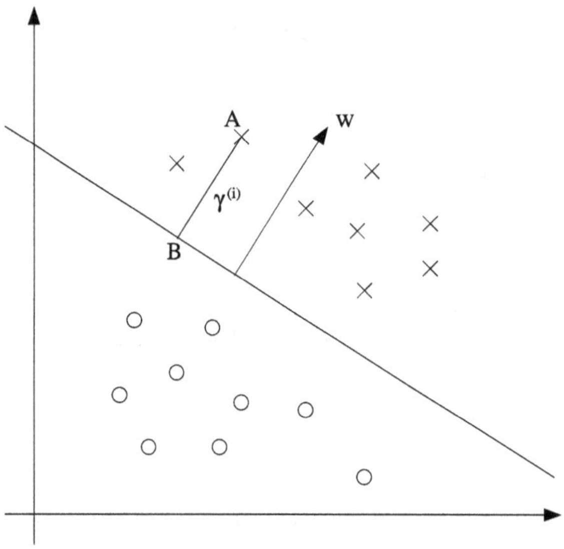

The decision boundary corresponding to (w, b) is shown, along with the vector w. Note that w is orthogonal (at 90°) to the separating hyperplane. (You should convince yourself that this must be the case.) Consider the point at A, which represents the input $x^{(i)}$ of some training example with label $y^{(i)} = 1$. Its distance to the decision boundary, $\gamma^{(i)}$, is given by the line segment AB.

How can we find the value of $\gamma^{(i)}$? Well, $w/||w||$ is a unit-length vector pointing in the same direction as w. Since A represents $x^{(i)}$, we therefore find that the point B is given by $x^{(i)} - \gamma^{(i)} \cdot w/||w||$. But this point lies on the decision boundary, and all points x on the decision boundary satisfy the equation $w^T x + b = 0$. Hence,

$$w^T \left(x^{(i)} - \gamma^{(i)} \frac{w}{||w||} \right) + b = 0.$$

Solving for $\gamma^{(i)}$ yields

$$\gamma^{(i)} = \frac{w^T x^{(i)} + b}{||w||} = \left(\frac{w}{||w||} \right)^T x^{(i)} + \frac{b}{||w||}.$$

This was worked out for the case of a positive training example at A in the figure, where being on the "positive" side of the decision boundary is good. More generally, we define the geometric margin of (w, b) with respect to a training example $(x^{(i)}, y^{(i)})$ to be

$$\gamma^{(i)} = y^{(i)} \left(\left(\frac{w}{||w||} \right)^T x^{(i)} + \frac{b}{||w||} \right).$$

Note that if $||w|| = 1$, then the functional margin equals the geometric margin—this thus gives us a way of relating these two different notions of margin. Also, the geometric margin is invariant to rescaling of the parameters; i.e., if we replace w with $2w$ and b with $2b$, then the geometric margin does not change. This will in fact come in handy later. Specifically, because of this invariance to the scaling of the parameters, when trying to fit w and b to training data, we can impose an arbitrary scaling constraint on w without changing anything important; for instance, we can demand that $||w|| = 1$, or $|w_1| = 5$, or $|w_1 + b| + |w_2| = 2$, and any of these can be satisfied simply by rescaling w and b.

Finally, given a training set $S = \{(x^{(i)}, y^{(i)}); i = 1, \ldots, n\}$, we also define the geometric margin of (w, b) with respect to S to be the smallest of the geometric margins on the individual training examples:

$$\gamma = \min_{i=1,\ldots,n} \gamma^{(i)}.$$

6.4 The optimal margin classifier (option reading)

Given a training set, it seems from our previous discussion that a natural desideratum is to try to find a decision boundary that maximizes the (geometric) margin, since this would reflect a very confident set of predictions on the training set and a good "fit" to the training data. Specifically, this will result in a classifier that separates the positive and the negative training examples with a "gap" (geometric margin).

For now, we will assume that we are given a training set that is linearly separable; i.e., that it is possible to separate the positive and negative examples using some separating hyperplane. How will we find the one that achieves the maximum geometric margin? We can pose the following optimization problem:

$$\begin{aligned} \max_{\gamma,w,b} \quad & \gamma \\ \text{s.t.} \quad & y^{(i)}(w^T x^{(i)} + b) \geq \gamma, \quad i = 1, \ldots, n \\ & ||w|| = 1. \end{aligned}$$

I.e., we want to maximize γ, subject to each training example having functional margin at least γ. The $||w|| = 1$ constraint moreover ensures that the functional margin equals to the geometric margin, so we are also guaranteed that all the geometric margins are at least γ. Thus, solving this problem will result in (w, b) with the largest possible geometric margin with respect to the training set.

If we could solve the optimization problem above, we'd be done. But the "$||w|| = 1$" constraint is a nasty (non-convex) one, and this problem certainly isn't in any format that we can plug into standard optimization software to solve. So, let's try transforming the problem into a nicer one. Consider:

$$\begin{aligned} \max_{\hat{\gamma},w,b} \quad & \frac{\hat{\gamma}}{||w||} \\ \text{s.t.} \quad & y^{(i)}(w^T x^{(i)} + b) \geq \hat{\gamma}, \quad i = 1, \ldots, n \end{aligned}$$

Here, we're going to maximize $\hat{\gamma}/||w||$, subject to the functional margins all being at least $\hat{\gamma}$. Since the geometric and functional margins are related by $\gamma = \hat{\gamma}/||w|$, this will give us the answer we want. Moreover, we've gotten rid of the constraint $||w|| = 1$ that we didn't like. The downside is that we now have a nasty (again, non-convex) objective $\frac{\hat{\gamma}}{||w||}$ function; and, we still don't have any off-the-shelf software that can solve this form of an optimization problem.

Let's keep going. Recall our earlier discussion that we can add an arbitrary scaling constraint on w and b without changing anything. This is the key idea we'll use now. We will introduce the scaling constraint that the functional margin of w, b with respect to the training set must be 1:

$$\hat{\gamma} = 1.$$

Since multiplying w and b by some constant results in the functional margin being multiplied by that same constant, this is indeed a scaling constraint, and can be satisfied by rescaling w, b. Plugging this into our problem above, and noting that maximizing $\hat{\gamma}/||w|| = 1/||w||$ is the same thing as minimizing $||w||^2$, we now have the following optimization problem:

$$\begin{aligned} \min_{w,b} \quad & \frac{1}{2}||w||^2 \\ \text{s.t.} \quad & y^{(i)}(w^T x^{(i)} + b) \geq 1, \quad i = 1, \ldots, n \end{aligned}$$

We've now transformed the problem into a form that can be efficiently solved. The above is an optimization problem with a convex quadratic objective and only linear constraints. Its solution gives us the **optimal margin classifier**. This optimization problem can be solved using commercial quadratic programming (QP) code.[1]

While we could call the problem solved here, what we will instead do is make a digression to talk about Lagrange duality. This will lead us to our optimization problem's dual form, which will play a key role in allowing us to use kernels to get optimal margin classifiers to work efficiently in very high dimensional spaces. The dual form will also allow us to derive an efficient algorithm for solving the above optimization problem that will typically do much better than generic QP software.

6.5 Lagrange duality (optional reading)

Let's temporarily put aside SVMs and maximum margin classifiers, and talk about solving constrained optimization problems.

Consider a problem of the following form:

$$\begin{aligned} \min_{w} \quad & f(w) \\ \text{s.t.} \quad & h_i(w) = 0, \quad i = 1, \ldots, l. \end{aligned}$$

Some of you may recall how the method of Lagrange multipliers can be used to solve it. (Don't worry if you haven't seen it before.) In this method, we define the **Lagrangian** to be

$$\mathcal{L}(w, \beta) = f(w) + \sum_{i=1}^{l} \beta_i h_i(w)$$

[1]You may be familiar with linear programming, which solves optimization problems that have linear objectives and linear constraints. QP software is also widely available, which allows convex quadratic objectives and linear constraints.

Here, the β_i's are called the **Lagrange multipliers**. We would then find and set $\mathcal{L}$'s partial derivatives to zero:

$$\frac{\partial \mathcal{L}}{\partial w_i} = 0; \quad \frac{\partial \mathcal{L}}{\partial \beta_i} = 0,$$

and solve for w and β.

In this section, we will generalize this to constrained optimization problems in which we may have inequality as well as equality constraints. Due to time constraints, we won't really be able to do the theory of Lagrange duality justice in this class,[2] but we will give the main ideas and results, which we will then apply to our optimal margin classifier's optimization problem.

Consider the following, which we'll call the **primal** optimization problem:

$$\begin{aligned} \min_w \quad & f(w) \\ \text{s.t.} \quad & g_i(w) \leq 0, \quad i = 1, \ldots, k \\ & h_i(w) = 0, \quad i = 1, \ldots, l. \end{aligned}$$

To solve it, we start by defining the **generalized Lagrangian**

$$\mathcal{L}(w, \alpha, \beta) = f(w) + \sum_{i=1}^{k} \alpha_i g_i(w) + \sum_{i=1}^{l} \beta_i h_i(w).$$

Here, the α_i's and β_i's are the Lagrange multipliers. Consider the quantity

$$\theta_{\mathcal{P}}(w) = \max_{\alpha, \beta \,:\, \alpha_i \geq 0} \mathcal{L}(w, \alpha, \beta).$$

Here, the "$\mathcal{P}$" subscript stands for "primal." Let some w be given. If w violates any of the primal constraints (i.e., if either $g_i(w) > 0$ or $h_i(w) \neq 0$ for some i), then you should be able to verify that

$$\begin{aligned} \theta_{\mathcal{P}}(w) &= \max_{\alpha, \beta \,:\, \alpha_i \geq 0} f(w) + \sum_{i=1}^{k} \alpha_i g_i(w) + \sum_{i=1}^{l} \beta_i h_i(w) && (6.1) \\ &= \infty. && (6.2) \end{aligned}$$

Conversely, if the constraints are indeed satisfied for a particular value of w, then $\theta_{\mathcal{P}}(w) = f(w)$. Hence,

$$\theta_{\mathcal{P}}(w) = \begin{cases} f(w) & \text{if } w \text{ satisfies primal constraints} \\ \infty & \text{otherwise.} \end{cases}$$

---

[2]Readers interested in learning more about this topic are encouraged to read, e.g., R. T. Rockarfeller (1970), Convex Analysis, Princeton University Press.

Thus, $\theta_{\mathcal{P}}$ takes the same value as the objective in our problem for all values of w that satisfies the primal constraints, and is positive infinity if the constraints are violated. Hence, if we consider the minimization problem

$$\min_w \theta_{\mathcal{P}}(w) = \min_w \max_{\alpha,\beta\,:\,\alpha_i\geq 0} \mathcal{L}(w,\alpha,\beta),$$

we see that it is the same problem (i.e., and has the same solutions as) our original, primal problem. For later use, we also define the optimal value of the objective to be $p^* = \min_w \theta_{\mathcal{P}}(w)$; we call this the **value** of the primal problem.

Now, let's look at a slightly different problem. We define

$$\theta_{\mathcal{D}}(\alpha,\beta) = \min_w \mathcal{L}(w,\alpha,\beta).$$

Here, the "$\mathcal{D}$" subscript stands for "dual." Note also that whereas in the definition of $\theta_{\mathcal{P}}$ we were optimizing (maximizing) with respect to α, β, here we are minimizing with respect to w.

We can now pose the **dual** optimization problem:

$$\max_{\alpha,\beta\,:\,\alpha_i\geq 0} \theta_{\mathcal{D}}(\alpha,\beta) = \max_{\alpha,\beta\,:\,\alpha_i\geq 0} \min_w \mathcal{L}(w,\alpha,\beta).$$

This is exactly the same as our primal problem shown above, except that the order of the "max" and the "min" are now exchanged. We also define the optimal value of the dual problem's objective to be $d^* = \max_{\alpha,\beta\,:\,\alpha_i\geq 0} \theta_{\mathcal{D}}(w)$.

How are the primal and the dual problems related? It can easily be shown that

$$d^* = \max_{\alpha,\beta\,:\,\alpha_i\geq 0} \min_w \mathcal{L}(w,\alpha,\beta) \leq \min_w \max_{\alpha,\beta\,:\,\alpha_i\geq 0} \mathcal{L}(w,\alpha,\beta) = p^*.$$

(You should convince yourself of this; this follows from the "max min" of a function always being less than or equal to the "min max.") However, under certain conditions, we will have

$$d^* = p^*,$$

so that we can solve the dual problem in lieu of the primal problem. Let's see what these conditions are.

Suppose f and the g_i's are convex,[3] and the h_i's are affine.[4] Suppose further that the constraints g_i are (strictly) feasible; this means that there exists some w so that $g_i(w) < 0$ for all i.

---

[3]When f has a Hessian, then it is convex if and only if the Hessian is positive semi-definite. For instance, $f(w) = w^T w$ is convex; similarly, all linear (and affine) functions are also convex. (A function f can also be convex without being differentiable, but we won't need those more general definitions of convexity here.)

[4]I.e., there exists a_i, b_i, so that $h_i(w) = a_i^T w + b_i$. "Affine" means the same thing as linear, except that we also allow the extra intercept term b_i.

Under our above assumptions, there must exist w^*, α^*, β^* so that w^* is the solution to the primal problem, α^*, β^* are the solution to the dual problem, and moreover $p^* = d^* = \mathcal{L}(w^*, \alpha^*, \beta^*)$. Moreover, w^*, α^* and β^* satisfy the **Karush-Kuhn-Tucker (KKT) conditions**, which are as follows:

$$\begin{aligned}
\frac{\partial}{\partial w_i}\mathcal{L}(w^*, \alpha^*, \beta^*) &= 0, \;\; i = 1, \ldots, d & (6.3)\\
\frac{\partial}{\partial \beta_i}\mathcal{L}(w^*, \alpha^*, \beta^*) &= 0, \;\; i = 1, \ldots, l & (6.4)\\
\alpha_i^* g_i(w^*) &= 0, \;\; i = 1, \ldots, k & (6.5)\\
g_i(w^*) &\leq 0, \;\; i = 1, \ldots, k & (6.6)\\
\alpha^* &\geq 0, \;\; i = 1, \ldots, k & (6.7)
\end{aligned}$$

Moreover, if some w^*, α^*, β^* satisfy the KKT conditions, then it is also a solution to the primal and dual problems.

We draw attention to Equation (6.5), which is called the KKT **dual complementarity** condition. Specifically, it implies that if $\alpha_i^* > 0$, then $g_i(w^*) = 0$. (I.e., the "$g_i(w) \leq 0$" constraint is **active**, meaning it holds with equality rather than with inequality.) Later on, this will be key for showing that the SVM has only a small number of "support vectors"; the KKT dual complementarity condition will also give us our convergence test when we talk about the SMO algorithm.

6.6 Optimal margin classifiers: the dual form (option reading)

Note: *The equivalence of optimization problem* (6.8) *and the optimization problem* (6.12)*, and the relationship between the primary and dual variables in equation* (6.10) *are the most important take home messages of this section.*

Previously, we posed the following (primal) optimization problem for finding the optimal margin classifier:

$$\begin{aligned}
\min_{w,b} \;\; & \frac{1}{2}||w||^2 & (6.8)\\
\text{s.t.} \;\; & y^{(i)}(w^T x^{(i)} + b) \geq 1, \;\; i = 1, \ldots, n
\end{aligned}$$

We can write the constraints as

$$g_i(w) = -y^{(i)}(w^T x^{(i)} + b) + 1 \leq 0.$$

We have one such constraint for each training example. Note that from the KKT dual complementarity condition, we will have $\alpha_i > 0$ only for the training examples that have functional margin exactly equal to one (i.e., the ones corresponding to constraints that hold with equality, $g_i(w) = 0$). Consider the figure below, in which a maximum margin separating hyperplane is shown by the solid line.

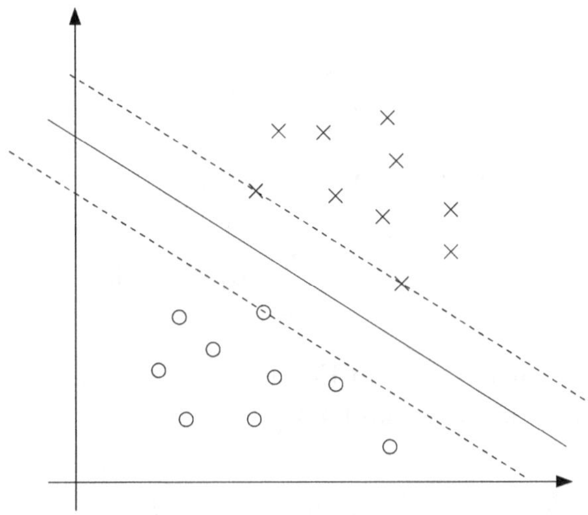

The points with the smallest margins are exactly the ones closest to the decision boundary; here, these are the three points (one negative and two positive examples) that lie on the dashed lines parallel to the decision boundary. Thus, only three of the α_i's—namely, the ones corresponding to these three training examples—will be non-zero at the optimal solution to our optimization problem. These three points are called the **support vectors** in this problem. The fact that the number of support vectors can be much smaller than the size the training set will be useful later.

Let's move on. Looking ahead, as we develop the dual form of the problem, one key idea to watch out for is that we'll try to write our algorithm in terms of only the inner product $\langle x^{(i)}, x^{(j)} \rangle$ (think of this as $(x^{(i)})^T x^{(j)}$) between points in the input feature space. The fact that we can express our algorithm in terms of these inner products will be key when we apply the kernel trick.

When we construct the Lagrangian for our optimization problem we have:

$$\mathcal{L}(w, b, \alpha) = \frac{1}{2}||w||^2 - \sum_{i=1}^{n} \alpha_i \left[y^{(i)}(w^T x^{(i)} + b) - 1 \right]. \tag{6.9}$$

Note that there're only "α_i" but no "β_i" Lagrange multipliers, since the problem has only inequality constraints.

Let's find the dual form of the problem. To do so, we need to first minimize $\mathcal{L}(w, b, \alpha)$ with respect to w and b (for fixed α), to get $\theta_{\mathcal{D}}$, which we'll do by setting the derivatives of $\mathcal{L}$ with respect to w and b to zero. We have:

$$\nabla_w \mathcal{L}(w, b, \alpha) = w - \sum_{i=1}^{n} \alpha_i y^{(i)} x^{(i)} = 0$$

This implies that

$$w = \sum_{i=1}^{n} \alpha_i y^{(i)} x^{(i)}. \tag{6.10}$$

As for the derivative with respect to b, we obtain

$$\frac{\partial}{\partial b} \mathcal{L}(w, b, \alpha) = \sum_{i=1}^{n} \alpha_i y^{(i)} = 0. \tag{6.11}$$

If we take the definition of w in Equation (6.10) and plug that back into the Lagrangian (Equation 6.9), and simplify, we get

$$\mathcal{L}(w, b, \alpha) = \sum_{i=1}^{n} \alpha_i - \frac{1}{2} \sum_{i,j=1}^{n} y^{(i)} y^{(j)} \alpha_i \alpha_j (x^{(i)})^T x^{(j)} - b \sum_{i=1}^{n} \alpha_i y^{(i)}.$$

But from Equation (6.11), the last term must be zero, so we obtain

$$\mathcal{L}(w, b, \alpha) = \sum_{i=1}^{n} \alpha_i - \frac{1}{2} \sum_{i,j=1}^{n} y^{(i)} y^{(j)} \alpha_i \alpha_j (x^{(i)})^T x^{(j)}.$$

Recall that we got to the equation above by minimizing $\mathcal{L}$ with respect to w and b. Putting this together with the constraints $\alpha_i \geq 0$ (that we always had) and the constraint (6.11), we obtain the following dual optimization problem:

$$\begin{aligned} \max_\alpha \quad & W(\alpha) = \sum_{i=1}^{n} \alpha_i - \frac{1}{2} \sum_{i,j=1}^{n} y^{(i)} y^{(j)} \alpha_i \alpha_j \langle x^{(i)}, x^{(j)} \rangle. \qquad (6.12) \\ \text{s.t.} \quad & \alpha_i \geq 0, \quad i = 1, \ldots, n \\ & \sum_{i=1}^{n} \alpha_i y^{(i)} = 0, \end{aligned}$$

You should also be able to verify that the conditions required for $p^* = d^*$ and the KKT conditions (Equations 6.3–6.7) to hold are indeed satisfied in our optimization problem. Hence, we can solve the dual in lieu of solving the primal problem. Specifically, in the dual problem above, we have a maximization problem in which the parameters are the α_i's. We'll talk later about the specific algorithm that we're going to use to solve the dual problem, but if we are indeed able to solve it (i.e., find the α's that maximize $W(\alpha)$ subject to the constraints), then we can use Equation (6.10) to go back and find the optimal w's as a function of the α's. Having found w^*, by considering the primal problem, it is also straightforward to find the optimal value for the intercept term b as

$$b^* = -\frac{\max_{i:y^{(i)}=-1} w^{*T}x^{(i)} + \min_{i:y^{(i)}=1} w^{*T}x^{(i)}}{2}. \tag{6.13}$$

(Check for yourself that this is correct.)

Before moving on, let's also take a more careful look at Equation (6.10), which gives the optimal value of w in terms of (the optimal value of) α. Suppose we've fit our model's parameters to a training set, and now wish to make a prediction at a new point input x. We would then calculate $w^Tx + b$, and predict $y = 1$ if and only if this quantity is bigger than zero. But using (6.10), this quantity can also be written:

$$\begin{aligned} w^Tx + b &= \left(\sum_{i=1}^{n} \alpha_i y^{(i)} x^{(i)}\right)^T x + b & (6.14)\\ &= \sum_{i=1}^{n} \alpha_i y^{(i)} \langle x^{(i)}, x\rangle + b. & (6.15)\end{aligned}$$

Hence, if we've found the α_i's, in order to make a prediction, we have to calculate a quantity that depends only on the inner product between x and the points in the training set. Moreover, we saw earlier that the α_i's will all be zero except for the support vectors. Thus, many of the terms in the sum above will be zero, and we really need to find only the inner products between x and the support vectors (of which there is often only a small number) in order calculate (6.15) and make our prediction.

By examining the dual form of the optimization problem, we gained significant insight into the structure of the problem, and were also able to write the entire algorithm in terms of only inner products between input feature vectors. In the next section, we will exploit this property to apply the kernels to our classification problem. The resulting algorithm, **support vector machines**, will be able to efficiently learn in very high dimensional spaces.

6.7 Regularization and the non-separable case (optional reading)

The derivation of the SVM as presented so far assumed that the data is linearly separable. While mapping data to a high dimensional feature space via ϕ does generally increase the likelihood that the data is separable, we can't guarantee that it always will be so. Also, in some cases it is not clear that finding a separating hyperplane is exactly what we'd want to do, since that might be susceptible to outliers. For instance, the left figure below shows an optimal margin classifier, and when a single outlier is added in the upper-left region (right figure), it causes the decision boundary to make a dramatic swing, and the resulting classifier has a much smaller margin.

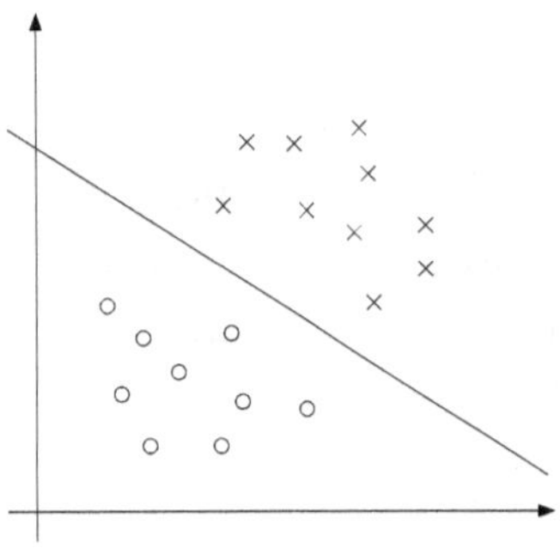

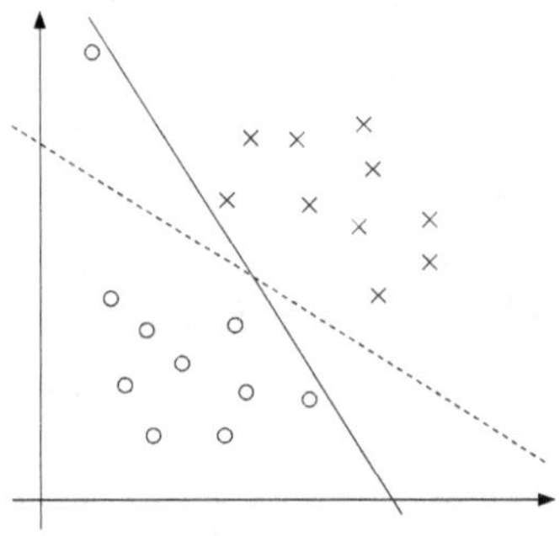

To make the algorithm work for non-linearly separable datasets as well as be less sensitive to outliers, we reformulate our optimization (using ℓ_1 **regularization**) as follows:

$$\begin{aligned} \min_{\gamma,w,b} \quad & \frac{1}{2}||w||^2 + C\sum_{i=1}^{n} \xi_i \\ \text{s.t.} \quad & y^{(i)}(w^T x^{(i)} + b) \geq 1 - \xi_i, \quad i = 1, \ldots, n \\ & \xi_i \geq 0, \quad i = 1, \ldots, n. \end{aligned}$$

Thus, examples are now permitted to have (functional) margin less than 1, and if an example has functional margin $1 - \xi_i$ (with $\xi > 0$), we would pay a cost of the objective function being increased by $C\xi_i$. The parameter C controls the relative weighting between the twin goals of making the $||w||^2$ small (which we saw earlier makes the margin large) and of ensuring that most examples have functional margin at least 1.

As before, we can form the Lagrangian:

$$\mathcal{L}(w,b,\xi,\alpha,r) = \frac{1}{2}w^Tw + C\sum_{i=1}^n \xi_i - \sum_{i=1}^n \alpha_i \left[y^{(i)}(x^Tw+b) - 1 + \xi_i\right] - \sum_{i=1}^n r_i\xi_i.$$

Here, the α_i's and r_i's are our Lagrange multipliers (constrained to be ≥ 0). We won't go through the derivation of the dual again in detail, but after setting the derivatives with respect to w and b to zero as before, substituting them back in, and simplifying, we obtain the following dual form of the problem:

$$\begin{aligned} \max_\alpha \quad & W(\alpha) = \sum_{i=1}^n \alpha_i - \frac{1}{2}\sum_{i,j=1}^n y^{(i)}y^{(j)}\alpha_i\alpha_j\langle x^{(i)}, x^{(j)}\rangle \\ \text{s.t.} \quad & 0 \leq \alpha_i \leq C, \;\; i = 1,\ldots,n \\ & \sum_{i=1}^n \alpha_i y^{(i)} = 0, \end{aligned}$$

As before, we also have that w can be expressed in terms of the α_i's as given in Equation (6.10), so that after solving the dual problem, we can continue to use Equation (6.15) to make our predictions. Note that, somewhat surprisingly, in adding ℓ_1 regularization, the only change to the dual problem is that what was originally a constraint that $0 \leq \alpha_i$ has now become $0 \leq \alpha_i \leq C$. The calculation for b^* also has to be modified (Equation 6.13 is no longer valid); see the comments in the next section/Platt's paper.

Also, the KKT dual-complementarity conditions (which in the next section will be useful for testing for the convergence of the SMO algorithm) are:

$$\alpha_i = 0 \;\Rightarrow\; y^{(i)}(w^Tx^{(i)} + b) \geq 1 \tag{6.16}$$
$$\alpha_i = C \;\Rightarrow\; y^{(i)}(w^Tx^{(i)} + b) \leq 1 \tag{6.17}$$
$$0 < \alpha_i < C \;\Rightarrow\; y^{(i)}(w^Tx^{(i)} + b) = 1. \tag{6.18}$$

Now, all that remains is to give an algorithm for actually solving the dual problem, which we will do in the next section.

6.8 The SMO algorithm (optional reading)

The SMO (sequential minimal optimization) algorithm, due to John Platt, gives an efficient way of solving the dual problem arising from the derivation of the SVM. Partly to motivate the SMO algorithm, and partly because it's interesting in its own right, let's first take another digression to talk about the coordinate ascent algorithm.

6.8.1 Coordinate ascent

Consider trying to solve the unconstrained optimization problem

$$\max_{\alpha} W(\alpha_1, \alpha_2, \ldots, \alpha_n).$$

Here, we think of W as just some function of the parameters α_i's, and for now ignore any relationship between this problem and SVMs. We've already seen two optimization algorithms, gradient ascent and Newton's method. The new algorithm we're going to consider here is called **coordinate ascent**:

Loop until convergence: {

For $i = 1, \ldots, n$, {

$\alpha_i := \arg\max_{\hat{\alpha}_i} W(\alpha_1, \ldots, \alpha_{i-1}, \hat{\alpha}_i, \alpha_{i+1}, \ldots, \alpha_n).$

}

}

Thus, in the innermost loop of this algorithm, we will hold all the variables except for some α_i fixed, and reoptimize W with respect to just the parameter α_i. In the version of this method presented here, the inner-loop reoptimizes the variables in order $\alpha_1, \alpha_2, \ldots, \alpha_n, \alpha_1, \alpha_2, \ldots$. (A more sophisticated version might choose other orderings; for instance, we may choose the next variable to update according to which one we expect to allow us to make the largest increase in $W(\alpha)$.)

When the function W happens to be of such a form that the "arg max" in the inner loop can be performed efficiently, then coordinate ascent can be a fairly efficient algorithm. Here's a picture of coordinate ascent in action:

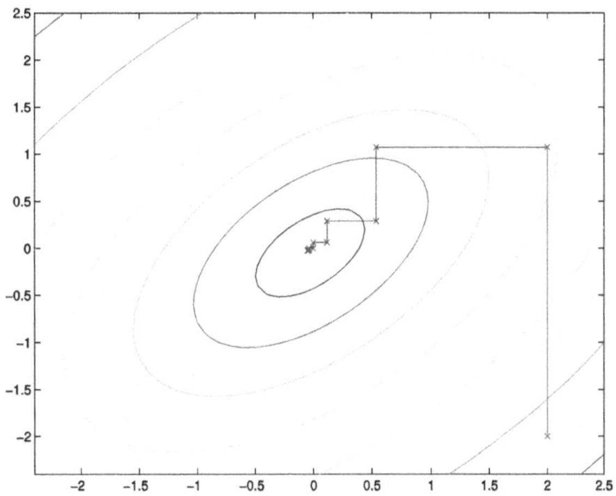

The ellipses in the figure are the contours of a quadratic function that we want to optimize. Coordinate ascent was initialized at $(2, -2)$, and also plotted in the figure is the path that it took on its way to the global maximum. Notice that on each step, coordinate ascent takes a step that's parallel to one of the axes, since only one variable is being optimized at a time.

6.8.2 SMO

We close off the discussion of SVMs by sketching the derivation of the SMO algorithm.

Here's the (dual) optimization problem that we want to solve:

$$\begin{aligned} \max_\alpha \quad & W(\alpha) = \sum_{i=1}^n \alpha_i - \frac{1}{2}\sum_{i,j=1}^n y^{(i)}y^{(j)}\alpha_i\alpha_j\langle x^{(i)}, x^{(j)}\rangle. && (6.19)\\ \text{s.t.} \quad & 0 \le \alpha_i \le C, \;\; i = 1, \dots, n && (6.20)\\ & \sum_{i=1}^n \alpha_i y^{(i)} = 0. && (6.21) \end{aligned}$$

Let's say we have set of α_i's that satisfy the constraints (6.20-6.21). Now, suppose we want to hold $\alpha_2, \dots, \alpha_n$ fixed, and take a coordinate ascent step and reoptimize the objective with respect to α_1. Can we make any progress? The answer is no, because the constraint (6.21) ensures that

$$\alpha_1 y^{(1)} = -\sum_{i=2}^n \alpha_i y^{(i)}.$$

Or, by multiplying both sides by $y^{(1)}$, we equivalently have

$$\alpha_1 = -y^{(1)} \sum_{i=2}^{n} \alpha_i y^{(i)}.$$

(This step used the fact that $y^{(1)} \in \{-1, 1\}$, and hence $(y^{(1)})^2 = 1$.) Hence, α_1 is exactly determined by the other α_i's, and if we were to hold $\alpha_2, \ldots, \alpha_n$ fixed, then we can't make any change to α_1 without violating the constraint (6.21) in the optimization problem.

Thus, if we want to update some subject of the α_i's, we must update at least two of them simultaneously in order to keep satisfying the constraints. This motivates the SMO algorithm, which simply does the following:

Repeat till convergence {

1. Select some pair α_i and α_j to update next (using a heuristic that tries to pick the two that will allow us to make the biggest progress towards the global maximum).
2. Reoptimize $W(\alpha)$ with respect to α_i and α_j, while holding all the other α_k's $(k \neq i, j)$ fixed.

}

To test for convergence of this algorithm, we can check whether the KKT conditions (Equations 6.16-6.18) are satisfied to within some *tol*. Here, *tol* is the convergence tolerance parameter, and is typically set to around 0.01 to 0.001. (See the paper and pseudocode for details.)

The key reason that SMO is an efficient algorithm is that the update to α_i, α_j can be computed very efficiently. Let's now briefly sketch the main ideas for deriving the efficient update.

Let's say we currently have some setting of the α_i's that satisfy the constraints (6.20-6.21), and suppose we've decided to hold $\alpha_3, \ldots, \alpha_n$ fixed, and want to reoptimize $W(\alpha_1, \alpha_2, \ldots, \alpha_n)$ with respect to α_1 and α_2 (subject to the constraints). From (6.21), we require that

$$\alpha_1 y^{(1)} + \alpha_2 y^{(2)} = -\sum_{i=3}^{n} \alpha_i y^{(i)}.$$

Since the right hand side is fixed (as we've fixed $\alpha_3, \ldots \alpha_n$), we can just let it be denoted by some constant ζ:

$$\alpha_1 y^{(1)} + \alpha_2 y^{(2)} = \zeta. \tag{6.22}$$

We can thus picture the constraints on α_1 and α_2 as follows:

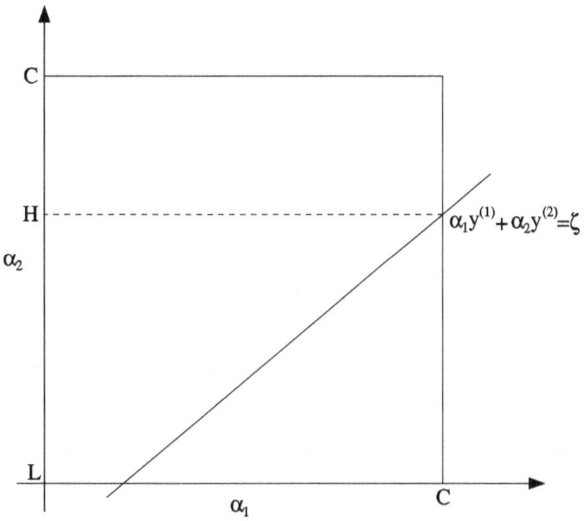

From the constraints (6.20), we know that α_1 and α_2 must lie within the box $[0, C] \times [0, C]$ shown. Also plotted is the line $\alpha_1 y^{(1)} + \alpha_2 y^{(2)} = \zeta$, on which we know α_1 and α_2 must lie. Note also that, from these constraints, we know $L \leq \alpha_2 \leq H$; otherwise, (α_1, α_2) can't simultaneously satisfy both the box and the straight line constraint. In this example, $L = 0$. But depending on what the line $\alpha_1 y^{(1)} + \alpha_2 y^{(2)} = \zeta$ looks like, this won't always necessarily be the case; but more generally, there will be some lower-bound L and some upper-bound H on the permissible values for α_2 that will ensure that α_1, α_2 lie within the box $[0, C] \times [0, C]$.

Using Equation (6.22), we can also write α_1 as a function of α_2:

$$\alpha_1 = (\zeta - \alpha_2 y^{(2)}) y^{(1)}.$$

(Check this derivation yourself; we again used the fact that $y^{(1)} \in \{-1, 1\}$ so that $(y^{(1)})^2 = 1$.) Hence, the objective $W(\alpha)$ can be written

$$W(\alpha_1, \alpha_2, \ldots, \alpha_n) = W((\zeta - \alpha_2 y^{(2)}) y^{(1)}, \alpha_2, \ldots, \alpha_n).$$

Treating $\alpha_3, \ldots, \alpha_n$ as constants, you should be able to verify that this is just some quadratic function in α_2. I.e., this can also be expressed in the form $a\alpha_2^2 + b\alpha_2 + c$ for some appropriate a, b, and c. If we ignore the "box" constraints (6.20) (or, equivalently, that $L \leq \alpha_2 \leq H$), then we can easily maximize this quadratic function by setting its derivative to zero and solving. We'll let $\alpha_2^{new,unclipped}$ denote the resulting value of α_2. You should also be able to convince yourself that if we had instead wanted to maximize W with respect to α_2 but subject to the box constraint, then we can find the resulting value optimal simply by taking $\alpha_2^{new,unclipped}$ and "clipping" it to lie in the

$[L, H]$ interval, to get

$$\alpha_2^{new} = \begin{cases} H & \text{if } \alpha_2^{new,unclipped} > H \\ \alpha_2^{new,unclipped} & \text{if } L \leq \alpha_2^{new,unclipped} \leq H \\ L & \text{if } \alpha_2^{new,unclipped} < L \end{cases}$$

Finally, having found the α_2^{new}, we can use Equation (6.22) to go back and find the optimal value of α_1^{new}.

There're a couple more details that are quite easy but that we'll leave you to read about yourself in Platt's paper: One is the choice of the heuristics used to select the next α_i, α_j to update; the other is how to update b as the SMO algorithm is run.

Part II

Deep learning

Chapter 7

Deep learning

We now begin our study of deep learning. In this set of notes, we give an overview of neural networks, discuss vectorization and discuss training neural networks with backpropagation.

7.1 Supervised learning with non-linear models

In the supervised learning setting (predicting y from the input x), suppose our model/hypothesis is $h_\theta(x)$. In the past lectures, we have considered the cases when $h_\theta(x) = \theta^\top x$ (in linear regression) or $h_\theta(x) = \theta^\top \phi(x)$ (where $\phi(x)$ is the feature map). A commonality of these two models is that they are linear in the parameters θ. Next we will consider learning general family of models that are **non-linear in both** the parameters θ and the inputs x. The most common non-linear models are neural networks, which we will define staring from the next section. For this section, it suffices to think $h_\theta(x)$ as an abstract non-linear model.[1]

Suppose $\{(x^{(i)}, y^{(i)})\}_{i=1}^n$ are the training examples. We will define the nonlinear model and the loss/cost function for learning it.

Regression problems. For simplicity, we start with the case where the output is a real number, that is, $y^{(i)} \in \mathbb{R}$, and thus the model h_θ also outputs a real number $h_\theta(x) \in \mathbb{R}$. We define the least square cost function for the

[1]If a concrete example is helpful, perhaps think about the model $h_\theta(x) = \theta_1^2 x_1^2 + \theta_2^2 x_2^2 + \cdots + \theta_d^2 x_d^2$ in this subsection, even though it's not a neural network.

i-th example $(x^{(i)}, y^{(i)})$ as

$$J^{(i)}(\theta) = \frac{1}{2}(h_\theta(x^{(i)}) - y^{(i)})^2\,, \tag{7.1}$$

and define the mean-square cost function for the dataset as

$$J(\theta) = \frac{1}{n}\sum_{i=1}^{n} J^{(i)}(\theta)\,, \tag{7.2}$$

which is same as in linear regression except that we introduce a constant $1/n$ in front of the cost function to be consistent with the convention. Note that multiplying the cost function with a scalar will not change the local minima or global minima of the cost function. Also note that the underlying parameterization for $h_\theta(x)$ is different from the case of linear regression, even though the form of the cost function is the same mean-squared loss. Throughout the notes, we use the words "loss" and "cost" interchangeably.

Binary classification. Next we define the model and loss function for binary classification. Suppose the inputs $x \in \mathbb{R}^d$. Let $\bar{h}_\theta : \mathbb{R}^d \to \mathbb{R}$ be a parameterized model (the analog of $\theta^\top x$ in logistic linear regression). We call the output $\bar{h}_\theta(x) \in \mathbb{R}$ the logit. Analogous to Section 2.1, we use the logistic function $g(\cdot)$ to turn the logit $\bar{h}_\theta(x)$ to a probability $h_\theta(x) \in [0, 1]$:

$$h_\theta(x) = g(\bar{h}_\theta(x)) = 1/(1 + \exp(-\bar{h}_\theta(x))\,. \tag{7.3}$$

We model the conditional distribution of y given x and θ by

$$\begin{aligned} P(y = 1 \mid x; \theta) &= h_\theta(x) \\ P(y = 0 \mid x; \theta) &= 1 - h_\theta(x) \end{aligned}$$

Following the same derivation in Section 2.1 and using the derivation in Remark 2.1.1, the negative likelihood loss function is equal to:

$$J^{(i)}(\theta) = -\log p(y^{(i)} \mid x^{(i)}; \theta) = \ell_{\text{logistic}}(\bar{h}_\theta(x^{(i)}), y^{(i)}) \tag{7.4}$$

As done in equation (7.2), the total loss function is also defined as the average of the loss function over individual training examples, $J(\theta) = \frac{1}{n}\sum_{i=1}^{n} J^{(i)}(\theta)$.

Multi-class classification. Following Section 2.3, we consider a classification problem where the response variable y can take on any one of k values, i.e. $y \in \{1, 2, \ldots, k\}$. Let $\bar{h}_\theta : \mathbb{R}^d \to \mathbb{R}^k$ be a parameterized model. We call the outputs $\bar{h}_\theta(x) \in \mathbb{R}^k$ the logits. Each logit corresponds to the prediction for one of the k classes. Analogous to Section 2.3, we use the softmax function to turn the logits $\bar{h}_\theta(x)$ into a probability vector with non-negative entries that sum up to 1:

$$P(y = j \mid x; \theta) = \frac{\exp(\bar{h}_\theta(x)_j)}{\sum_{s=1}^{k} \exp(\bar{h}_\theta(x)_s)}, \tag{7.5}$$

where $\bar{h}_\theta(x)_s$ denotes the s-th coordinate of $\bar{h}_\theta(x)$.

Similarly to Section 2.3, the loss function for a single training example $(x^{(i)}, y^{(i)})$ is its negative log-likelihood:

$$J^{(i)}(\theta) = -\log p(y^{(i)} \mid x^{(i)}; \theta) = -\log \left(\frac{\exp(\bar{h}_\theta(x^{(i)})_{y^{(i)}})}{\sum_{s=1}^{k} \exp(\bar{h}_\theta(x^{(i)})_s)} \right). \tag{7.6}$$

Using the notations of Section 2.3, we can simply write in an abstract way:

$$J^{(i)}(\theta) = \ell_{\text{ce}}(\bar{h}_\theta(x^{(i)}), y^{(i)}). \tag{7.7}$$

The loss function is also defined as the average of the loss function of individual training examples, $J(\theta) = \frac{1}{n} \sum_{i=1}^{n} J^{(i)}(\theta)$.

We also note that the approach above can also be generated to any conditional probabilistic model where we have an exponential distribution for y, Exponential-family$(y; \eta)$, where $\eta = \bar{h}_\theta(x)$ is a parameterized nonlinear function of x. However, the most widely used situations are the three cases discussed above.

Optimizers (SGD). Commonly, people use gradient descent (GD), stochastic gradient (SGD), or their variants to optimize the loss function $J(\theta)$. GD's update rule can be written as[2]

$$\theta := \theta - \alpha \nabla_\theta J(\theta) \tag{7.8}$$

where $\alpha > 0$ is often referred to as the learning rate or step size. Next, we introduce a version of the SGD (Algorithm 1), which is lightly different from that in the first lecture notes.

[2]Recall that, as defined in the previous lecture notes, we use the notation "$a := b$" to denote an operation (in a computer program) in which we *set* the value of a variable a to be equal to the value of b. In other words, this operation overwrites a with the value of b. In contrast, we will write "$a = b$" when we are asserting a statement of fact, that the value of a is equal to the value of b.

Algorithm 1 Stochastic Gradient Descent

Hyperparameter: learning rate α, number of total iteration n_{iter}.
Initialize θ randomly.
for $i = 1$ to n_{iter} **do**
    Sample j uniformly from $\{1, \ldots, n\}$, and update θ by

$$\theta := \theta - \alpha \nabla_\theta J^{(j)}(\theta) \tag{7.9}$$

Oftentimes computing the gradient of B examples simultaneously for the parameter θ can be faster than computing B gradients separately due to hardware parallelization. Therefore, a mini-batch version of SGD is most commonly used in deep learning, as shown in Algorithm 2. There are also other variants of the SGD or mini-batch SGD with slightly different sampling schemes.

Algorithm 2 Mini-batch Stochastic Gradient Descent

Hyperparameters: learning rate α, batch size B, # iterations n_{iter}.
Initialize θ randomly
for $i = 1$ to n_{iter} **do**
    Sample B examples $j_1, \ldots, j_B$ (without replacement) uniformly from $\{1, \ldots, n\}$, and update θ by

$$\theta := \theta - \frac{\alpha}{B} \sum_{k=1}^{B} \nabla_\theta J^{(j_k)}(\theta) \tag{7.10}$$

With these generic algorithms, a typical deep learning model is learned with the following steps. 1. Define a neural network parametrization $h_\theta(x)$, which we will introduce in Section 7.2, and 2. write the backpropagation algorithm to compute the gradient of the loss function $J^{(j)}(\theta)$ efficiently, which will be covered in Section 7.4, and 3. run SGD or mini-batch SGD (or other gradient-based optimizers) with the loss function $J(\theta)$.

7.2 Neural networks

Neural networks refer to a broad type of non-linear models/parametrizations $\bar{h}_\theta(x)$ that involve combinations of matrix multiplications and other entry-wise non-linear operations. To have a unified treatment for regression problem and classification problem, here we consider $\bar{h}_\theta(x)$ as the output of the neural network. For regression problem, the final prediction $h_\theta(x) = \bar{h}_\theta(x)$, and for classification problem, $\bar{h}_\theta(x)$ is the logits and the predicted probability will be $h_\theta(x) = 1/(1+\exp(-\bar{h}_\theta(x))$ (see equation 7.3) for binary classification or $h_\theta(x) = \text{softmax}(\bar{h}_\theta(x))$ for multi-class classification (see equation 7.5).

We will start small and slowly build up a neural network, step by step.

A Neural Network with a Single Neuron. Recall the housing price prediction problem from before: given the size of the house, we want to predict the price. We will use it as a running example in this subsection.

Previously, we fit a straight line to the graph of size vs. housing price. Now, instead of fitting a straight line, we wish to prevent negative housing prices by setting the absolute minimum price as zero. This produces a "kink" in the graph as shown in Figure 7.1. How do we represent such a function with a single kink as $\bar{h}_\theta(x)$ with unknown parameter? (After doing so, we can invoke the machinery in Section 7.1.)

We define a parameterized function $\bar{h}_\theta(x)$ with input x, parameterized by θ, which outputs the price of the house y. Formally, $\bar{h}_\theta : x \to y$. Perhaps one of the simplest parametrization would be

$$\bar{h}_\theta(x) = \max(wx + b, 0), \text{ where } \theta = (w, b) \in \mathbb{R}^2 \tag{7.11}$$

Here $\bar{h}_\theta(x)$ returns a single value: $(wx+b)$ or zero, whichever is greater. In the context of neural networks, the function $\max\{t, 0\}$ is called a ReLU (pronounced "ray-lu"), or rectified linear unit, and often denoted by $\text{ReLU}(t) \triangleq \max\{t, 0\}$.

Generally, a one-dimensional non-linear function that maps $\mathbb{R}$ to $\mathbb{R}$ such as ReLU is often referred to as an **activation function**. The model $\bar{h}_\theta(x)$ is said to have a single neuron partly because it has a single non-linear activation function. (We will discuss more about why a non-linear activation is called neuron.)

When the input $x \in \mathbb{R}^d$ has multiple dimensions, a neural network with a single neuron can be written as

$$\bar{h}_\theta(x) = \text{ReLU}(w^\top x + b), \text{ where } w \in \mathbb{R}^d,\ b \in \mathbb{R}, \text{ and } \theta = (w, b) \tag{7.12}$$

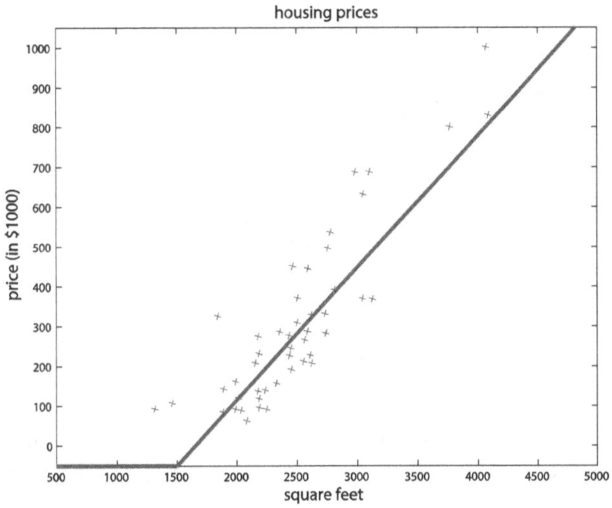

Figure 7.1: Housing prices with a "kink" in the graph.

The term b is often referred to as the "bias", and the vector w is referred to as the weight vector. Such a neural network has 1 layer. (We will define what multiple layers mean in the sequel.)

Stacking Neurons. A more complex neural network may take the single neuron described above and "stack" them together such that one neuron passes its output as input into the next neuron, resulting in a more complex function.

Let us now deepen the housing prediction example. In addition to the size of the house, suppose that you know the number of bedrooms, the zip code and the wealth of the neighborhood. Building neural networks is analogous to Lego bricks: you take individual bricks and stack them together to build complex structures. The same applies to neural networks: we take individual neurons and stack them together to create complex neural networks.

Given these features (size, number of bedrooms, zip code, and wealth), we might then decide that the price of the house depends on the maximum family size it can accommodate. Suppose the family size is a function of the size of the house and number of bedrooms (see Figure 7.2). The zip code may provide additional information such as how walkable the neighborhood is (i.e., can you walk to the grocery store or do you need to drive everywhere). Combining the zip code with the wealth of the neighborhood may predict the quality of the local elementary school. Given these three derived features (family size, walkable, school quality), we may conclude that the price of the home ultimately depends on these three features.

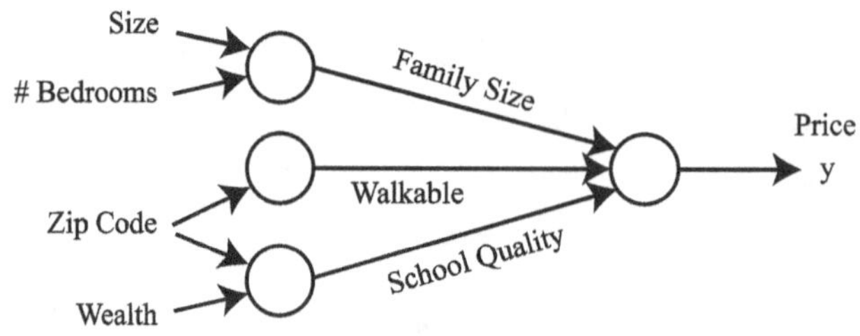

Figure 7.2: Diagram of a small neural network for predicting housing prices.

Formally, the input to a neural network is a set of input features x_1, x_2, x_3, x_4. We denote the intermediate variables for "family size", "walkable", and "school quality" by a_1, a_2, a_3 (these a_i's are often referred to as "hidden units" or "hidden neurons"). We represent each of the a_i's as a neural network with a single neuron with a subset of $x_1, \ldots, x_4$ as inputs. Then as in Figure 7.1, we will have the parameterization:

$$
\begin{aligned}
a_1 &= \mathrm{ReLU}(\theta_1 x_1 + \theta_2 x_2 + \theta_3) \\
a_2 &= \mathrm{ReLU}(\theta_4 x_3 + \theta_5) \\
a_3 &= \mathrm{ReLU}(\theta_6 x_3 + \theta_7 x_4 + \theta_8)
\end{aligned}
$$

where $(\theta_1, \cdots, \theta_8)$ are parameters. Now we represent the final output $\bar{h}_\theta(x)$ as another linear function with a_1, a_2, a_3 as inputs, and we get[3]

$$
\bar{h}_\theta(x) = \theta_9 a_1 + \theta_{10} a_2 + \theta_{11} a_3 + \theta_{12} \tag{7.13}
$$

where θ contains all the parameters $(\theta_1, \cdots, \theta_{12})$.

Now we represent the output as a quite complex function of x with parameters θ. Then you can use this parametrization $\bar{h}_\theta$ with the machinery of Section 7.1 to learn the parameters θ.

Inspiration from Biological Neural Networks. As the name suggests, artificial neural networks were inspired by biological neural networks. The hidden units $a_1, \ldots, a_m$ correspond to the neurons in a biological neural network, and the parameters θ_i's correspond to the synapses. However, it's unclear how similar the modern deep artificial neural networks are to the biological ones. For example, perhaps not many neuroscientists think biological

[3]Typically, for multi-layer neural network, at the end, near the output, we don't apply ReLU, especially when the output is not necessarily a positive number.

neural networks could have 1000 layers, while some modern artificial neural networks do (we will elaborate more on the notion of layers.) Moreover, it's an open question whether human brains update their neural networks in a way similar to the way that computer scientists learn artificial neural networks (using backpropagation, which we will introduce in the next section.).

Two-layer Fully-Connected Neural Networks. We constructed the neural network in equation (7.13) using a significant amount of prior knowledge/belief about how the "family size", "walkable", and "school quality" are determined by the inputs. We implicitly assumed that we know the family size is an important quantity to look at and that it can be determined by only the "size" and "# bedrooms". Such a prior knowledge might not be available for other applications. It would be more flexible and general to have a generic parameterization. A simple way would be to write the intermediate variable a_1 as a function of all $x_1, \dots, x_4$:

$$\begin{aligned} a_1 &= \mathrm{ReLU}(w_1^\top x + b_1), \text{ where } w_1 \in \mathbb{R}^4 \text{ and } b_1 \in \mathbb{R} \\ a_2 &= \mathrm{ReLU}(w_2^\top x + b_2), \text{ where } w_2 \in \mathbb{R}^4 \text{ and } b_2 \in \mathbb{R} \\ a_3 &= \mathrm{ReLU}(w_3^\top x + b_3), \text{ where } w_3 \in \mathbb{R}^4 \text{ and } b_3 \in \mathbb{R} \end{aligned} \tag{7.14}$$

We still define $\bar{h}_\theta(x)$ using equation (7.13) with a_1, a_2, a_3 being defined as above. Thus we have a so-called **fully-connected neural network** because all the intermediate variables a_i's depend on all the inputs x_i's.

For full generality, a two-layer fully-connected neural network with m hidden units and d dimensional input $x \in \mathbb{R}^d$ is defined as

$$\forall j \in [1, ..., m], \quad z_j = {w_j^{[1]}}^\top x + b_j^{[1]} \text{ where } w_j^{[1]} \in \mathbb{R}^d, b_j^{[1]} \in \mathbb{R} \tag{7.15}$$

$$\begin{aligned} a_j &= \mathrm{ReLU}(z_j), \\ a &= [a_1, \dots, a_m]^\top \in \mathbb{R}^m \end{aligned}$$

$$\bar{h}_\theta(x) = {w^{[2]}}^\top a + b^{[2]} \text{ where } w^{[2]} \in \mathbb{R}^m, b^{[2]} \in \mathbb{R}, \tag{7.16}$$

Note that by default the vectors in $\mathbb{R}^d$ are viewed as column vectors, and in particular a is a column vector with components $a_1, a_2, ..., a_m$. The indices $^{[1]}$ and $^{[2]}$ are used to distinguish two sets of parameters: the $w_j^{[1]}$'s (each of which is a vector in $\mathbb{R}^d$) and $w^{[2]}$ (which is a vector in $\mathbb{R}^m$). We will have more of these later.

Vectorization. Before we introduce neural networks with more layers and more complex structures, we will simplify the expressions for neural networks with more matrix and vector notations. Another important motivation of vectorization is the speed perspective in the implementation. In order to implement a neural network efficiently, one must be careful when using for loops. The most natural way to implement equation (7.15) in code is perhaps to use a for loop. In practice, the dimensionalities of the inputs and hidden units are high. As a result, code will run very slowly if you use for loops. Leveraging the parallelism in GPUs is/was crucial for the progress of deep learning.

This gave rise to *vectorization*. Instead of using for loops, vectorization takes advantage of matrix algebra and highly optimized numerical linear algebra packages (e.g., BLAS) to make neural network computations run quickly. Before the deep learning era, a for loop may have been sufficient on smaller datasets, but modern deep networks and state-of-the-art datasets will be infeasible to run with for loops.

We vectorize the two-layer fully-connected neural network as below. We define a weight matrix $W^{[1]}$ in $\mathbb{R}^{m\times d}$ as the concatenation of all the vectors $w_j^{[1]}$'s in the following way:

$$W^{[1]} = \begin{bmatrix} \text{---} & {w_1^{[1]}}^\top & \text{---} \\ \text{---} & {w_2^{[1]}}^\top & \text{---} \\ & \vdots & \\ \text{---} & {w_m^{[1]}}^\top & \text{---} \end{bmatrix} \in \mathbb{R}^{m\times d} \tag{7.17}$$

Now by the definition of matrix vector multiplication, we can write $z = [z_1, \dots, z_m]^\top \in \mathbb{R}^m$ as

$$\underbrace{\begin{bmatrix} z_1 \\ \vdots \\ \vdots \\ z_m \end{bmatrix}}_{z\in\mathbb{R}^{m\times 1}} = \underbrace{\begin{bmatrix} \text{---} & {w_1^{[1]}}^\top & \text{---} \\ \text{---} & {w_2^{[1]}}^\top & \text{---} \\ & \vdots & \\ \text{---} & {w_m^{[1]}}^\top & \text{---} \end{bmatrix}}_{W^{[1]}\in\mathbb{R}^{m\times d}} \underbrace{\begin{bmatrix} x_1 \\ x_2 \\ \vdots \\ x_d \end{bmatrix}}_{x\in\mathbb{R}^{d\times 1}} + \underbrace{\begin{bmatrix} b_1^{[1]} \\ b_2^{[1]} \\ \vdots \\ b_m^{[1]} \end{bmatrix}}_{b^{[1]}\in\mathbb{R}^{m\times 1}} \tag{7.18}$$

Or succinctly,

$$z = W^{[1]}x + b^{[1]} \tag{7.19}$$

We remark again that a vector in $\mathbb{R}^d$ in this notes, following the conventions previously established, is automatically viewed as a column vector, and can also be viewed as a $d \times 1$ dimensional matrix. (Note that this is different from numpy where a vector is viewed as a row vector in broadcasting.)

Computing the activations $a \in \mathbb{R}^m$ from $z \in \mathbb{R}^m$ involves an element-wise non-linear application of the ReLU function, which can be computed in parallel efficiently. Overloading ReLU for element-wise application of ReLU (meaning, for a vector $t \in \mathbb{R}^d$, $\mathrm{ReLU}(t)$ is a vector such that $\mathrm{ReLU}(t)_i = \mathrm{ReLU}(t_i)$), we have

$$a = \mathrm{ReLU}(z) \tag{7.20}$$

Define $W^{[2]} = [w^{[2]^\top}] \in \mathbb{R}^{1\times m}$ similarly. Then, the model in equation (7.16) can be summarized as

$$\begin{aligned} a &= \mathrm{ReLU}(W^{[1]}x + b^{[1]}) \\ \bar{h}_\theta(x) &= W^{[2]}a + b^{[2]} \end{aligned} \tag{7.21}$$

Here θ consists of $W^{[1]}, W^{[2]}$ (often referred to as the weight matrices) and $b^{[1]}, b^{[2]}$ (referred to as the biases). The collection of $W^{[1]}, b^{[1]}$ is referred to as the first layer, and $W^{[2]}, b^{[2]}$ the second layer. The activation a is referred to as the hidden layer. A two-layer neural network is also called one-hidden-layer neural network.

Multi-layer fully-connected neural networks. With this succinct notations, we can stack more layers to get a deeper fully-connected neural network. Let r be the number of layers (weight matrices). Let $W^{[1]}, \ldots, W^{[r]}, b^{[1]}, \ldots, b^{[r]}$ be the weight matrices and biases of all the layers. Then a multi-layer neural network can be written as

$$\begin{aligned} a^{[1]} &= \mathrm{ReLU}(W^{[1]}x + b^{[1]}) \\ a^{[2]} &= \mathrm{ReLU}(W^{[2]}a^{[1]} + b^{[2]}) \\ &\cdots \\ a^{[r-1]} &= \mathrm{ReLU}(W^{[r-1]}a^{[r-2]} + b^{[r-1]}) \\ \bar{h}_\theta(x) &= W^{[r]}a^{[r-1]} + b^{[r]} \end{aligned} \tag{7.22}$$

We note that the weight matrices and biases need to have compatible dimensions for the equations above to make sense. If $a^{[k]}$ has dimension m_k, then the weight matrix $W^{[k]}$ should be of dimension $m_k \times m_{k-1}$, and the bias $b^{[k]} \in \mathbb{R}^{m_k}$. Moreover, $W^{[1]} \in \mathbb{R}^{m_1\times d}$ and $W^{[r]} \in \mathbb{R}^{1\times m_{r-1}}$.

The total number of neurons in the network is $m_1 + \cdots + m_r$, and the total number of parameters in this network is $(d+1)m_1 + (m_1+1)m_2 + \cdots + (m_{r-1}+1)m_r$.

Sometimes for notational consistency we also write $a^{[0]} = x$, and $a^{[r]} = h_\theta(x)$. Then we have simple recursion that

$$a^{[k]} = \text{ReLU}(W^{[k]}a^{[k-1]} + b^{[k]}), \forall k = 1, \ldots, r-1 \tag{7.23}$$

Note that this would have be true for $k = r$ if there were an additional ReLU in equation (7.22), but often people like to make the last layer linear (aka without a ReLU) so that negative outputs are possible and it's easier to interpret the last layer as a linear model. (More on the interpretability at the "connection to kernel method" paragraph of this section.)

Other activation functions. The activation function ReLU can be replaced by many other non-linear function $\sigma(\cdot)$ that maps $\mathbb{R}$ to $\mathbb{R}$ such as

$$\sigma(z) = \frac{1}{1+e^{-z}} \qquad \text{(sigmoid)} \tag{7.24}$$

$$\sigma(z) = \frac{e^z - e^{-z}}{e^z + e^{-z}} \qquad \text{(tanh)} \tag{7.25}$$

$$\sigma(z) = \max\{z, \gamma z\}, \gamma \in (0,1) \qquad \text{(leaky ReLU)} \tag{7.26}$$

$$\sigma(z) = \frac{z}{2}\left[1 + \text{erf}(\frac{z}{\sqrt{2}})\right] \qquad \text{(GELU)} \tag{7.27}$$

$$\sigma(z) = \frac{1}{\beta}\log(1 + \exp(\beta z)), \beta > 0 \qquad \text{(Softplus)} \tag{7.28}$$

The activation functions are plotted in Figure 7.3. Sigmoid and tanh are less and less used these days partly because their are bounded from both sides and the gradient of them vanishes as z goes to both positive and negative infinity (whereas all the other activation functions still have gradients as the input goes to positive infinity.) Softplus is not used very often either in practice and can be viewed as a smoothing of the ReLU so that it has a proper second order derivative. GELU and leaky ReLU are both variants of ReLU but they have some non-zero gradient even when the input is negative. GELU (or its slight variant) is used in NLP models such as BERT and GPT (which we will discuss in Chapter 14.)

Why do we not use the identity function for $\sigma(z)$? That is, why not use $\sigma(z) = z$? Assume for sake of argument that $b^{[1]}$ and $b^{[2]}$ are zeros.

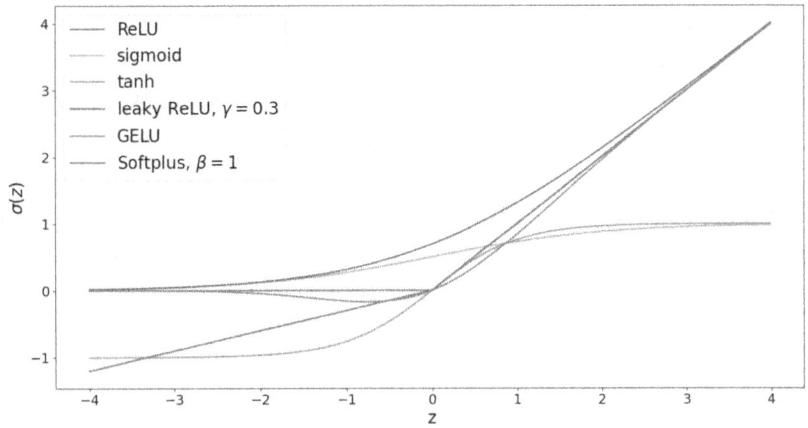

Figure 7.3: Activation functions in deep learning.

Suppose $\sigma(z) = z$, then for two-layer neural network, we have that

$$\begin{aligned}
\bar{h}_\theta(x) &= W^{[2]}a^{[1]} && (7.29)\\
&= W^{[2]}\sigma(z^{[1]}) && \text{by definition} \quad (7.30)\\
&= W^{[2]}z^{[1]} && \text{since } \sigma(z) = z \quad (7.31)\\
&= W^{[2]}W^{[1]}x && \text{from Equation (7.18)} \quad (7.32)\\
&= \tilde{W}x && \text{where } \tilde{W} = W^{[2]}W^{[1]} \quad (7.33)
\end{aligned}$$

Notice how $W^{[2]}W^{[1]}$ collapsed into $\tilde{W}$.

This is because applying a linear function to another linear function will result in a linear function over the original input (i.e., you can construct a $\tilde{W}$ such that $\tilde{W}x = W^{[2]}W^{[1]}x$). This loses much of the representational power of the neural network as often times the output we are trying to predict has a non-linear relationship with the inputs. Without non-linear activation functions, the neural network will simply perform linear regression.

Connection to the Kernel Method. In the previous lectures, we covered the concept of feature maps. Recall that the main motivation for feature maps is to represent functions that are non-linear in the input x by $\theta^\top \phi(x)$, where θ are the parameters and $\phi(x)$, the feature map, is a handcrafted function non-linear in the raw input x. The performance of the learning algorithms can significantly depends on the choice of the feature map $\phi(x)$. Oftentimes people use domain knowledge to design the feature map $\phi(x)$ that suits the particular applications. The process of choosing the feature maps is often referred to as **feature engineering**.

We can view deep learning as a way to automatically learn the right feature map (sometimes also referred to as "the representation") as follows. Suppose we denote by β the collection of the parameters in a fully-connected neural networks (equation (7.22)) except those in the last layer. Then we can abstract right $a^{[r-1]}$ as a function of the input x and the parameters in β: $a^{[r-1]} = \phi_\beta(x)$. Now we can write the model as

$$\bar{h}_\theta(x) = W^{[r]}\phi_\beta(x) + b^{[r]} \tag{7.34}$$

When β is fixed, then $\phi_\beta(\cdot)$ can viewed as a feature map, and therefore $\bar{h}_\theta(x)$ is just a linear model over the features $\phi_\beta(x)$. However, we will train the neural networks, both the parameters in β and the parameters $W^{[r]}, b^{[r]}$ are optimized, and therefore we are not learning a linear model in the feature space, but also learning a good feature map $\phi_\beta(\cdot)$ itself so that it's possible to predict accurately with a linear model on top of the feature map. Therefore, deep learning tends to depend less on the domain knowledge of the particular applications and requires often less feature engineering. The penultimate layer $a^{[r]}$ is often (informally) referred to as the learned features or representations in the context of deep learning.

In the example of house price prediction, a fully-connected neural network does not need us to specify the intermediate quantity such "family size", and may automatically discover some useful features in the last penultimate layer (the activation $a^{[r-1]}$), and use them to linearly predict the housing price. Often the feature map / representation obtained from one datasets (that is, the function $\phi_\beta(\cdot)$ can be also useful for other datasets, which indicates they contain essential information about the data. However, oftentimes, the neural network will discover complex features which are very useful for predicting the output but may be difficult for a human to understand or interpret. This is why some people refer to neural networks as a *black box*, as it can be difficult to understand the features it has discovered.

7.3 Modules in Modern Neural Networks

The multi-layer neural network introduced in equation (7.22) of Section 7.2 is often called multi-layer perceptron (MLP) these days. Modern neural networks used in practice are often much more complex and consist of multiple building blocks or multiple layers of building blocks. In this section, we will introduce some of the other building blocks and discuss possible ways to combine them.

First, each matrix multiplication can be viewed as a building block. Consider a matrix multiplication operation with parameters (W, b) where W is the weight matrix and b is the bias vector, operating on an input z,

$$\mathrm{MM}_{W,b}(z) = Wz + b\,. \tag{7.35}$$

Note that we implicitly assume all the dimensions are chosen to be compatible. We will also drop the subscripts under MM when they are clear in the context or just for convenience when they are not essential to the discussion.

Then, the MLP can be written as as a composition of multiple matrix multiplication modules and nonlinear activation modules (which can also be viewed as a building block):

$$\mathrm{MLP}(x) = \mathrm{MM}_{W^{[r]},b^{[r]}}(\sigma(\mathrm{MM}_{W^{[r-1]},b^{[r-1]}}(\sigma(\cdots \mathrm{MM}_{W^{[1]},b^{[1]}}(x))))). \tag{7.36}$$

Alternatively, when we drop the subscripts that indicate the parameters for convenience, we can write

$$\mathrm{MLP}(x) = \mathrm{MM}(\sigma(\mathrm{MM}\sigma(\cdots \mathrm{MM}(x)))). \tag{7.37}$$

Note that in this lecture notes, by default, all the modules have different sets of parameters, and the dimensions of the parameters are chosen such that the composition is meaningful.

Larger modules can be defined via smaller modules as well, e.g., one activation layer σ and a matrix multiplication layer MM are often combined and called a "layer" in many papers. People often draw the architecture with the basic modules in a figure by indicating the dependency between these modules. E.g., see an illustration of an MLP in Figure 7.4, Left.

Residual connections. One of the very influential neural network architecture for vision application is ResNet, which uses the residual connections that are essentially used in almost all large-scale deep learning architectures these days. Using our notation above, a very much simplified residual block can be defined as

$$\mathrm{Res}(z) = z + \sigma(\mathrm{MM}(\sigma(\mathrm{MM}(z)))). \tag{7.38}$$

A much simplified ResNet is a composition of many residual blocks followed by a matrix multiplication,

$$\text{ResNet-S}(x) = \mathrm{MM}(\mathrm{Res}(\mathrm{Res}(\cdots \mathrm{Res}(x)))). \tag{7.39}$$

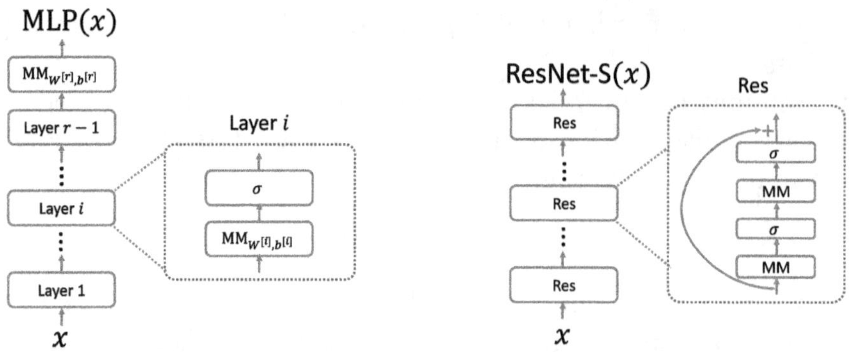

Figure 7.4: Illustrative Figures for Architecture. **Left**: An MLP with r layers. **Right**: A residual network.

We also draw the dependency of these modules in Figure 7.4, Right.

We note that the ResNet-S is still not the same as the ResNet architecture introduced in the seminal paper [He et al., 2016] because ResNet uses convolution layers instead of vanilla matrix multiplication, and adds batch normalization between convolutions and activations. We will introduce convolutional layers and some variants of batch normalization below. ResNet-S and layer normalization are part of the Transformer architecture that are widely used in modern large language models.

Layer normalization. Layer normalization, denoted by LN in this text, is a module that maps a vector $z \in \mathbb{R}^m$ to a more normalized vector $\mathrm{LN}(z) \in \mathbb{R}^m$. It is oftentimes used after the nonlinear activations.

We first define a sub-module of the layer normalization, denoted by LN-S.

$$\text{LN-S}(z) = \begin{bmatrix} \frac{z_1-\hat{\mu}}{\hat{\sigma}} \\ \frac{z_2-\hat{\mu}}{\hat{\sigma}} \\ \vdots \\ \frac{z_m-\hat{\mu}}{\hat{\sigma}} \end{bmatrix}, \tag{7.40}$$

where $\hat{\mu} = \frac{\sum_{i=1}^m z_i}{m}$ is the empirical mean of the vector z and $\hat{\sigma} = \sqrt{\frac{\sum_{i=1}^m (z_i-\hat{\mu}^2)}{m}}$ is the empirical standard deviation of the entries of z.[4] Intuitively, LN-S(z) is a vector that is normalized to having empirical mean zero and empirical standard deviation 1.

[4]Note that we divide by m instead of $m-1$ in the empirical standard deviation here because we are interested in making the output of LN-S(z) have sum of squares equal to 1 (as opposed to estimating the standard deviation in statistics.)

Oftentimes zero mean and standard deviation 1 is not the most desired normalization scheme, and thus layernorm introduces to parameters learnable scalars β and γ as the desired mean and standard deviation, and use an affine transformation to turn the output of LN-S(z) into a vector with mean β and standard deviation γ.

$$\mathrm{LN}(z) = \beta + \gamma \cdot \text{LN-S}(z) = \begin{bmatrix} \beta + \gamma\left(\frac{z_1 - \hat{\mu}}{\hat{\sigma}}\right) \\ \beta + \gamma\left(\frac{z_2 - \hat{\mu}}{\hat{\sigma}}\right) \\ \vdots \\ \beta + \gamma\left(\frac{z_m - \hat{\mu}}{\hat{\sigma}}\right) \end{bmatrix}. \tag{7.41}$$

Here the first occurrence of β should be technically interpreted as a vector with all the entries being β. in We also note that $\hat{\mu}$ and $\hat{\sigma}$ are also functions of z and shouldn't be treated as constants when computing the derivatives of layernorm. Moreover, β and γ are learnable parameters and thus layernorm is a parameterized module (as opposed to the activation layer which doesn't have any parameters.)

Scaling-invariant property. One important property of layer normalization is that it will make the model invariant to scaling of the parameters in the following sense. Suppose we consider composing LN with $\mathrm{MM}_{W,b}$ and get a subnetwork $\mathrm{LN}(\mathrm{MM}_{W,b}(z))$. Then, we have that the output of this subnetwork does not change when the parameter in $\mathrm{MM}_{W,b}$ is scaled:

$$\mathrm{LN}(\mathrm{MM}_{\alpha W,\alpha b}(z)) = \mathrm{LN}(\mathrm{MM}_{W,b}(z)), \forall \alpha > 0. \tag{7.42}$$

To see this, we first know that LN-S$(\cdot)$ is scale-invariant

$$\text{LN-S}(\alpha z) = \begin{bmatrix} \frac{\alpha z_1 - \alpha\hat{\mu}}{\alpha\hat{\sigma}} \\ \frac{\alpha z_2 - \alpha\hat{\mu}}{\alpha\hat{\sigma}} \\ \vdots \\ \frac{\alpha z_m - \alpha\hat{\mu}}{\alpha\hat{\sigma}} \end{bmatrix} = \begin{bmatrix} \frac{z_1 - \hat{\mu}}{\hat{\sigma}} \\ \frac{z_2 - \hat{\mu}}{\hat{\sigma}} \\ \vdots \\ \frac{z_m - \hat{\mu}}{\hat{\sigma}} \end{bmatrix} = \text{LN-S}(z). \tag{7.43}$$

Then we have

$$\begin{aligned} \mathrm{LN}(\mathrm{MM}_{\alpha W,\alpha b}(z)) &= \beta + \gamma\text{LN-S}(\mathrm{MM}_{\alpha W,\alpha b}(z)) && (7.44) \\ &= \beta + \gamma\text{LN-S}(\alpha\mathrm{MM}_{W,b}(z)) && (7.45) \\ &= \beta + \gamma\text{LN-S}(\mathrm{MM}_{W,b}(z)) && (7.46) \\ &= \mathrm{LN}(\mathrm{MM}_{W,b}(z)). && (7.47) \end{aligned}$$

Due to this property, most of the modern DL architectures for large-scale computer vision and language applications have the following scale-invariant property w.r.t all the weights that are not at the last layer. Suppose the network f has last layer' weights W_{last}, and all the rest of the weights are denote by W. Then, we have $f_{W_{\text{last}},\alpha W}(x) = f_{W_{\text{last}},W}(x)$ for all $\alpha > 0$. Here, the last layers weights are special because there are typically no layernorm or batchnorm after the last layer's weights.

Other normalization layers. There are several other normalization layers that aim to normalize the intermediate layers of the neural networks to a more fixed and controllable scaling, such as batch-normalization [?], and group normalization [?]. Batch normalization and group normalization are more often used in computer vision applications whereas layer norm is used more often in language applications.

Convolutional Layers. Convolutional Neural Networks are neural networks that consist of convolution layers (and many other modules), and are particularly useful for computer vision applications. For the simplicity of exposition, we focus on 1-D convolution in this text and only briefly mention 2-D convolution informally at the end of this subsection. (2-D convolution is more suitable for images which have two dimensions. 1-D convolution is also used in natural language processing.)

We start by introducing a simplified version of the 1-D convolution layer, denoted by Conv1D-S($\cdot$) which is a type of matrix multiplication layer with a special structure. The parameters of Conv1D-S are a filter vector $w \in \mathbb{R}^k$ where k is called the filter size (oftentimes $k \ll m$), and a bias scalar b. Oftentimes the filter is also called a kernel (but it does not have much to do with the kernel in kernel method.) For simplicity, we assume $k = 2\ell + 1$ is an odd number. We first pad zeros to the input vector z in the sense that we let $z_{1-\ell} = z_{1-\ell+1} = .. = z_0 = 0$ and $z_{m+1} = z_{m+2} = .. = z_{m+\ell} = 0$, and treat z as an $(m + 2\ell)$-dimension vector. Conv1D-S outputs a vector of dimension $\mathbb{R}^m$ where each output dimension is a linear combination of subsets of z_j's with coefficients from w,

$$\text{Conv1D-S}(z)_i = w_1 z_{i-\ell} + w_2 z_{i-\ell+1} + \cdots + w_{2\ell+1} z_{i+\ell} = \sum_{j=1}^{2\ell+1} w_j z_{i-\ell+(j-1)}. \tag{7.48}$$

Therefore, one can view Conv1D-S as a matrix multiplication with shared parameters: Conv1D-S$(z) = Qz$, where

$$Q = \begin{bmatrix} w_{\ell+1} & \cdots & w_{2\ell+1} & 0 & 0 & \cdots & \cdots & \cdots & \cdots & \cdots & \cdots & 0 \\ w_{\ell} & \cdots & w_{2\ell} & w_{2\ell+1} & 0 & \cdots & \cdots & \cdots & \cdots & \cdots & \cdots & 0 \\ \vdots & & & & & & & & & & & \\ w_1 & \cdots & w_{\ell+1} & \cdots & \cdots & \cdots & w_{2\ell+1} & 0 & \cdots & \cdots & \cdots & 0 \\ 0 & w_1 & \cdots & \cdots & \cdots & \cdots & w_{2\ell} & w_{2\ell+1} & 0 & \cdots & \cdots & 0 \\ \vdots & & & & & & & & & & & \\ \vdots & & & & & & & & & & & \\ 0 & \cdots & \cdots & \cdots & \cdots & \cdots & 0 & w_1 & \cdots & & \cdots & w_{2\ell+1} \\ \vdots & & & & & & & & & & & \\ 0 & \cdots & \cdots & \cdots & \cdots & \cdots & \cdots & \cdots & 0 & w_1 & \cdots & w_{\ell+1} \end{bmatrix}. \tag{7.49}$$

Note that $Q_{i,j} = Q_{i-1,j-1}$ for all $i, j \in \{2, \ldots, m\}$, and thus convoluation is a matrix multiplication with parameter sharing. We also note that computing the convolution only takes $O(km)$ times but computing a generic matrix multiplication takes $O(m^2)$ time. Convolution has k parameters but generic matrix multiplication will have m^2 parameters. Thus convolution is supposed to be much more efficient than a generic matrix multiplication (as long as the additional structure imposed does not hurt the flexibility of the model to fit the data).

We also note that in practice there are many variants of the convolutional layers that we define here, e.g., there are other ways to pad zeros or sometimes the dimension of the output of the convolutional layers could be different from the input. We omit some of this subtleties here for simplicity.

The convolutional layers used in practice have also many "channels" and the simplified version above corresponds to the 1-channel version. Formally, Conv1D takes in C vectors $z_1, \ldots, z_C \in \mathbb{R}^m$ as inputs, where C is referred to as the number of channels. In other words, the more general version, denoted by Conv1D, takes in a matrix as input, which is the concatenation of $z_1, \ldots, z_C$ and has dimension $m \times C$. It can output C' vectors of dimension m, denoted by Conv1D$(z)_1, \ldots,$ Conv1D$(z)_{C'}$, where C' is referred to as the output channel, or equivalently a matrix of dimension $m \times C'$. Each of the output is a sum of the simplified convolutions applied on various channels.

$$\forall i \in [C'], \text{Conv1D}(z)_i = \sum_{j=1}^{C} \text{Conv1D-S}_{i,j}(z_j). \tag{7.50}$$

Note that each Conv1D-S$_{i,j}$ are modules with different parameters, and thus the total number of parameters is k (the number of parameters in a Conv1D-S) $\times CC'$ (the number of Conv1D-S$_{i,j}$'s) $= kCC'$. In contrast, a generic linear mapping from $\mathbb{R}^{m \times C}$ and $\mathbb{R}^{m \times C'}$ has m^2CC' parameters. The parameters can also be represented as a three-dimensional tensor of dimension $k \times C \times C'$.

2-D convolution (brief). A 2-D convolution with one channel, denoted by Conv2D-S, is analogous to the Conv1D-S, but takes a 2-dimensional input $z \in \mathbb{R}^{m\times m}$ and applies a filter of size $k \times k$, and outputs Conv2D-S$(z) \in \mathbb{R}^{m\times m}$. The full 2-D convolutional layer, denoted by Conv2D, takes in a sequence of matrices $z_1, \dots, z_C \in \mathbb{R}^{m\times m}$, or equivalently a 3-D tensor $z = (z_1, \dots, z_C) \in \mathbb{R}^{m\times m\times C}$ and outputs a sequence of matrices, $\text{Conv2D}(z)_1, \dots, \text{Conv2D}(z)_{C'} \in \mathbb{R}^{m\times m}$, which can also be viewed as a 3D tensor in $\mathbb{R}^{m\times m\times C'}$. Each channel of the output is sum of the outcomes of applying Conv2D-S layers on all the input channels.

$$\forall i \in [C'], \text{Conv2D}(z)_i = \sum_{j=1}^{C} \text{Conv2D-S}_{i,j}(z_j). \tag{7.51}$$

Because there are CC' number of Conv2D-S modules and each of the Conv2D-S module has k^2 parameters, the total number of parameters is $CC'k^2$. The parameters can also be viewed as a 4D tensor of dimension $C \times C' \times k \times k$.

7.4 Backpropagation

In this section, we introduce backpropgation or auto-differentiation, which computes the gradient of the loss $\nabla J(\theta)$ efficiently. We will start with an informal theorem that states that as long as a *real-valued function* f can be efficiently computed/evaluated by a differentiable network or circuit, then its gradient can be efficiently computed in a similar time. We will then show how to do this concretely for neural networks.

Because the formality of the general theorem is not the main focus here, we will introduce the terms with informal definitions. By a differentiable circuit or a differentiable network, we mean a composition of a sequence of differentiable arithmetic operations (additions, subtraction, multiplication, divisions, etc) and elementary differentiable functions (ReLU, exp, log, sin, cos, etc.). Let the size of the circuit be the total number of such operations and elementary functions. We assume that each of the operations and functions, and their derivatives or partial derivatives ecan be computed in $O(1)$ time.

Theorem 7.4.1: *[backpropagation or auto-differentiation, informally stated] Suppose a differentiable circuit of size N computes a real-valued function*

$f : \mathbb{R}^\ell \to \mathbb{R}$. Then, the gradient ∇f can be computed in time $O(N)$, by a circuit of size $O(N)$.[5]

We note that the loss function $J^{(j)}(\theta)$ for j-th example can be indeed computed by a sequence of operations and functions involving additions, subtraction, multiplications, and non-linear activations. Thus the theorem suggests that we should be able to compute the $\nabla J^{(j)}(\theta)$ in a similar time to that for computing $J^{(j)}(\theta)$ itself. This does not only apply to the fully-connected neural network introduced in the Section 7.2, but also many other types of neural networks that uses more advance modules.

We remark that auto-differentiation or backpropagation is already implemented in all the deep learning packages such as tensorflow and pytorch, and thus in practice, in most of cases a researcher does not need to write their backpropagation algorithms. However, understanding it is very helpful for gaining insights into the working of deep learning.

Organization of the rest of the section. In Section 7.4.1, we will start reviewing the basic Chain rule with a new perspective that is particularly useful for understanding backpropgation. Section 7.4.2 will introduce the general strategy for backpropagation. Section 7.4.2 will discuss how to compute the so-called backward function for basic modules used in neural networks, and Section 7.4.4 will put everything together to get a concrete backprop algorithm for MLPs.

7.4.1 Preliminaries on partial derivatives

Suppose a *scalar variable* J depend on some variables z (which could be a scalar, matrix, or high-order tensor), we write $\frac{\partial J}{\partial z}$ as the partial derivatives of J w.r.t to the variable z. We stress that the convention here is that $\frac{\partial J}{\partial z}$ has exactly the same dimension as z itself. For example, if $z \in \mathbb{R}^{m\times n}$, then $\frac{\partial J}{\partial z} \in \mathbb{R}^{m\times n}$, and the (i, j)-entry of $\frac{\partial J}{\partial z}$ is equal to $\frac{\partial J}{\partial z_{ij}}$.

Remark 7.4.2: When both J and z are not scalars, the partial derivatives of J w.r.t z becomes either a matrix or tensor and the notation becomes somewhat tricky. Besides the mathematical or notational challenges in dealing

[5]We note if the output of the function f does not depend on some of the input coordinates, then we set by default the gradient w.r.t that coordinate to zero. Setting to zero does not count towards the total runtime here in our accounting scheme. This is why when $N \leq \ell$, we can compute the gradient in $O(N)$ time, which might be potentially even less than ℓ.

with these partial derivatives of multi-variate functions, they are also expensive to compute and store, and thus rarely explicitly constructed empirically. The experience of authors of this note is that it's generally more productive to think only about derivatives of scalar function w.r.t to vector, matrices, or tensors. For example, in this note, we will not deal with derivatives of multi-variate functions.

Chain rule. We review the chain rule in calculus but with a perspective and notions that are more relevant for auto-differentiation.

Consider a scalar variable J which is obtained by the composition of f and g on some variable z,

$$\begin{aligned} & z \in \mathbb{R}^m \\ & u = g(z) \in \mathbb{R}^n \\ & J = f(u) \in \mathbb{R}\,. \end{aligned} \tag{7.52}$$

The same derivations below can be easily extend to the cases when z and u are matrices or tensors; but we insist that the final variable J is a scalar. (See also Remark 7.4.2.) Let $u = (u_1, \ldots, u_n)$ and let $g(z) = (g_1(z), \cdots, g_n(z))$. Then, the standard chain rule gives us that

$$\forall i \in \{1, \ldots, m\}, \quad \frac{\partial J}{\partial z_i} = \sum_{j=1}^{n} \frac{\partial J}{\partial u_j} \cdot \frac{\partial g_j}{\partial z_i}\,. \tag{7.53}$$

Alternatively, when z and u are both vectors, in a vectorized notation:

$$\frac{\partial J}{\partial z} = \begin{bmatrix} \frac{\partial g_1}{\partial z_1} & \cdots & \frac{\partial g_n}{\partial z_1} \\ \vdots & \ddots & \vdots \\ \frac{\partial g_1}{\partial z_m} & \cdots & \frac{\partial g_n}{\partial z_m} \end{bmatrix} \cdot \frac{\partial J}{\partial u}\,. \tag{7.54}$$

In other words, the backward function is always a linear map from $\frac{\partial J}{\partial u}$ to $\frac{\partial J}{\partial z}$, though note that the mapping itself can depend on z in complex ways. The matrix on the RHS of (7.54) is actually the transpose of the Jacobian matrix of the function g. However, we do not discuss in-depth about Jacobian matrices to avoid complications. Part of the reason is that when z is a matrix (or tensor), to write an analog of equation (7.54), one has to either flatten z into a vector or introduce additional notations on tensor-matrix product. In this sense, equation (7.53) is more convenient and effective to use in all cases. For example, when $z \in \mathbb{R}^{r \times s}$ is a matrix, we can easily rewrite equation (7.53) to

$$\forall i, k, \quad \frac{\partial J}{\partial z_{ik}} = \sum_{j=1}^{n} \frac{\partial J}{\partial u_j} \cdot \frac{\partial g_j}{\partial z_{ik}} . \tag{7.55}$$

which will indeed be used in some of the derivations in Section 7.4.3.

Key interpretation of the chain rule. We can view the formula above (equation (7.53) or (7.54)) as a way to compute $\frac{\partial J}{\partial z}$ from $\frac{\partial J}{\partial u}$. Consider the following abstract problem. Suppose J depends on z via u as defined in equation (7.52). However, suppose the function f is not given or the function f is complex, but we are given the value of $\frac{\partial J}{\partial u}$. Then, the formula in equation (7.54) gives us a way to compute $\frac{\partial J}{\partial z}$ from $\frac{\partial J}{\partial u}$.

$$\frac{\partial J}{\partial u} \xrightarrow[\text{only requires info about } g(\cdot) \text{ and } z]{\text{chain rule, formula (7.54)}} \frac{\partial J}{\partial z} . \tag{7.56}$$

Moreover, this formula only involves knowledge about g (more precisely $\frac{\partial g_j}{\partial z_i}$). We will repeatedly use this fact in situations where g is a building blocks of a complex network f.

Empirically, it's often useful to modularized the mapping in (7.53) or (7.54) into a black-box, and mathematically it's also convenient to define a notation for it.[6] We use $\mathcal{B}[g, z]$ to define the function that maps $\frac{\partial J}{\partial u}$ to $\frac{\partial J}{\partial z}$, and write

$$\frac{\partial J}{\partial z} = \mathcal{B}[g, z]\left(\frac{\partial J}{\partial u}\right) . \tag{7.57}$$

We call $\mathcal{B}[g, z]$ the **backward function** for the module g. Note that when z is fixed, $\mathcal{B}[g, z]$ is merely a linear map from $\mathbb{R}^n$ to $\mathbb{R}^m$. Using equation (7.53), we have

$$(\mathcal{B}[g, z](v))_i = \sum_{j=1}^{m} \frac{\partial g_j}{\partial z_i} \cdot v_j . \tag{7.58}$$

Or in vectorized notation, using (7.54), we have

$$\mathcal{B}[g, z](v) = \begin{bmatrix} \frac{\partial g_1}{\partial z_1} & \cdots & \frac{\partial g_n}{\partial z_1} \\ \vdots & \ddots & \vdots \\ \frac{\partial g_1}{\partial z_m} & \cdots & \frac{\partial g_n}{\partial z_m} \end{bmatrix} \cdot v . \tag{7.59}$$

[6] e.g., the function is the .backward() method of the module in pytorch.

and therefore $\mathcal{B}[g,z]$ can be viewed as a matrix. However, in reality, z will be changing and thus the backward mapping has to be recomputed for different z's while g is often fixed. Thus, empirically, the backward function $\mathcal{B}[g,z](v)$ is often viewed as a function which takes in z (=the input to g) and v (=a vector that is supposed to be the gradient of some variable J w.r.t to the output of g) as the inputs, and outputs a vector that is supposed to be the gradient of J w.r.t to z.

7.4.2 General strategy of backpropagation

We discuss the general strategy of auto-differentiation in this section to build a high-level understanding. Then, we will instantiate the approach to concrete neural networks. We take the viewpoint that neural networks are complex compositions of small building blocks such as MM, σ, Conv2D, LN, etc., defined in Section 7.3. Note that the losses (e.g., mean-squared loss, or the cross-entropy loss) can also be abstractly viewed as additional modules. Thus, we can abstractly write the loss function J (on a single example (x,y)) as a composition of many modules:[7]

$$J = M_k(M_{k-1}(\cdots M_1(x)))\,. \tag{7.60}$$

For example, for a binary classification problem with a MLP $\bar{h}_\theta(x)$ (defined in equation (7.36) and (7.37)), the loss function has ber written in the form of equation (7.60) with $M_1 = \mathrm{MM}_{W^{[1]},b^{[1]}}$, $M_2 = \sigma$, $M_3 = \mathrm{MM}_{W^{[2]},b^{[2]}}$, $\dots$, and $M_{k-1} = \mathrm{MM}_{W^{[r]},b^{[r]}}$ and $M_k = \ell_{\text{logistic}}$.

We can see from this example that some modules involve parameters, and other modules might only involve a fixed set of operations. For generality, we assume that eachj M_i involves a set of parameters $\theta^{[i]}$, though $\theta^{[i]}$ could possibly be an empty set when M_i is a fixed operation such as the nonlinear activations. We will discuss more on the granularity of the modularization, but so far we assume all the modules M_i's are simple enough.

We introduce the intermediate variables for the computation in (7.60).

[7]Technically, we should write $J = M_k(M_{k-1}(\cdots M_1(x)), y)$. However, y is treated as a constant for the purpose of computing the derivatives w.r.t to the parameters, and thus we can view it as part of M_k for the sake of simplicity of notations.

Let

$$\begin{aligned} u^{[0]} &= x \\ u^{[1]} &= M_1(u^{[0]}) \\ u^{[2]} &= M_2(u^{[1]}) \\ &\vdots \\ J = u^{[k]} &= M_k(u^{[k-1]})\,. \end{aligned} \tag{F}$$

Backpropgation consists of two passes, the forward pass and backward pass. In the forward pass, the algorithm simply computes $u^{[1]}, \ldots, u^{[k]}$ from $i = 1, \ldots, k$, sequentially using the definition in (F), and **save all the intermediate variables** $u^{[i]}$'s in the memory.

In the **backward pass**, we first compute the derivatives w.r.t to the intermediate variables, that is, $\frac{\partial J}{\partial u^{[k]}}, \ldots, \frac{\partial J}{\partial u^{[1]}}$, sequentially in this backward order, and then compute the derivatives of the parameters $\frac{\partial J}{\partial \theta^{[i]}}$ from $\frac{\partial J}{\partial u^{[i]}}$ and $u^{[i-1]}$. These two type of computations can be also interleaved with each other because $\frac{\partial J}{\partial \theta^{[i]}}$ only depends on $\frac{\partial J}{\partial u^{[i]}}$ and $u^{[i-1]}$ but not any $\frac{\partial J}{\partial u^{[k]}}$ with $k < i$.

We first see why $\frac{\partial J}{\partial u^{[i-1]}}$ can be computed efficiently from $\frac{\partial J}{\partial u^{[i]}}$ and $u^{[i-1]}$ by invoking the discussion in Section 7.4.1 on the chain rule. We instantiate the discussion by setting $u = u^{[i]}$ and $z = u^{[i-1]}$, and $f(u) = M_k(M_{k-1}(\cdots M_{i+1}(u^{[i]})))$, and $g(\cdot) = M_i(\cdot)$. Note that f is very complex but we don't need any concrete information about f. Then, the conclusive equation (7.56) corresponds to

$$\frac{\partial J}{\partial u^{[i]}} \xrightarrow[\textbf{only requires info about } M_i(\cdot) \textbf{ and } u^{[i-1]}]{\text{chain rule}} \frac{\partial J}{\partial u^{[i-1]}}. \tag{7.61}$$

More precisely, we can write, following equation (7.57)

$$\frac{\partial J}{\partial u^{[i-1]}} = \mathcal{B}[M_i, u^{[i-1]}]\left(\frac{\partial J}{\partial u^{[i]}}\right). \tag{B1}$$

Instantiating the chain rule with $z = \theta^{[i]}$ and $u = u^{[i]}$, we also have

$$\frac{\partial J}{\partial \theta^{[i]}} = \mathcal{B}[M_i, \theta^{[i]}]\left(\frac{\partial J}{\partial u^{[i]}}\right). \tag{B2}$$

See Figure 7.5 for an illustration of the algorithm.

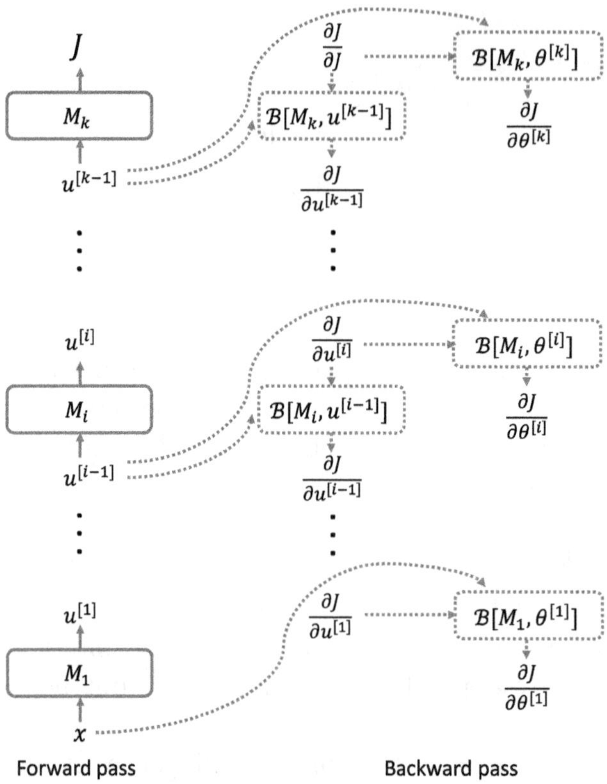

Figure 7.5: Back-propagation.

Remark 7.4.3: [Computational efficiency and granularity of the modules] The main underlying purpose of treating a complex network as compositions of small modules is that small modules tend to have efficiently implementable backward function. In fact, the backward functions of all the atomic modules such as addition, multiplication and ReLU can be computed as efficiently as the the evaluation of these modules (up to multiplicative constant factor). Using this fact, we can prove Theorem 7.4.1 by viewing neural networks as compositions of many atomic operations, and invoking the backpropagation discussed above. However, in practice, it's oftentimes more convenient to modularize the networks using modules on the level of matrix multiplication, layernorm, etc. As we will see, naive implementation of these operations' backward functions also have the same runtime as the evaluation of these functions.

7.4.3 Backward functions for basic modules

Using the general strategy in Section 7.4.2, it suffices to compute the backward function for all modules M_i's used in the networks. We compute the backward function for the basic module MM, activations σ, and loss functions in this section.

Backward function for MM. Suppose $\text{MM}_{W,b}(z) = Wz + b$ is a matrix multiplication module where $z \in \mathbb{R}^m$ and $W \in \mathbb{R}^{n\times m}$. Then, using equation (7.59), we have for $v \in \mathbb{R}^n$

$$\mathcal{B}[\text{MM}, z](v) = \begin{bmatrix} \frac{\partial (Wz+b)_1}{\partial z_1} & \cdots & \frac{\partial (Wz+b)_n}{\partial z_1} \\ \vdots & \ddots & \vdots \\ \frac{\partial (Wz+b)_1}{\partial z_m} & \cdots & \frac{\partial (Wz+b)_n}{\partial z_m} \end{bmatrix} v\,. \tag{7.62}$$

Using the fact that $\forall i \in [m], j \in [n], \frac{\partial (Wz+b)_j}{\partial z_i} = \frac{\partial b_j + \sum_{k=1}^m W_{jk} z_k}{\partial z_i} = W_{ji}$, we have

$$\mathcal{B}[\text{MM}, z](v) = W^\top v \in \mathbb{R}^m\,. \tag{7.63}$$

In the derivation above, we have treated MM as a function of z. If we treat MM as a function of W and b, then we can also compute the backward function for the parameter variables W and b. It's less convenient to use equation (7.59) because the variable W is a matrix and the matrix in (7.59) will be a 4-th order tensor that is challenging for us to mathematically write down. We use (7.58) instead:

$$(\mathcal{B}[\text{MM}, W](v))_{ij} = \sum_{k=1}^m \frac{\partial (Wz+b)_k}{\partial W_{ij}} \cdot v_k = \sum_{k=1}^m \frac{\partial \sum_{s=1}^m W_{ks} z_s}{\partial W_{ij}} \cdot v_k = v_i z_j\,. \tag{7.64}$$

In vectorized notation, we have

$$\mathcal{B}[\text{MM}, W](v) = v z^\top \in \mathbb{R}^{n\times m}\,. \tag{7.65}$$

Using equation (7.59) for the variable b, we have,

$$\mathcal{B}[\text{MM}, b](v) = \begin{bmatrix} \frac{\partial (Wz+b)_1}{\partial b_1} & \cdots & \frac{\partial (Wz+b)_n}{\partial b_1} \\ \vdots & \ddots & \vdots \\ \frac{\partial (Wz+b)_1}{\partial b_n} & \cdots & \frac{\partial (Wz+b)_n}{\partial b_n} \end{bmatrix} v = v\,. \tag{7.66}$$

Here we used that $\frac{\partial (Wz+b)_j}{\partial b_i} = 0$ if $i \neq j$ and $\frac{\partial (Wz+b)_j}{\partial b_i} = 1$ if $i = j$.

The computational efficiency for computing the backward function is $O(mn)$, the same as evaluating the result of matrix multiplication up to constant factor.

Backward function for the activations. Suppose $M(z) = \sigma(z)$ where σ is an element-wise activation function and $z \in \mathbb{R}^m$. Then, using equation (7.59), we have

$$\mathcal{B}[\sigma, z](v) = \begin{bmatrix} \frac{\partial \sigma(z_1)}{\partial z_1} & \cdots & \frac{\partial \sigma(z_m)}{\partial z_1} \\ \vdots & \ddots & \vdots \\ \frac{\partial \sigma(z_1)}{\partial z_m} & \cdots & \frac{\partial \sigma(z_m)}{\partial z_m} \end{bmatrix} v \tag{7.67}$$

$$= \operatorname{diag}(\sigma'(z_1), \cdots, \sigma'(z_m))v \tag{7.68}$$

$$= \sigma'(z) \odot v \in \mathbb{R}^m . \tag{7.69}$$

Here, we used the fact that $\frac{\partial \sigma(z_j)}{\partial z_i} = 0$ when $j \neq i$, $\operatorname{diag}(\lambda_1, \ldots, \lambda_m)$ denotes the diagonal matrix with $\lambda_1, \ldots, \lambda_m$ on the diagonal, and $\odot$ denotes the element-wise product of two vectors with the same dimension, and $\sigma'(\cdot)$ is the element-wise application of the derivative of the activation function σ.

Regarding computation efficiency, we note that at the first sight, equation (7.67) appears to indicate the backward function takes $O(m^2)$ time, but equation (7.69) shows that it's implementable in $O(m)$ time (which is the same as the time for evaluating of the function.) We are not supposed to be surprised by that the possibility of simplifying equation (7.67) to (7.69)—if we use smaller modules, that is, treating the vector-to-vector nonlinear activation as m scalar-to-scalar non-linear activation, then it's more obvious that the backward pass should have similar time to the forward pass.

Backward function for loss functions. When a module M takes in a vector z and outputs a scalar, by equation (7.59), the backward function takes in a scalar v and outputs a vector with entries $(\mathcal{B}[M, z](v))_i = \frac{\partial M}{\partial z_i} v$. Therefore, in vectorized notation, $\mathcal{B}[M, z](v) = \frac{\partial M}{\partial z} \cdot v$.

Recall that squared loss $\ell_{\text{MSE}}(z, y) = \frac{1}{2}(z - y)^2$. Thus, $\mathcal{B}[\ell_{\text{MSE}}, z](v) = \frac{\partial \frac{1}{2}(z-y)^2}{\partial z} \cdot v = (z - y) \cdot v$.

For logistics loss, by equation (2.6), we have

$$\mathcal{B}[\ell_{\text{logistic}}, t](v) = \frac{\partial \ell_{\text{logistic}}(t, y)}{\partial t} \cdot v = (1/(1 + \exp(-t)) - y) \cdot v . \tag{7.70}$$

For cross-entropy loss, by equation (2.17), we have

$$\mathcal{B}[\ell_{\text{ce}}, t](v) = \frac{\partial \ell_{\text{ce}}(t, y)}{\partial t} \cdot v = (\phi - e_y) \cdot v\,, \tag{7.71}$$

where $\phi = \text{softmax}(t)$.

7.4.4 Back-propagation for MLPs

Given the backward functions for every module needed in evaluating the loss of an MLP, we follow the strategy in Section 7.4.2 to compute the gradient of the loss w.r.t to the hidden activations and the parameters.

We consider the an r-layer MLP with a logistic loss. The loss function can be computed via a sequence of operations (that is, the forward pass),

$$\begin{aligned}
z^{[1]} &= \text{MM}_{W^{[1]}, b^{[1]}}(x), \\
a^{[1]} &= \sigma(z^{[1]}) \\
z^{[2]} &= \text{MM}_{W^{[2]}, b^{[2]}}(a^{[1]}) \\
a^{[2]} &= \sigma(z^{[2]}) \\
&\ \ \vdots \\
z^{[r]} &= \text{MM}_{W^{[r]}, b^{[r]}}(a^{[r-1]}) \\
J &= \ell_{\text{logistic}}(z^{[r]}, y)\,.
\end{aligned} \tag{7.72}$$

We apply the backward function sequentially in a backward order. First, we have that

$$\frac{\partial J}{\partial z^{[r]}} = \mathcal{B}[\ell_{\text{logistic}}, z^{[r]}]\left(\frac{\partial J}{\partial J}\right) = \mathcal{B}[\ell_{\text{logistic}}, z^{[r]}](1)\,. \tag{7.73}$$

Then, we iteratively compute $\frac{\partial J}{\partial a^{[i]}}$ and $\frac{\partial J}{\partial z^{[i]}}$'s by repeatedly invoking the chain rule (equation (7.58)),

$$\begin{aligned}
\frac{\partial J}{\partial a^{[r-1]}} &= \mathcal{B}[\text{MM}, a^{[r-1]}]\left(\frac{\partial J}{\partial z^{[r]}}\right) \\
\frac{\partial J}{\partial z^{[r-1]}} &= \mathcal{B}[\sigma, z^{[r-1]}]\left(\frac{\partial J}{\partial a^{[r-1]}}\right) \\
&\ \ \vdots \\
\frac{\partial J}{\partial z^{[1]}} &= \mathcal{B}[\sigma, z^{[1]}]\left(\frac{\partial J}{\partial a^{[1]}}\right)\,.
\end{aligned} \tag{7.74}$$

Numerically, we compute these quantities by repeatedly invoking equations (7.69) and (7.63) with different choices of variables.

We note that the intermediate values of $a^{[i]}$ and $z^{[i]}$ are used in the backpropagation (equation (7.74)), and therefore these values need to be stored in the memory after the forward pass.

Next, we compute the gradient of the parameters by invoking equations (7.65) and (7.66),

$$\begin{aligned}
\frac{\partial J}{\partial W^{[r]}} &= \mathcal{B}[\mathrm{MM}, W^{[r]}]\left(\frac{\partial J}{\partial z^{[r]}}\right) \\
\frac{\partial J}{\partial b^{[r]}} &= \mathcal{B}[\mathrm{MM}, b^{[r]}]\left(\frac{\partial J}{\partial z^{[r]}}\right) \\
&\vdots \\
\frac{\partial J}{\partial W^{[1]}} &= \mathcal{B}[\mathrm{MM}, W^{[1]}]\left(\frac{\partial J}{\partial z^{[1]}}\right) \\
\frac{\partial J}{\partial b^{[1]}} &= \mathcal{B}[\mathrm{MM}, b^{[1]}]\left(\frac{\partial J}{\partial z^{[1]}}\right) .
\end{aligned} \tag{7.75}$$

We also note that the block of computations in equations (7.75) can be interleaved with the block of computation in equations (7.74) because the $\frac{\partial J}{\partial W^{[i]}}$ and $\frac{\partial J}{\partial b^{[i]}}$ can be computed as soon as $\frac{\partial J}{\partial z^{[i]}}$ is computed.

Putting all of these together, and explicitly invoking the equations (7.72), (7.74) and (7.75), we have the following algorithm (Algorithm 3).

Algorithm 3 Back-propagation for multi-layer neural networks.

1: **Forward pass.** Compute and store the values of $a^{[k]}$'s, $z^{[k]}$'s, and J using the equations (7.72).

2: **Backward pass.** Compute the gradient of loss J with respect to $z^{[r]}$:

$$\frac{\partial J}{\partial z^{[r]}} = \mathcal{B}[\ell_{\text{logistic}}, z^{[r]}](1) = \left(1/(1+\exp(-z^{[r]})) - y\right) . \tag{7.76}$$

3: **for** $k = r-1$ to 0 **do**

4: Compute the gradient with respect to parameters $W^{[k+1]}$ and $b^{[k+1]}$.

$$\begin{aligned}\frac{\partial J}{\partial W^{[k+1]}} &= \mathcal{B}[\text{MM}, W^{[k+1]}]\left(\frac{\partial J}{\partial z^{[k+1]}}\right)\\ &= \frac{\partial J}{\partial z^{[k+1]}} a^{[k]\top} . \end{aligned} \tag{7.77}$$

$$\begin{aligned}\frac{\partial J}{\partial b^{[k+1]}} &= \mathcal{B}[\text{MM}, b^{[k+1]}]\left(\frac{\partial J}{\partial z^{[k+1]}}\right)\\ &= \frac{\partial J}{\partial z^{[k+1]}} . \end{aligned} \tag{7.78}$$

5: When $k \geq 1$, compute the gradient with respect to $z^{[k]}$ and $a^{[k]}$.

$$\begin{aligned}\frac{\partial J}{\partial a^{[k]}} &= \mathcal{B}[\sigma, a^{[k]}]\left(\frac{\partial J}{\partial z^{[k+1]}}\right)\\ &= W^{[k+1]\top} \frac{\partial J}{\partial z^{[k+1]}} . \end{aligned} \tag{7.79}$$

$$\begin{aligned}\frac{\partial J}{\partial z^{[k]}} &= \mathcal{B}[\sigma, z^{[k]}]\left(\frac{\partial J}{\partial a^{[k]}}\right)\\ &= \sigma'(z^{[k]}) \odot \frac{\partial J}{\partial a^{[k]}} . \end{aligned} \tag{7.80}$$

7.5 Vectorization over training examples

As we discussed in Section 7.1, in the implementation of neural networks, we will leverage the parallelism across the multiple examples. This means that we will need to write the forward pass (the evaluation of the outputs) of the neural network and the backward pass (backpropagation) for multiple training examples in matrix notation.

The basic idea. The basic idea is simple. Suppose you have a training set with three examples $x^{(1)}, x^{(2)}, x^{(3)}$. The first-layer activations for each example are as follows:

$$\begin{aligned} z^{[1](1)} &= W^{[1]}x^{(1)} + b^{[1]} \\ z^{[1](2)} &= W^{[1]}x^{(2)} + b^{[1]} \\ z^{[1](3)} &= W^{[1]}x^{(3)} + b^{[1]} \end{aligned}$$

Note the difference between square brackets $[\cdot]$, which refer to the layer number, and parenthesis $(\cdot)$, which refer to the training example number. Intuitively, one would implement this using a for loop. It turns out, we can vectorize these operations as well. First, define:

$$X = \begin{bmatrix} | & | & | \\ x^{(1)} & x^{(2)} & x^{(3)} \\ | & | & | \end{bmatrix} \in \mathbb{R}^{d\times 3} \tag{7.81}$$

Note that we are stacking training examples in columns and *not* rows. We can then combine this into a single unified formulation:

$$Z^{[1]} = \begin{bmatrix} | & | & | \\ z^{[1](1)} & z^{[1](2)} & z^{[1](3)} \\ | & | & | \end{bmatrix} = W^{[1]}X + b^{[1]} \tag{7.82}$$

You may notice that we are attempting to add $b^{[1]} \in \mathbb{R}^{4\times 1}$ to $W^{[1]}X \in \mathbb{R}^{4\times 3}$. Strictly following the rules of linear algebra, this is not allowed. In practice however, this addition is performed using *broadcasting*. We create an intermediate $\tilde{b}^{[1]} \in \mathbb{R}^{4\times 3}$:

$$\tilde{b}^{[1]} = \begin{bmatrix} | & | & | \\ b^{[1]} & b^{[1]} & b^{[1]} \\ | & | & | \end{bmatrix} \tag{7.83}$$

We can then perform the computation: $Z^{[1]} = W^{[1]}X + \tilde{b}^{[1]}$. Often times, it is not necessary to explicitly construct $\tilde{b}^{[1]}$. By inspecting the dimensions in (7.82), you can assume $b^{[1]} \in \mathbb{R}^{4\times 1}$ is correctly broadcast to $W^{[1]}X \in \mathbb{R}^{4\times 3}$.

The matricization approach as above can easily generalize to multiple layers, with one subtlety though, as discussed below.

Complications/Subtlety in the Implementation. All the deep learning packages or implementations put the data points in the rows of a data matrix. (If the data point itself is a matrix or tensor, then the data are concentrated along the zero-th dimension.) However, most of the deep learning papers use a similar notation to these notes where the data points are treated as column vectors.[8] There is a simple conversion to deal with the mismatch: in the implementation, all the columns become row vectors, row vectors become column vectors, all the matrices are transposed, and the orders of the matrix multiplications are flipped. In the example above, using the row major convention, the data matrix is $X \in \mathbb{R}^{3\times d}$, the first layer weight matrix has dimensionality $d \times m$ (instead of $m \times d$ as in the two layer neural net section), and the bias vector $b^{[1]} \in \mathbb{R}^{1\times m}$. The computation for the hidden activation becomes

$$Z^{[1]} = XW^{[1]} + b^{[1]} \in \mathbb{R}^{3\times m} \tag{7.84}$$

[8]The instructor suspects that this is mostly because in mathematics we naturally multiply a matrix to a vector on the left hand side.

Part III

Generalization and regularization

Chapter 8

Generalization

This chapter discusses tools to analyze and understand the generalization of machine learning models, i.e, their performances on unseen test examples. Recall that for supervised learning problems, given a training dataset $\{(x^{(i)}, y^{(i)})\}_{i=1}^n$, we typically learn a model h_θ by minimizing a loss/cost function $J(\theta)$, which encourages h_θ to fit the data. E.g., when the loss function is the least square loss (aka mean squared error), we have $J(\theta) = \frac{1}{n}\sum_{i=1}^n (y^{(i)} - h_\theta(x^{(i)}))^2$. This loss function for training purposes is oftentimes referred to as the **training** loss/error/cost.

However, minimizing the training loss is **not** our ultimate goal—it is merely our approach towards the goal of learning a predictive model. The most important evaluation metric of a model is the loss on unseen test examples, which is oftentimes referred to as the test error. Formally, we sample a test example (x, y) from the so-called test distribution $\mathcal{D}$, and measure the model's error on it, by, e.g., the mean squared error, $(h_\theta(x) - y)^2$. The expected loss/error over the randomness of the test example is called the test loss/error,[1]

$$L(\theta) = \mathbb{E}_{(x,y)\sim\mathcal{D}}[(y - h_\theta(x))^2] \tag{8.1}$$

Note that the measurement of the error involves computing the expectation, and in practice, it can be approximated by the average error on many sampled test examples, which are referred to as the test dataset. Note that the key difference here between training and test datasets is that the test examples

[1] In theoretical and statistical literature, we oftentimes call the uniform distribution over the training set $\{(x^{(i)}, y^{(i)})\}_{i=1}^n$, denoted by $\widehat{\mathcal{D}}$, an empirical distribution, and call $\mathcal{D}$ the population distribution. Partly because of this, the training loss is also referred to as the empirical loss/risk/error, and the test loss is also referred to as the population loss/risk/error.

are *unseen*, in the sense that the training procedure has not used the test examples. In classical statistical learning settings, the training examples are also drawn from the same distribution as the test distribution $\mathcal{D}$, but still the test examples are unseen by the learning procedure whereas the training examples are seen.[2]

Because of this key difference between training and test datasets, even if they are both drawn from the same distribution $\mathcal{D}$, the test error is not necessarily always close to the training error.[3] As a result, successfully minimizing the training error may not always lead to a small test error. We typically say the model **overfits** the data if the model predicts accurately on the training dataset but doesn't generalize well to other test examples, that is, if the training error is small but the test error is large. We say the model **underfits** the data if the training error is relatively large[4] (and in this case, typically the test error is also relatively large.)

This chapter studies how the test error is influenced by the learning procedure, especially the choice of model parameterizations. We will decompose the test error into "bias" and "variance" terms and study how each of them is affected by the choice of model parameterizations and their tradeoffs. Using the bias-variance tradeoff, we will discuss when overfitting and underfitting will occur and be avoided. We will also discuss the double descent phenomenon in Section 8.2 and some classical theoretical results in Section 8.3.

[2]These days, researchers have increasingly been more interested in the setting with "domain shift", that is, the training distribution and test distribution are different.

[3]the difference between test error and training error is often referred to as the generalization gap. The term *generalization error* in some literature means the test error, and in some other literature means the generalization gap.

[4]e.g., larger than the intrinsic noise level of the data in regression problems.

8.1 Bias-variance tradeoff

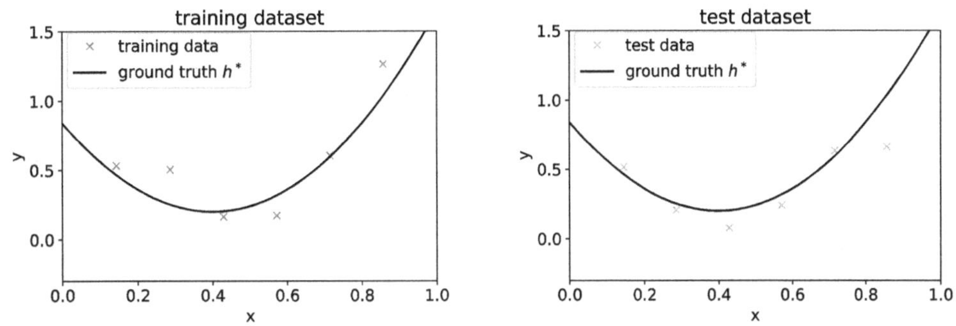

Figure 8.1: A running example of training and test dataset for this section.

As an illustrating example, we consider the following training dataset and test dataset, which are also shown in Figure 8.1. The training inputs $x^{(i)}$'s are randomly chosen and the outputs $y^{(i)}$ are generated by $y^{(i)} = h^\star(x^{(i)}) + \xi^{(i)}$ where the function $h^\star(\cdot)$ is a quadratic function and is shown in Figure 8.1 as the solid line, and $\xi^{(i)}$ is the a observation noise assumed to be generated from $\sim N(0, \sigma^2)$. A test example (x, y) also has the same input-output relationship $y = h^\star(x) + \xi$ where $\xi \sim N(0, \sigma^2)$. It's impossible to predict the noise ξ, and therefore essentially our goal is to recover the function $h^\star(\cdot)$.

We will consider the test error of learning various types of models. When talking about linear regression, we discussed the problem of whether to fit a "simple" model such as the linear "$y = \theta_0 + \theta_1 x$," or a more "complex" model such as the polynomial "$y = \theta_0 + \theta_1 x + \cdots \theta_5 x^5$."

We start with fitting a linear model, as shown in Figure 8.2. The best fitted linear model cannot predict y from x accurately even on the training dataset, let alone on the test dataset. This is because the true relationship between y and x is not linear—any linear model is far away from the true function $h^\star(\cdot)$. As a result, the training error is large and this is a typical situation of *underfitting*.

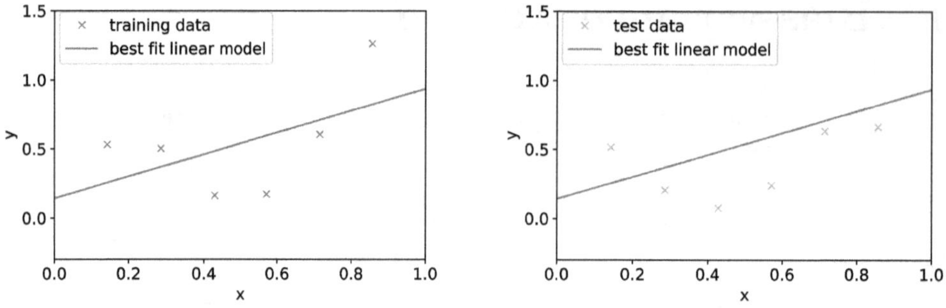

Figure 8.2: The best fit linear model has large training and test errors.

The issue cannot be mitigated with more training examples—even with a very large amount of, or even infinite training examples, the best fitted linear model is still inaccurate and fails to capture the structure of the data (Figure 8.3). Even if the noise is not present in the training data, the issue still occurs (Figure 8.4). Therefore, the fundamental bottleneck here is the linear model family's inability to capture the structure in the data—linear models cannot represent the true quadratic function $h^\star$—, but not the lack of the data. Informally, we define the **bias** of a model to be the test error even if we were to fit it to a very (say, infinitely) large training dataset. Thus, in this case, the linear model suffers from large bias, and underfits (i.e., fails to capture structure exhibited by) the data.

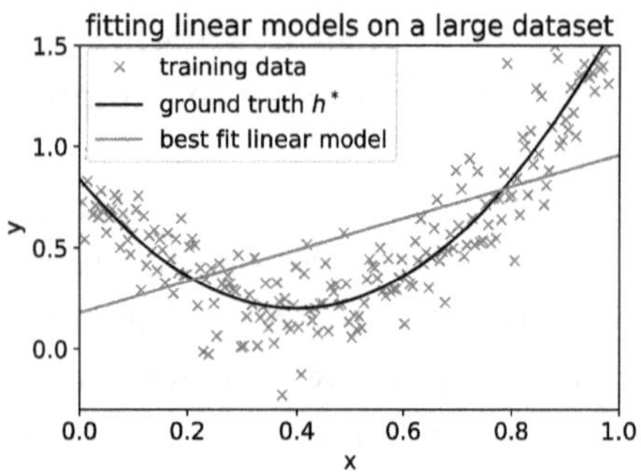

Figure 8.3: The best fit linear model on a much larger dataset still has a large training error.

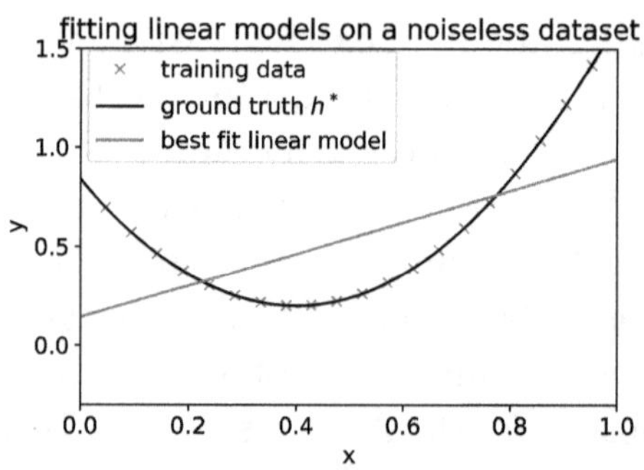

Figure 8.4: The best fit linear model on a noiseless dataset also has a large training/test error.

Next, we fit a 5th-degree polynomial to the data. Figure 8.5 shows that it fails to learn a good model either. However, the failure pattern is different from the linear model case. Specifically, even though the learnt 5th-degree polynomial did a very good job predicting $y^{(i)}$'s from $x^{(i)}$'s for training examples, it does not work well on test examples (Figure 8.5). In other words, the model learnt from the training set does not *generalize* well to other test examples—the test error is high. Contrary to the behavior of linear models, the bias of the 5-th degree polynomials is small—if we were to fit a 5-th degree polynomial to an extremely large dataset, the resulting model would be close to a quadratic function and be accurate (Figure 8.6). This is because the family of 5-th degree polynomials contains all the quadratic functions (setting $\theta_5 = \theta_4 = \theta_3 = 0$ results in a quadratic function), and, therefore, 5-th degree polynomials are in principle capable of capturing the structure of the data.

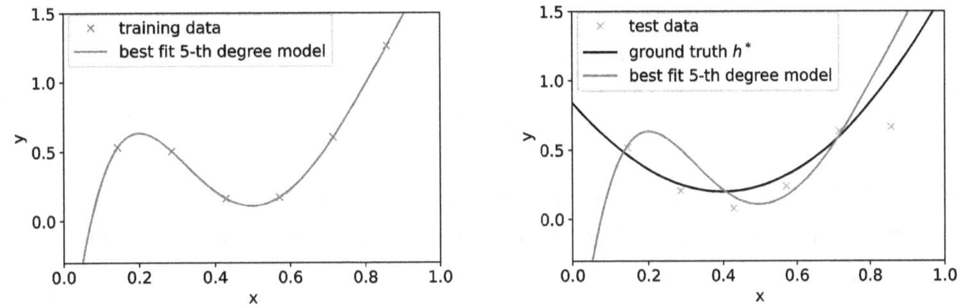

Figure 8.5: Best fit 5-th degree polynomial has zero training error, but still has a large test error and does not recover the the ground truth. This is a classic situation of overfitting.

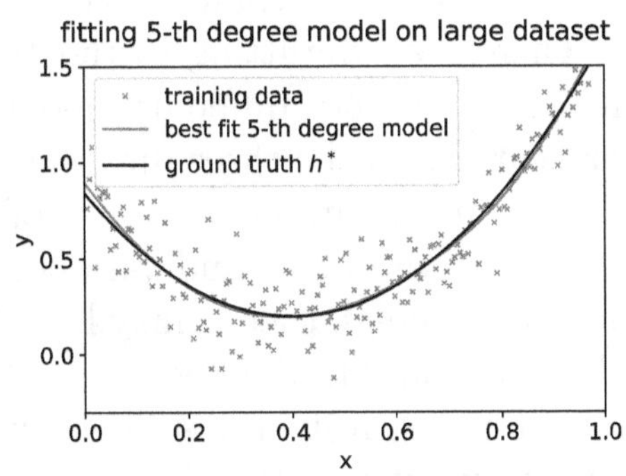

Figure 8.6: The best fit 5-th degree polynomial on a huge dataset nearly recovers the ground-truth—suggesting that the culprit in Figure 8.5 is the variance (or lack of data) but not bias.

The failure of fitting 5-th degree polynomials can be captured by another component of the test error, called **variance** of a model fitting procedure. Specifically, when fitting a 5-th degree polynomial as in Figure 8.7, there is a large risk that we're fitting patterns in the data that happened to be present in our *small, finite* training set, but that do not reflect the wider pattern of the relationship between x and y. These "spurious" patterns in the training set are (mostly) due to the observation noise $\xi^{(i)}$, and fitting these spurious patters results in a model with large test error. In this case, we say the model has a large variance.

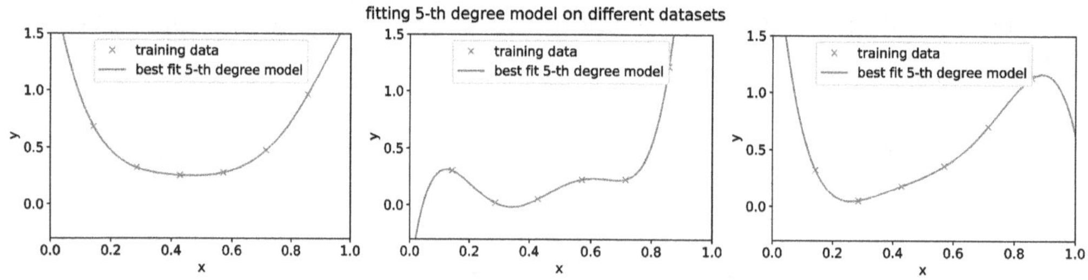

Figure 8.7: The best fit 5-th degree models on three different datasets generated from the same distribution behave quite differently, suggesting the existence of a large variance.

The variance can be intuitively (and mathematically, as shown in Section 8.1.1) characterized by the amount of variations across models learnt on multiple different training datasets (drawn from the same underlying distribution). The "spurious patterns" are specific to the randomness of the noise (and inputs) in a particular dataset, and thus are different across multiple training datasets. Therefore, overfitting to the "spurious patterns" of multiple datasets should result in very different models. Indeed, as shown in Figure 8.7, the models learned on the three different training datasets are quite different, overfitting to the "spurious patterns" of each datasets.

Often, there is a tradeoff between bias and variance. If our model is too "simple" and has very few parameters, then it may have large bias (but small variance), and it typically may suffer from underfittng. If it is too "complex" and has very many parameters, then it may suffer from large variance (but have smaller bias), and thus overfitting. See Figure 8.8 for a typical tradeoff between bias and variance.

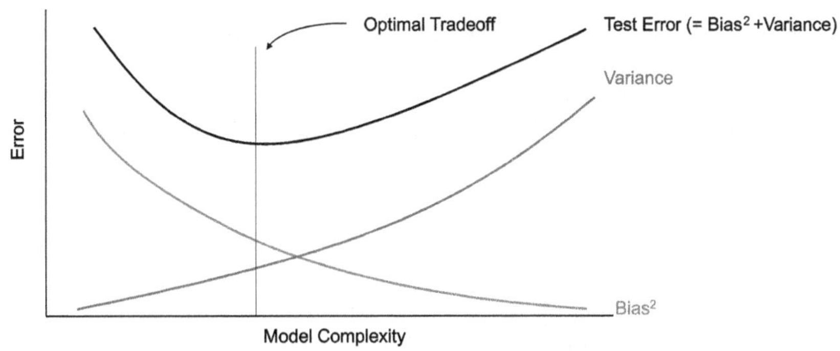

Figure 8.8: An illustration of the typical bias-variance tradeoff.

As we will see formally in Section 8.1.1, the test error can be decomposed as a summation of bias and variance. This means that the test error will have a convex curve as the model complexity increases, and in practice we should tune the model complexity to achieve the best tradeoff. For instance, in the example above, fitting a quadratic function does better than either of the extremes of a first or a 5-th degree polynomial, as shown in Figure 8.9.

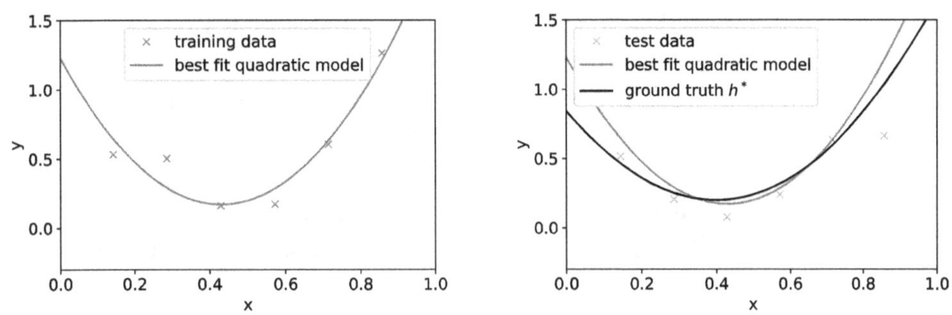

Figure 8.9: Best fit quadratic model has small training and test error because quadratic model achieves a better tradeoff.

Interestingly, the bias-variance tradeoff curves or the test error curves do not universally follow the shape in Figure 8.8, at least not universally when the model complexity is simply measured by the number of parameters. (We will discuss the so-called double descent phenomenon in Section 8.2.) Nevertheless, the principle of bias-variance tradeoff is perhaps still the first resort when analyzing and predicting the behavior of test errors.

8.1.1 A mathematical decomposition (for regression)

To formally state the bias-variance tradeoff for regression problems, we consider the following setup (which is an extension of the beginning paragraph of Section 8.1).

- Draw a training dataset $S = \{x^{(i)}, y^{(i)}\}_{i=1}^n$ such that $y^{(i)} = h^\star(x^{(i)}) + \xi^{(i)}$ where $\xi^{(i)} \in N(0, \sigma^2)$.
- Train a model on the dataset S, denoted by $\hat{h}_S$.
- Take a test example (x, y) such that $y = h^\star(x) + \xi$ where $\xi \sim N(0, \sigma^2)$, and measure the expected test error (averaged over the random draw of the training set S and the randomness of ξ)[5][6]

$$\text{MSE}(x) = \mathbb{E}_{S,\xi}[(y - h_S(x))^2] \tag{8.2}$$

We will decompose the MSE into a bias and variance term. We start by stating a following simple mathematical tool that will be used twice below.

Claim 8.1.1: Suppose A and B are two independent real random variables and $\mathbb{E}[A] = 0$. Then, $\mathbb{E}[(A + B)^2] = \mathbb{E}[A^2] + \mathbb{E}[B^2]$.

As a corollary, because a random variable A is independent with a constant c, when $\mathbb{E}[A] = 0$, we have $\mathbb{E}[(A + c)^2] = \mathbb{E}[A^2] + c^2$.

The proof of the claim follows from expanding the square: $\mathbb{E}[(A+B)^2] = \mathbb{E}[A^2] + \mathbb{E}[B^2] + 2\mathbb{E}[AB] = \mathbb{E}[A^2] + \mathbb{E}[B^2]$. Here we used the independence to show that $\mathbb{E}[AB] = \mathbb{E}[A]\mathbb{E}[B] = 0$.

Using Claim 8.1.1 with $A = \xi$ and $B = h^\star(x) - \hat{h}_S(x)$, we have

$$\begin{aligned}
\text{MSE}(x) = \mathbb{E}[(y - h_S(x))^2] &= \mathbb{E}[(\xi + (h^\star(x) - h_S(x)))^2] && (8.3)\\
&= \mathbb{E}[\xi^2] + \mathbb{E}[(h^\star(x) - h_S(x))^2] && \text{(by Claim 8.1.1)}\\
&= \sigma^2 + \mathbb{E}[(h^\star(x) - h_S(x))^2] && (8.4)
\end{aligned}$$

Then, let's define $h_{\text{avg}}(x) = \mathbb{E}_S[h_S(x)]$ as the "average model"—the model obtained by drawing an infinite number of datasets, training on them, and averaging their predictions on x. Note that h_{avg} is a hypothetical model for analytical purposes that can not be obtained in reality (because we don't

[5]For simplicity, the test input x is considered to be fixed here, but the same conceptual message holds when we average over the choice of x's.

[6]The subscript under the expectation symbol is to emphasize the variables that are considered as random by the expectation operation.

have infinite number of datasets). It turns out that for many cases, h_{avg} is (approximately) equal to the the model obtained by training on a *single* dataset with infinite samples. Thus, we can also intuitively interpret h_{avg} this way, which is consistent with our intuitive definition of bias in the previous subsection.

We can further decompose $\text{MSE}(x)$ by letting $c = h^\star(x) - h_{\text{avg}}(x)$ (which is a constant that does not depend on the choice of S!) and $A = h_{\text{avg}}(x) - h_S(x)$ in the corollary part of Claim 8.1.1:

$$\begin{aligned}
\text{MSE}(x) &= \sigma^2 + \mathbb{E}[(h^\star(x) - h_S(x))^2] &(8.5)\\
&= \sigma^2 + (h^\star(x) - h_{\text{avg}}(x))^2 + \mathbb{E}[(h_{\text{avg}} - h_S(x))^2] &(8.6)\\
&= \underbrace{\sigma^2}_{\text{unavoidable}} + \underbrace{(h^\star(x) - h_{\text{avg}}(x))^2}_{\triangleq\ \text{bias}^2} + \underbrace{\text{var}(h_S(x))}_{\triangleq\ \text{variance}} &(8.7)
\end{aligned}$$

We call the second term the bias (square) and the third term the variance. As discussed before, the bias captures the part of the error that are introduced due to the lack of expressivity of the model. Recall that h_{avg} can be thought of as the best possible model learned even with infinite data. Thus, the bias is not due to the lack of data, but is rather caused by that the family of models fundamentally cannot approximate the $h^\star$. For example, in the illustrating example in Figure 8.2, because any linear model cannot approximate the true quadratic function $h^\star$, neither can h_{avg}, and thus the bias term has to be large.

The variance term captures how the random nature of the finite dataset introduces errors in the learned model. It measures the sensitivity of the learned model to the randomness in the dataset. It often decreases as the size of the dataset increases.

There is nothing we can do about the first term σ^2 as we can not predict the noise ξ by definition.

Finally, we note that the bias-variance decomposition for classification is much less clear than for regression problems. There have been several proposals, but there is as yet no agreement on what is the "right" and/or the most useful formalism.

8.2 The double descent phenomenon

Model-wise double descent. Recent works have demonstrated that the test error can present a "double descent" phenomenon in a range of machine learning models including linear models and deep neural networks.[7] The conventional wisdom, as discussed in Section 8.1, is that as we increase the model complexity, the test error first decreases and then increases, as illustrated in Figure 8.8. However, in many cases, we empirically observe that the test error can have a second descent—it first decreases, then increases to a peak around when the model size is large enough to fit all the training data very well, and then decreases again in the so-called overparameterized regime, where the number of parameters is larger than the number of data points. See Figure 8.10 for an illustration of the typical curves of test errors against model complexity (measured by the number of parameters). To some extent, the overparameterized regime with the second descent is considered as new to the machine learning community—partly because lightly-regularized, overparameterized models are only extensively used in the deep learning era. A practical implication of the phenomenon is that one should not hold back from scaling into and experimenting with over-parametrized models because the test error may well decrease again to a level even smaller than the previous lowest point. Actually, in many cases, larger overparameterized models always lead to a better test performance (meaning there won't be a second ascent after the second descent).

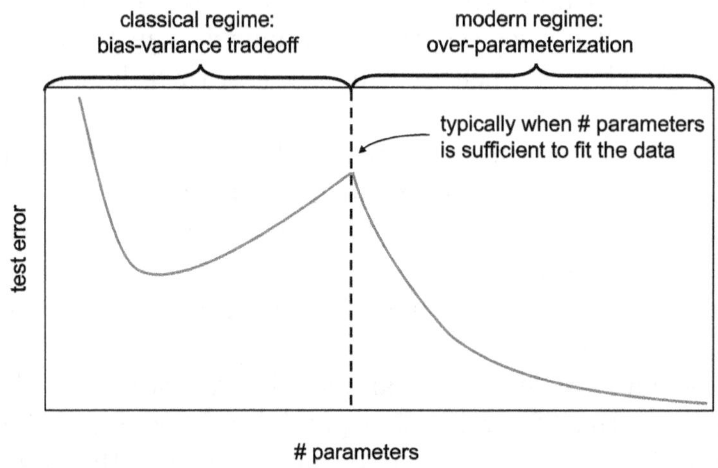

Figure 8.10: A typical model-wise double descent phenomenon. As the number of parameters increases, the test error first decreases when the number of parameters is smaller than the training data. Then in the overparameterized regime, the test error decreases again.

[7]The discovery of the phenomenon perhaps dates back to Opper [1995, 2001], and has been recently popularized by Belkin et al. [2020], Hastie et al. [2019], etc.

Sample-wise double descent. A priori, we would expect that more training examples always lead to smaller test errors—more samples give strictly more information for the algorithm to learn from. However, recent work [Nakkiran, 2019] observes that the test error is not monotonically decreasing as we increase the sample size. Instead, as shown in Figure 8.11, the test error decreases, and then increases and peaks around when the number of examples (denoted by n) is similar to the number of parameters (denoted by d), and then decreases again. We refer to this as the sample-wise double descent phenomenon. To some extent, sample-wise double descent and model-wise double descent are essentially describing similar phenomena—the test error is peaked when $n \approx d$.

Explanation and mitigation strategy. The sample-wise double descent, or, in particular, the peak of test error at $n \approx d$, suggests that the existing training algorithms evaluated in these experiments are far from optimal when $n \approx d$. We will be better off by tossing away some examples and run the algorithms with a smaller sample size to steer clear of the peak. In other words, in principle, there are other algorithms that can achieve smaller test error when $n \approx d$, but the algorithms evaluated in these experiments fail to do so. The sub-optimality of the learning procedure appears to be the culprit of the peak in both sample-wise and model-wise double descent.

Indeed, with an optimally-tuned regularization (which will be discussed more in Section 9), the test error in the $n \approx d$ regime can be dramatically improved, and the model-wise and sample-wise double descent are both mitigated. See Figure 8.11.

The intuition above only explains the peak in the model-wise and sample-wise double descent, but does not explain the second descent in the model-wise double descent—why overparameterized models are able to generalize so well. The theoretical understanding of overparameterized models is an active research area with many recent advances. A typical explanation is that the commonly-used optimizers such as gradient descent provide an implicit regularization effect (which will be discussed in more detail in Section 9.2). In other words, even in the overparameterized regime and with an unregularized loss function, the model is still implicitly regularized, and thus exhibits a better test performance than an arbitrary solution that fits the data. For example, for linear models, when $n \ll d$, the gradient descent optimizer with zero initialization finds the *minimum norm* solution that fits the data (instead of an arbitrary solution that fits the data), and the minimum norm regularizer turns out to be a sufficiently good for the overparameterized regime (but it's not a good regularizer when $n \approx d$, resulting in the peak of test error).

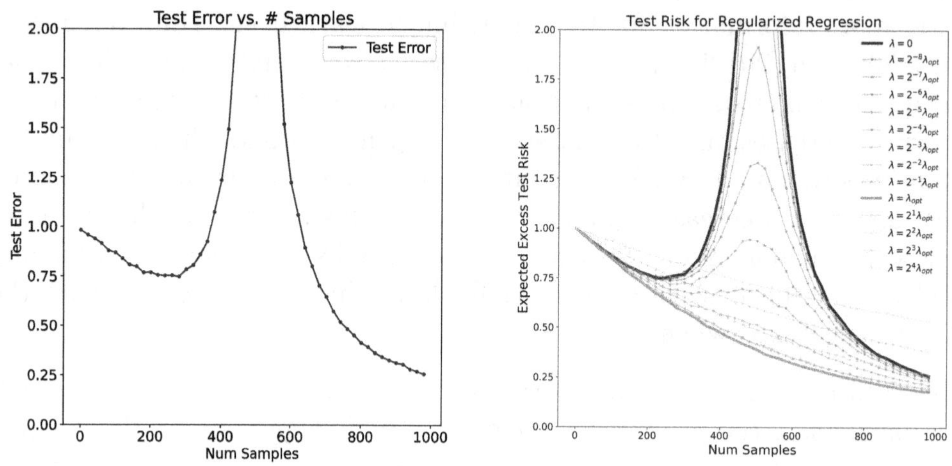

Figure 8.11: **Left:** The sample-wise double descent phenomenon for linear models. **Right:** The sample-wise double descent with different regularization strength for linear models. Using the optimal regularization parameter λ (optimally tuned for each n, shown in green solid curve) mitigates double descent. **Setup:** The data distribution of (x, y) is $x \sim \mathcal{N}(0, I_d)$ and $y \sim x^\top \beta + \mathcal{N}(0, \sigma^2)$ where $d = 500, \sigma = 0.5$ and $\|\beta\|_2 = 1$.[8]

Finally, we also remark that the double descent phenomenon has been mostly observed when the model complexity is measured by the number of parameters. It is unclear if and when the number of parameters is the best complexity measure of a model. For example, in many situations, the norm of the models is used as a complexity measure. As shown in Figure 8.12 right, for a particular linear case, if we plot the test error against the norm of the learnt model, the double descent phenomenon no longer occurs. This is partly because the norm of the learned model is also peaked around $n \approx d$ (See Figure 8.12 (middle) or Belkin et al. [2019], Mei and Montanari [2022], and discussions in Section 10.8 of James et al. [2021]). For deep neural networks, the correct complexity measure is even more elusive. The study of double descent phenomenon is an active research topic.

[8]The figure is reproduced from Figure 1 of Nakkiran et al. [2020]. Similar phenomenon are also observed in Hastie et al. [2022], Mei and Montanari [2022]

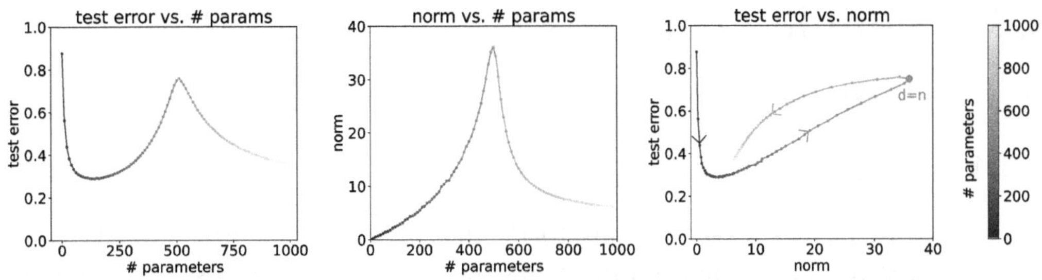

Figure 8.12: **Left:** The double descent phenomenon, where the number of parameters is used as the model complexity. **Middle:** The norm of the learned model is peaked around $n \approx d$. **Right:** The test error against the norm of the learnt model. The color bar indicate the number of parameters and the arrows indicates the direction of increasing model size. Their relationship are closer to the convention wisdom than to a double descent. **Setup:** We consider a linear regression with a fixed dataset of size $n = 500$. The input x is a random ReLU feature on Fashion-MNIST, and output $y \in \mathbb{R}^{10}$ is the one-hot label. This is the same setting as in Section 5.2 of Nakkiran et al. [2020].

8.3 Sample complexity bounds (optional readings)

8.3.1 Preliminaries

In this set of notes, we begin our foray into learning theory. Apart from being interesting and enlightening in its own right, this discussion will also help us hone our intuitions and derive rules of thumb about how to best apply learning algorithms in different settings. We will also seek to answer a few questions: First, can we make formal the bias/variance tradeoff that was just discussed? This will also eventually lead us to talk about model selection methods, which can, for instance, automatically decide what order polynomial to fit to a training set. Second, in machine learning it's really generalization error that we care about, but most learning algorithms fit their models to the training set. Why should doing well on the training set tell us anything about generalization error? Specifically, can we relate error on the training set to generalization error? Third and finally, are there conditions under which we can actually prove that learning algorithms will work well?

We start with two simple but very useful lemmas.

Lemma. (The union bound). Let $A_1, A_2, \ldots, A_k$ be k different events (that may not be independent). Then

$$P(A_1 \cup \cdots \cup A_k) \leq P(A_1) + \ldots + P(A_k).$$

In probability theory, the union bound is usually stated as an axiom (and thus we won't try to prove it), but it also makes intuitive sense: The probability of any one of k events happening is at most the sum of the probabilities of the k different events.

Lemma. (Hoeffding inequality) Let $Z_1, \ldots, Z_n$ be n independent and identically distributed (iid) random variables drawn from a Bernoulli(ϕ) distribution. I.e., $P(Z_i = 1) = \phi$, and $P(Z_i = 0) = 1 - \phi$. Let $\hat{\phi} = (1/n) \sum_{i=1}^{n} Z_i$ be the mean of these random variables, and let any $\gamma > 0$ be fixed. Then

$$P(|\phi - \hat{\phi}| > \gamma) \leq 2 \exp(-2\gamma^2 n)$$

This lemma (which in learning theory is also called the **Chernoff bound**) says that if we take $\hat{\phi}$—the average of n Bernoulli(ϕ) random variables—to be our estimate of ϕ, then the probability of our being far from the true value is small, so long as n is large. Another way of saying this is that if you have a biased coin whose chance of landing on heads is ϕ, then if you toss it n

times and calculate the fraction of times that it came up heads, that will be a good estimate of ϕ with high probability (if n is large).

Using just these two lemmas, we will be able to prove some of the deepest and most important results in learning theory.

To simplify our exposition, let's restrict our attention to binary classification in which the labels are $y \in \{0, 1\}$. Everything we'll say here generalizes to other problems, including regression and multi-class classification.

We assume we are given a training set $S = \{(x^{(i)}, y^{(i)}); i = 1, \ldots, n\}$ of size n, where the training examples $(x^{(i)}, y^{(i)})$ are drawn iid from some probability distribution $\mathcal{D}$. For a hypothesis h, we define the **training error** (also called the **empirical risk** or **empirical error** in learning theory) to be

$$\hat{\varepsilon}(h) = \frac{1}{n} \sum_{i=1}^{n} 1\{h(x^{(i)}) \neq y^{(i)}\}.$$

This is just the fraction of training examples that h misclassifies. When we want to make explicit the dependence of $\hat{\varepsilon}(h)$ on the training set S, we may also write this a $\hat{\varepsilon}_S(h)$. We also define the generalization error to be

$$\varepsilon(h) = P_{(x,y)\sim\mathcal{D}}(h(x) \neq y).$$

I.e. this is the probability that, if we now draw a new example (x, y) from the distribution $\mathcal{D}$, h will misclassify it.

Note that we have assumed that the training data was drawn from the *same* distribution $\mathcal{D}$ with which we're going to evaluate our hypotheses (in the definition of generalization error). This is sometimes also referred to as one of the **PAC** assumptions.[9]

Consider the setting of linear classification, and let $h_\theta(x) = 1\{\theta^T x \geq 0\}$. What's a reasonable way of fitting the parameters θ? One approach is to try to minimize the training error, and pick

$$\hat{\theta} = \arg\min_{\theta} \hat{\varepsilon}(h_\theta).$$

We call this process **empirical risk minimization** (ERM), and the resulting hypothesis output by the learning algorithm is $\hat{h} = h_{\hat{\theta}}$. We think of ERM as the most "basic" learning algorithm, and it will be this algorithm that we

[9]PAC stands for "probably approximately correct," which is a framework and set of assumptions under which numerous results on learning theory were proved. Of these, the assumption of training and testing on the same distribution, and the assumption of the independently drawn training examples, were the most important.

focus on in these notes. (Algorithms such as logistic regression can also be viewed as approximations to empirical risk minimization.)

In our study of learning theory, it will be useful to abstract away from the specific parameterization of hypotheses and from issues such as whether we're using a linear classifier. We define the **hypothesis class** $\mathcal{H}$ used by a learning algorithm to be the set of all classifiers considered by it. For linear classification, $\mathcal{H} = \{h_\theta : h_\theta(x) = 1\{\theta^T x \geq 0\}, \theta \in \mathbb{R}^{d+1}\}$ is thus the set of all classifiers over $\mathcal{X}$ (the domain of the inputs) where the decision boundary is linear. More broadly, if we were studying, say, neural networks, then we could let $\mathcal{H}$ be the set of all classifiers representable by some neural network architecture.

Empirical risk minimization can now be thought of as a minimization over the class of functions $\mathcal{H}$, in which the learning algorithm picks the hypothesis:

$$\hat{h} = \arg\min_{h \in \mathcal{H}} \hat{\varepsilon}(h)$$

8.3.2 The case of finite $\mathcal{H}$

Let's start by considering a learning problem in which we have a finite hypothesis class $\mathcal{H} = \{h_1, \ldots, h_k\}$ consisting of k hypotheses. Thus, $\mathcal{H}$ is just a set of k functions mapping from $\mathcal{X}$ to $\{0, 1\}$, and empirical risk minimization selects $\hat{h}$ to be whichever of these k functions has the smallest training error.

We would like to give guarantees on the generalization error of $\hat{h}$. Our strategy for doing so will be in two parts: First, we will show that $\hat{\varepsilon}(h)$ is a reliable estimate of $\varepsilon(h)$ for all h. Second, we will show that this implies an upper-bound on the generalization error of $\hat{h}$.

Take any one, fixed, $h_i \in \mathcal{H}$. Consider a Bernoulli random variable Z whose distribution is defined as follows. We're going to sample $(x, y) \sim \mathcal{D}$. Then, we set $Z = 1\{h_i(x) \neq y\}$. I.e., we're going to draw one example, and let Z indicate whether h_i misclassifies it. Similarly, we also define $Z_j = 1\{h_i(x^{(j)}) \neq y^{(j)}\}$. Since our training set was drawn iid from $\mathcal{D}$, Z and the Z_j's have the same distribution.

We see that the misclassification probability on a randomly drawn example—that is, $\varepsilon(h)$—is exactly the expected value of Z (and Z_j). Moreover, the training error can be written

$$\hat{\varepsilon}(h_i) = \frac{1}{n} \sum_{j=1}^{n} Z_j.$$

Thus, $\hat{\varepsilon}(h_i)$ is exactly the mean of the n random variables Z_j that are drawn iid from a Bernoulli distribution with mean $\varepsilon(h_i)$. Hence, we can apply the

Hoeffding inequality, and obtain

$$P(|\varepsilon(h_i) - \hat{\varepsilon}(h_i)| > \gamma) \leq 2\exp(-2\gamma^2 n).$$

This shows that, for our particular h_i, training error will be close to generalization error with high probability, assuming n is large. But we don't just want to guarantee that $\varepsilon(h_i)$ will be close to $\hat{\varepsilon}(h_i)$ (with high probability) for just only one particular h_i. We want to prove that this will be true simultaneously for *all* $h \in \mathcal{H}$. To do so, let A_i denote the event that $|\varepsilon(h_i) - \hat{\varepsilon}(h_i)| > \gamma$. We've already shown that, for any particular A_i, it holds true that $P(A_i) \leq 2\exp(-2\gamma^2 n)$. Thus, using the union bound, we have that

$$\begin{aligned} P(\exists\, h \in \mathcal{H}.|\varepsilon(h_i) - \hat{\varepsilon}(h_i)| > \gamma) &= P(A_1 \cup \cdots \cup A_k) \\ &\leq \sum_{i=1}^{k} P(A_i) \\ &\leq \sum_{i=1}^{k} 2\exp(-2\gamma^2 n) \\ &= 2k\exp(-2\gamma^2 n) \end{aligned}$$

If we subtract both sides from 1, we find that

$$\begin{aligned} P(\neg\exists\, h \in \mathcal{H}.|\varepsilon(h_i) - \hat{\varepsilon}(h_i)| > \gamma) &= P(\forall h \in \mathcal{H}.|\varepsilon(h_i) - \hat{\varepsilon}(h_i)| \leq \gamma) \\ &\geq 1 - 2k\exp(-2\gamma^2 n) \end{aligned}$$

(The "$\neg$" symbol means "not.") So, with probability at least $1 - 2k\exp(-2\gamma^2 n)$, we have that $\varepsilon(h)$ will be within γ of $\hat{\varepsilon}(h)$ for all $h \in \mathcal{H}$. This is called a *uniform convergence* result, because this is a bound that holds simultaneously for all (as opposed to just one) $h \in \mathcal{H}$.

In the discussion above, what we did was, for particular values of n and γ, give a bound on the probability that for some $h \in \mathcal{H}$, $|\varepsilon(h) - \hat{\varepsilon}(h)| > \gamma$. There are three quantities of interest here: n, γ, and the probability of error; we can bound either one in terms of the other two.

For instance, we can ask the following question: Given γ and some $\delta > 0$, how large must n be before we can guarantee that with probability at least $1 - \delta$, training error will be within γ of generalization error? By setting $\delta = 2k\exp(-2\gamma^2 n)$ and solving for n, [you should convince yourself this is the right thing to do!], we find that if

$$n \geq \frac{1}{2\gamma^2} \log \frac{2k}{\delta},$$

then with probability at least $1-\delta$, we have that $|\varepsilon(h)-\hat{\varepsilon}(h)| \leq \gamma$ for all $h \in \mathcal{H}$. (Equivalently, this shows that the probability that $|\varepsilon(h)-\hat{\varepsilon}(h)| > \gamma$ for some $h \in \mathcal{H}$ is at most δ.) This bound tells us how many training examples we need in order make a guarantee. The training set size n that a certain method or algorithm requires in order to achieve a certain level of performance is also called the algorithm's **sample complexity**.

The key property of the bound above is that the number of training examples needed to make this guarantee is only *logarithmic* in k, the number of hypotheses in $\mathcal{H}$. This will be important later.

Similarly, we can also hold n and δ fixed and solve for γ in the previous equation, and show [again, convince yourself that this is right!] that with probability $1-\delta$, we have that for all $h \in \mathcal{H}$,

$$|\hat{\varepsilon}(h)-\varepsilon(h)| \leq \sqrt{\frac{1}{2n}\log\frac{2k}{\delta}}.$$

Now, let's assume that uniform convergence holds, i.e., that $|\varepsilon(h)-\hat{\varepsilon}(h)| \leq \gamma$ for all $h \in \mathcal{H}$. What can we prove about the generalization of our learning algorithm that picked $\hat{h} = \arg\min_{h\in\mathcal{H}} \hat{\varepsilon}(h)$?

Define $h^* = \arg\min_{h\in\mathcal{H}} \varepsilon(h)$ to be the best possible hypothesis in $\mathcal{H}$. Note that h^* is the best that we could possibly do given that we are using $\mathcal{H}$, so it makes sense to compare our performance to that of h^*. We have:

$$\begin{aligned}
\varepsilon(\hat{h}) &\leq \hat{\varepsilon}(\hat{h}) + \gamma \\
&\leq \hat{\varepsilon}(h^*) + \gamma \\
&\leq \varepsilon(h^*) + 2\gamma
\end{aligned}$$

The first line used the fact that $|\varepsilon(\hat{h})-\hat{\varepsilon}(\hat{h})| \leq \gamma$ (by our uniform convergence assumption). The second used the fact that $\hat{h}$ was chosen to minimize $\hat{\varepsilon}(h)$, and hence $\hat{\varepsilon}(\hat{h}) \leq \hat{\varepsilon}(h)$ for all h, and in particular $\hat{\varepsilon}(\hat{h}) \leq \hat{\varepsilon}(h^*)$. The third line used the uniform convergence assumption again, to show that $\hat{\varepsilon}(h^*) \leq \varepsilon(h^*) + \gamma$. So, what we've shown is the following: If uniform convergence occurs, then the generalization error of $\hat{h}$ is at most 2γ worse than the best possible hypothesis in $\mathcal{H}$!

Let's put all this together into a theorem.

Theorem. Let $|\mathcal{H}| = k$, and let any n, δ be fixed. Then with probability at least $1-\delta$, we have that

$$\varepsilon(\hat{h}) \leq \left(\min_{h\in\mathcal{H}} \varepsilon(h)\right) + 2\sqrt{\frac{1}{2n}\log\frac{2k}{\delta}}.$$

This is proved by letting γ equal the $\sqrt{\cdot}$ term, using our previous argument that uniform convergence occurs with probability at least $1-\delta$, and then noting that uniform convergence implies $\varepsilon(h)$ is at most 2γ higher than $\varepsilon(h^*) = \min_{h\in\mathcal{H}} \varepsilon(h)$ (as we showed previously).

This also quantifies what we were saying previously saying about the bias/variance tradeoff in model selection. Specifically, suppose we have some hypothesis class $\mathcal{H}$, and are considering switching to some much larger hypothesis class $\mathcal{H}' \supseteq \mathcal{H}$. If we switch to $\mathcal{H}'$, then the first term $\min_h \varepsilon(h)$ can only decrease (since we'd then be taking a min over a larger set of functions). Hence, by learning using a larger hypothesis class, our "bias" can only decrease. However, if k increases, then the second $2\sqrt{\cdot}$ term would also increase. This increase corresponds to our "variance" increasing when we use a larger hypothesis class.

By holding γ and δ fixed and solving for n like we did before, we can also obtain the following sample complexity bound:

Corollary. Let $|\mathcal{H}| = k$, and let any δ, γ be fixed. Then for $\varepsilon(\hat{h}) \leq \min_{h\in\mathcal{H}} \varepsilon(h) + 2\gamma$ to hold with probability at least $1-\delta$, it suffices that

$$\begin{aligned} n &\geq \frac{1}{2\gamma^2}\log\frac{2k}{\delta} \\ &= O\left(\frac{1}{\gamma^2}\log\frac{k}{\delta}\right), \end{aligned}$$

8.3.3 The case of infinite $\mathcal{H}$

We have proved some useful theorems for the case of finite hypothesis classes. But many hypothesis classes, including any parameterized by real numbers (as in linear classification) actually contain an infinite number of functions. Can we prove similar results for this setting?

Let's start by going through something that is *not* the "right" argument. *Better and more general arguments exist*, but this will be useful for honing our intuitions about the domain.

Suppose we have an $\mathcal{H}$ that is parameterized by d real numbers. Since we are using a computer to represent real numbers, and IEEE double-precision floating point (`double`'s in C) uses 64 bits to represent a floating point number, this means that our learning algorithm, assuming we're using double-precision floating point, is parameterized by $64d$ bits. Thus, our hypothesis class really consists of at most $k = 2^{64d}$ different hypotheses. From the Corollary at the end of the previous section, we therefore find that, to guarantee

$\varepsilon(\hat{h}) \le \varepsilon(h^*) + 2\gamma$, with to hold with probability at least $1-\delta$, it suffices that $n \ge O\left(\frac{1}{\gamma^2}\log\frac{2^{64d}}{\delta}\right) = O\left(\frac{d}{\gamma^2}\log\frac{1}{\delta}\right) = O_{\gamma,\delta}(d)$. (The γ, δ subscripts indicate that the last big-O is hiding constants that may depend on γ and δ.) Thus, the number of training examples needed is at most *linear* in the parameters of the model.

The fact that we relied on 64-bit floating point makes this argument not entirely satisfying, but the conclusion is nonetheless roughly correct: If what we try to do is minimize training error, then in order to learn "well" using a hypothesis class that has d parameters, generally we're going to need on the order of a linear number of training examples in d.

(At this point, it's worth noting that these results were proved for an algorithm that uses empirical risk minimization. Thus, while the linear dependence of sample complexity on d does generally hold for most discriminative learning algorithms that try to minimize training error or some approximation to training error, these conclusions do not always apply as readily to discriminative learning algorithms. Giving good theoretical guarantees on many non-ERM learning algorithms is still an area of active research.)

The other part of our previous argument that's slightly unsatisfying is that it relies on the parameterization of $\mathcal{H}$. Intuitively, this doesn't seem like it should matter: We had written the class of linear classifiers as $h_\theta(x) = 1\{\theta_0 + \theta_1 x_1 + \cdots \theta_d x_d \ge 0\}$, with $n+1$ parameters $\theta_0, \ldots, \theta_d$. But it could also be written $h_{u,v}(x) = 1\{(u_0^2 - v_0^2) + (u_1^2 - v_1^2)x_1 + \cdots (u_d^2 - v_d^2)x_d \ge 0\}$ with $2d+2$ parameters u_i, v_i. Yet, both of these are just defining the same $\mathcal{H}$: The set of linear classifiers in d dimensions.

To derive a more satisfying argument, let's define a few more things.

Given a set $S = \{x^{(i)}, \ldots, x^{(\mathbf{D})}\}$ (no relation to the training set) of points $x^{(i)} \in \mathcal{X}$, we say that $\mathcal{H}$ **shatters** S if $\mathcal{H}$ can realize any labeling on S. I.e., if for any set of labels $\{y^{(1)}, \ldots, y^{(\mathbf{D})}\}$, there exists some $h \in \mathcal{H}$ so that $h(x^{(i)}) = y^{(i)}$ for all $i = 1, \ldots \mathbf{D}$.

Given a hypothesis class $\mathcal{H}$, we then define its **Vapnik-Chervonenkis dimension**, written VC($\mathcal{H}$), to be the size of the largest set that is shattered by $\mathcal{H}$. (If $\mathcal{H}$ can shatter arbitrarily large sets, then VC($\mathcal{H}$) $= \infty$.)

For instance, consider the following set of three points:

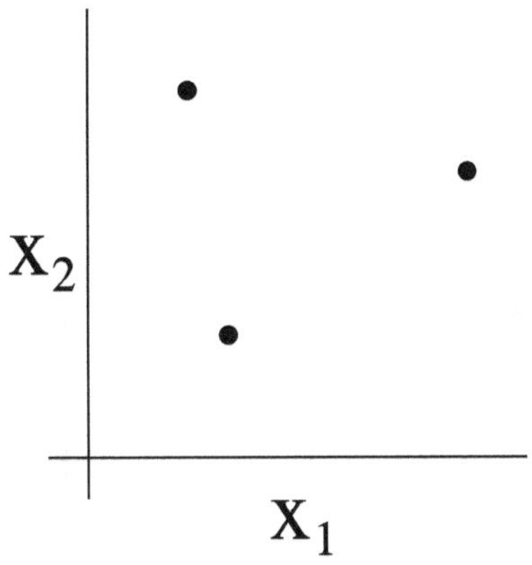

Can the set $\mathcal{H}$ of linear classifiers in two dimensions ($h(x) = 1\{\theta_0+\theta_1 x_1+\theta_2 x_2 \geq 0\}$) can shatter the set above? The answer is yes. Specifically, we see that, for any of the eight possible labelings of these points, we can find a linear classifier that obtains "zero training error" on them:

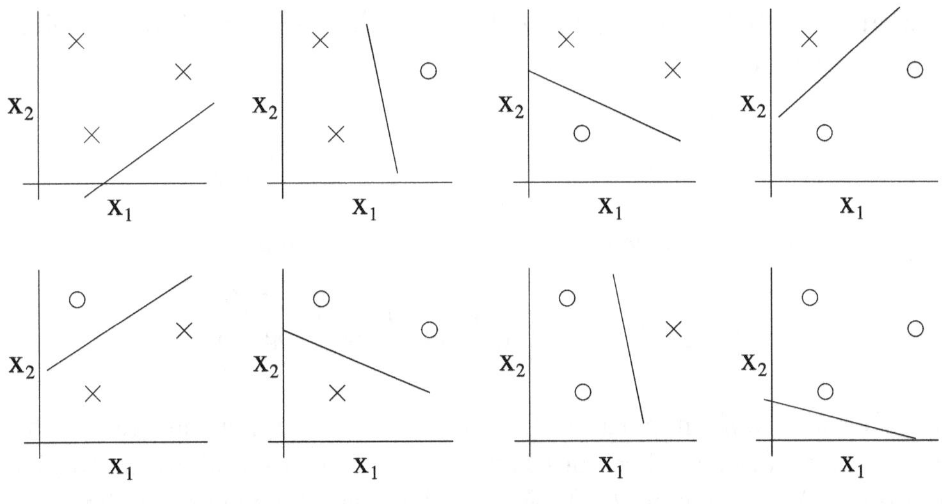

Moreover, it is possible to show that there is no set of 4 points that this hypothesis class can shatter. Thus, the largest set that $\mathcal{H}$ can shatter is of size 3, and hence $\mathrm{VC}(\mathcal{H}) = 3$.

Note that the VC dimension of $\mathcal{H}$ here is 3 even though there may be sets of size 3 that it cannot shatter. For instance, if we had a set of three points lying in a straight line (left figure), then there is no way to find a linear separator for the labeling of the three points shown below (right figure):

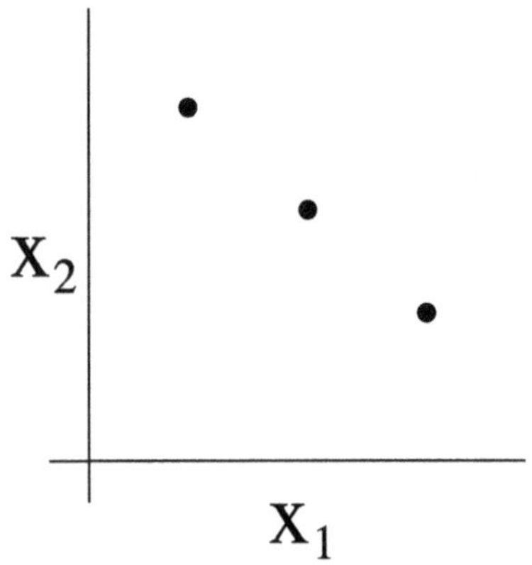

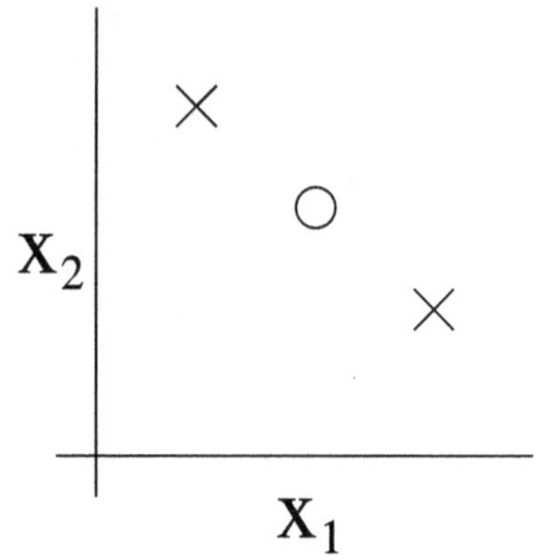

In order words, under the definition of the VC dimension, in order to prove that VC($\mathcal{H}$) is at least **D**, we need to show only that there's at least *one* set of size **D** that $\mathcal{H}$ can shatter.

The following theorem, due to Vapnik, can then be shown. (This is, many would argue, the most important theorem in all of learning theory.)

Theorem. Let $\mathcal{H}$ be given, and let $\mathbf{D} = \mathrm{VC}(\mathcal{H})$. Then with probability at least $1 - \delta$, we have that for all $h \in \mathcal{H}$,

$$|\varepsilon(h) - \hat{\varepsilon}(h)| \leq O\left(\sqrt{\frac{\mathbf{D}}{n}\log\frac{n}{\mathbf{D}} + \frac{1}{n}\log\frac{1}{\delta}}\right).$$

Thus, with probability at least $1 - \delta$, we also have that:

$$\varepsilon(\hat{h}) \leq \varepsilon(h^*) + O\left(\sqrt{\frac{\mathbf{D}}{n}\log\frac{n}{\mathbf{D}} + \frac{1}{n}\log\frac{1}{\delta}}\right).$$

In other words, if a hypothesis class has finite VC dimension, then uniform convergence occurs as n becomes large. As before, this allows us to give a bound on $\varepsilon(h)$ in terms of $\varepsilon(h^*)$. We also have the following corollary:

Corollary. For $|\varepsilon(h) - \hat{\varepsilon}(h)| \leq \gamma$ to hold for all $h \in \mathcal{H}$ (and hence $\varepsilon(\hat{h}) \leq \varepsilon(h^*) + 2\gamma$) with probability at least $1 - \delta$, it suffices that $n = O_{\gamma,\delta}(\mathbf{D})$.

In other words, the number of training examples needed to learn "well" using $\mathcal{H}$ is linear in the VC dimension of $\mathcal{H}$. It turns out that, for "most" hypothesis classes, the VC dimension (assuming a "reasonable" parameterization) is also roughly linear in the number of parameters. Putting these together, we conclude that for a given hypothesis class $\mathcal{H}$ (and for an algorithm that tries to minimize training error), the number of training examples needed to achieve generalization error close to that of the optimal classifier is usually roughly linear in the number of parameters of $\mathcal{H}$.

Chapter 9

Regularization and model selection

9.1 Regularization

Recall that as discussed in Section 8.1, overftting is typically a result of using too complex models, and we need to choose a proper model complexity to achieve the optimal bias-variance tradeoff. When the model complexity is measured by the number of parameters, we can vary the size of the model (e.g., the width of a neural net). However, the correct, informative complexity measure of the models can be a function of the parameters (e.g., ℓ_2 norm of the parameters), which may not necessarily depend on the number of parameters. In such cases, we will use regularization, an important technique in machine learning, control the model complexity and prevent overfitting.

Regularization typically involves adding an additional term, called a regularizer and denoted by $R(\theta)$ here, to the training loss/cost function:

$$J_\lambda(\theta) = J(\theta) + \lambda R(\theta) \tag{9.1}$$

Here J_λ is often called the regularized loss, and $\lambda \geq 0$ is called the regularization parameter. The regularizer $R(\theta)$ is a nonnegative function (in almost all cases). In classical methods, $R(\theta)$ is purely a function of the parameter θ, but some modern approach allows $R(\theta)$ to depend on the training dataset.[1]

The regularizer $R(\theta)$ is typically chosen to be some measure of the complexity of the model θ. Thus, when using the regularized loss, we aim to find a model that both fit the data (a small loss $J(\theta)$) and have a small

[1]Here our notations generally omit the dependency on the training dataset for simplicity—we write $J(\theta)$ even though it obviously needs to depend on the training dataset.

model complexity (a small $R(\theta)$). The balance between the two objectives is controlled by the regularization parameter λ. When $\lambda = 0$, the regularized loss is equivalent to the original loss. When λ is a sufficiently small positive number, minimizing the regularized loss is effectively minimizing the original loss with the regularizer as the tie-breaker. When the regularizer is extremely large, then the original loss is not effective (and likely the model will have a large bias.)

The most commonly used regularization is perhaps ℓ_2 regularization, where $R(\theta) = \frac{1}{2}\|\theta\|_2^2$. It encourages the optimizer to find a model with small ℓ_2 norm. In deep learning, it's oftentimes referred to as **weight decay**, because gradient descent with learning rate η on the regularized loss $R_\lambda(\theta)$ is equivalent to shrinking/decaying θ by a scalar factor of $1 - \eta\lambda$ and then applying the standard gradient

$$\begin{aligned} \theta &\leftarrow \theta - \eta \nabla J_\lambda(\theta) = \theta - \eta\lambda\theta - \eta\nabla J(\theta) \\ &= \underbrace{(1 - \lambda\eta)\theta}_{\text{decaying weights}} \; - \eta \nabla J(\theta) \end{aligned} \tag{9.2}$$

Besides encouraging simpler models, regularization can also impose inductive biases or structures on the model parameters. For example, suppose we had a prior belief that the number of non-zeros in the ground-truth model parameters is small,[2]—which is oftentimes called sparsity of the model—, we can impose a regularization on the number of non-zeros in θ, denoted by $\|\theta\|_0$, to leverage such a prior belief. Imposing additional structure of the parameters narrows our search space and makes the complexity of the model family smaller,—e.g., the family of sparse models can be thought of as having lower complexity than the family of all models—, and thus tends to lead to a better generalization. On the other hand, imposing additional structure may risk increasing the bias. For example, if we regularize the sparsity strongly but no sparse models can predict the label accurately, we will suffer from large bias (analogously to the situation when we use linear models to learn data than can only be represented by quadratic functions in Section 8.1.)

The sparsity of the parameters is not a continuous function of the parameters, and thus we cannot optimize it with (stochastic) gradient descent. A common relaxation is to use $R(\theta) = \|\theta\|_1$ as a continuous surrogate.[3]

---

[2]For linear models, this means the model just uses a few coordinates of the inputs to make an accurate prediction.

[3]There has been a rich line of theoretical work that explains why $\|\theta\|_1$ is a good surrogate for encouraging sparsity, but it's beyond the scope of this course. An intuition is: assuming the parameter is on the unit sphere, the parameter with smallest ℓ_1 norm also

The $R(\theta) = \|\theta\|_1$ (also called LASSO) and $R(\theta) = \frac{1}{2}\|\theta\|_2^2$ are perhaps among the most commonly used regularizers for linear models. Other norm and powers of norms are sometimes also used. The ℓ_2 norm regularization is much more commonly used with kernel methods because ℓ_1 regularization is typically not compatible with the kernel trick (the optimal solution cannot be written as functions of inner products of features.)

In deep learning, the most commonly used regularizer is ℓ_2 regularization or weight decay. Other common ones include dropout, data augmentation, regularizing the spectral norm of the weight matrices, and regularizing the Lipschitzness of the model, etc. Regularization in deep learning is an active research area, and it's known that there is another implicit source of regularization, as discussed in the next section.

9.2 Implicit regularization effect (optional reading)

The implicit regularization effect of optimizers, or implicit bias or algorithmic regularization, is a new concept/phenomenon observed in the deep learning era. It largely refers to that the optimizers can implicitly impose structures on parameters beyond what has been imposed by the regularized loss.

In most classical settings, the loss or regularized loss has a unique global minimum, and thus any reasonable optimizer should converge to that global minimum and cannot impose any additional preferences. However, in deep learning, oftentimes the loss or regularized loss has more than one (approximate) global minima, and difference optimizers may converge to different global minima. Though these global minima have the same or similar training losses, they may be of different nature and have dramatically different generalization performance. See Figures 9.1 and 9.2 and its caption for an illustration and some experiment results. For example, it's possible that one global minimum gives a much more Lipschitz or sparse model than others and thus has a better test error. It turns out that many commonly-used optimizers (or their components) prefer or bias towards finding global minima of certain properties, leading to a better test performance.

---

happen to be the sparsest parameter with only 1 non-zero coordinate. Thus, sparsity and ℓ_1 norm gives the same extremal points to some extent.

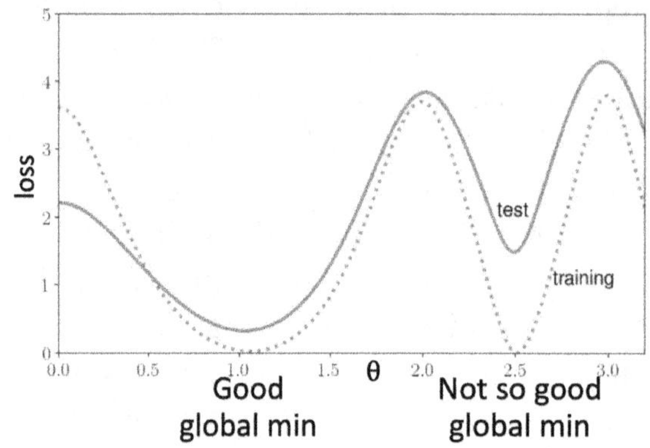

Figure 9.1: An Illustration that different global minima of the training loss can have different test performance.

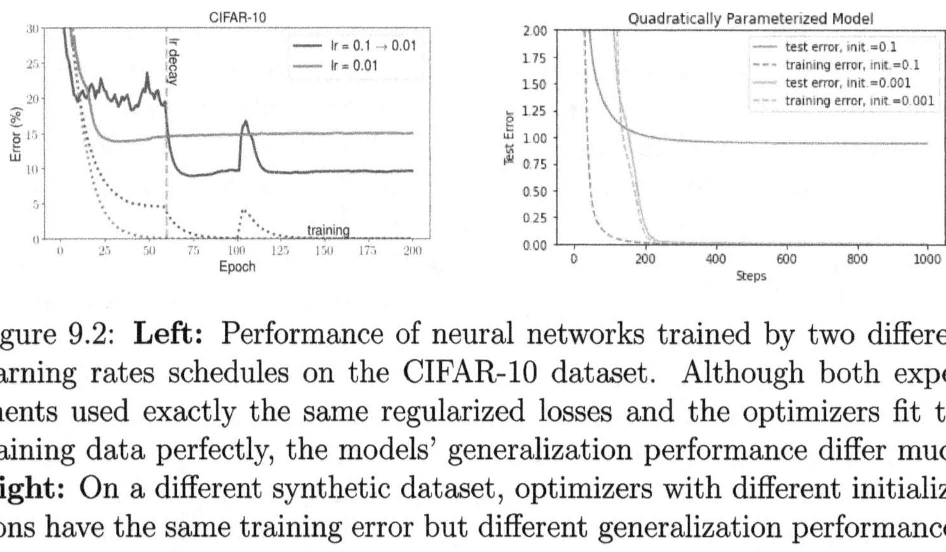

Figure 9.2: **Left:** Performance of neural networks trained by two different learning rates schedules on the CIFAR-10 dataset. Although both experiments used exactly the same regularized losses and the optimizers fit the training data perfectly, the models' generalization performance differ much. **Right:** On a different synthetic dataset, optimizers with different initializations have the same training error but different generalization performance.[4]

In summary, the takehome message here is that the choice of optimizer does not only affect minimizing the training loss, but also imposes implicit regularization and affects the generalization of the model. Even if your current optimizer already converges to a small training error perfectly, you may still need to tune your optimizer for a better generalization, .

[4]The setting is the same as in Woodworth et al. [2020], HaoChen et al. [2020]

One may wonder which components of the optimizers bias towards what type of global minima and what type of global minima may generalize better. These are open questions that researchers are actively investigating. Empirical and theoretical research have offered some clues and heuristics. In many (but definitely far from all) situations, among those setting where optimization can succeed in minimizing the training loss, the use of larger initial learning rate, smaller initialization, smaller batch size, and momentum appears to help with biasing towards more generalizable solutions. A conjecture (that can be proven in certain simplified case) is that stochasticity in the optimization process help the optimizer to find flatter global minima (global minima where the curvature of the loss is small), and flat global minima tend to give more Lipschitz models and better generalization. Characterizing the implicit regularization effect formally is still a challenging open research question.

9.3 Model selection via cross validation

Suppose we are trying select among several different models for a learning problem. For instance, we might be using a polynomial regression model $h_\theta(x) = g(\theta_0 + \theta_1 x + \theta_2 x^2 + \cdots + \theta_k x^k)$, and wish to decide if k should be 0, 1, ..., or 10. How can we automatically select a model that represents a good tradeoff between the twin evils of bias and variance[5]? Alternatively, suppose we want to automatically choose the bandwidth parameter τ for locally weighted regression, or the parameter C for our ℓ_1-regularized SVM. How can we do that?

For the sake of concreteness, in these notes we assume we have some finite set of models $\mathcal{M} = \{M_1, \ldots, M_d\}$ that we're trying to select among. For instance, in our first example above, the model M_i would be an i-th degree polynomial regression model. (The generalization to infinite $\mathcal{M}$ is not hard.[6]) Alternatively, if we are trying to decide between using an SVM, a neural network or logistic regression, then $\mathcal{M}$ may contain these models.

[5]Given that we said in the previous set of notes that bias and variance are two very different beasts, some readers may be wondering if we should be calling them "twin" evils here. Perhaps it'd be better to think of them as non-identical twins. The phrase "the fraternal twin evils of bias and variance" doesn't have the same ring to it, though.

[6]If we are trying to choose from an infinite set of models, say corresponding to the possible values of the bandwidth $\tau \in \mathbb{R}^+$, we may discretize τ and consider only a finite number of possible values for it. More generally, most of the algorithms described here can all be viewed as performing optimization search in the space of models, and we can perform this search over infinite model classes as well.

Cross validation. Lets suppose we are, as usual, given a training set S. Given what we know about empirical risk minimization, here's what might initially seem like a algorithm, resulting from using empirical risk minimization for model selection:

1. Train each model M_i on S, to get some hypothesis h_i.
2. Pick the hypotheses with the smallest training error.

This algorithm does *not* work. Consider choosing the degree of a polynomial. The higher the degree of the polynomial, the better it will fit the training set S, and thus the lower the training error. Hence, this method will always select a high-variance, high-degree polynomial model, which we saw previously is often poor choice.

Here's an algorithm that works better. In **hold-out cross validation** (also called **simple cross validation**), we do the following:

1. Randomly split S into S_{train} (say, 70% of the data) and S_{cv} (the remaining 30%). Here, S_{cv} is called the hold-out cross validation set.
2. Train each model M_i on S_{train} only, to get some hypothesis h_i.
3. Select and output the hypothesis h_i that had the smallest error $\hat{\varepsilon}_{S_{\text{cv}}}(h_i)$ on the hold out cross validation set. (Here $\hat{\varepsilon}_{S_{\text{cv}}}(h)$ denotes the average error of h on the set of examples in S_{cv}.) The error on the hold out validation set is also referred to as the validation error.

By testing/validating on a set of examples S_{cv} that the models were not trained on, we obtain a better estimate of each hypothesis h_i's true generalization/test error. Thus, this approach is essentially picking the model with the smallest estimated generalization/test error. The size of the validation set depends on the total number of available examples. Usually, somewhere between $1/4 - 1/3$ of the data is used in the hold out cross validation set, and 30% is a typical choice. However, when the total dataset is huge, validation set can be a smaller fraction of the total examples as long as the absolute number of validation examples is decent. For example, for the ImageNet dataset that has about 1M training images, the validation set is sometimes set to be 50K images, which is only about 5% of the total examples.

Optionally, step 3 in the algorithm may also be replaced with selecting the model M_i according to $\arg\min_i \hat{\varepsilon}_{S_{\text{cv}}}(h_i)$, and then retraining M_i on the entire training set S. (This is often a good idea, with one exception being learning algorithms that are be very sensitive to perturbations of the initial conditions and/or data. For these methods, M_i doing well on S_{train} does not necessarily mean it will also do well on S_{cv}, and it might be better to forgo this retraining step.)

The disadvantage of using hold out cross validation is that it "wastes" about 30% of the data. Even if we were to take the optional step of retraining the model on the entire training set, it's still as if we're trying to find a good model for a learning problem in which we had $0.7n$ training examples, rather than n training examples, since we're testing models that were trained on only $0.7n$ examples each time. While this is fine if data is abundant and/or cheap, in learning problems in which data is scarce (consider a problem with $n = 20$, say), we'd like to do something better.

Here is a method, called **k-fold cross validation**, that holds out less data each time:

1. Randomly split S into k disjoint subsets of m/k training examples each. Lets call these subsets $S_1, \ldots, S_k$.

2. For each model M_i, we evaluate it as follows:

   For $j = 1, \ldots, k$

   Train the model M_i on $S_1 \cup \cdots \cup S_{j-1} \cup S_{j+1} \cup \cdots S_k$ (i.e., train on all the data except S_j) to get some hypothesis h_{ij}.

   Test the hypothesis h_{ij} on S_j, to get $\hat{\varepsilon}_{S_j}(h_{ij})$.

   The estimated generalization error of model M_i is then calculated as the average of the $\hat{\varepsilon}_{S_j}(h_{ij})$'s (averaged over j).

3. Pick the model M_i with the lowest estimated generalization error, and retrain that model on the entire training set S. The resulting hypothesis is then output as our final answer.

A typical choice for the number of folds to use here would be $k = 10$. While the fraction of data held out each time is now $1/k$—much smaller than before—this procedure may also be more computationally expensive than hold-out cross validation, since we now need train to each model k times.

While $k = 10$ is a commonly used choice, in problems in which data is really scarce, sometimes we will use the extreme choice of $k = m$ in order to leave out as little data as possible each time. In this setting, we would repeatedly train on all but one of the training examples in S, and test on that held-out example. The resulting $m = k$ errors are then averaged together to obtain our estimate of the generalization error of a model. This method has its own name; since we're holding out one training example at a time, this method is called **leave-one-out cross validation.**

Finally, even though we have described the different versions of cross validation as methods for selecting a model, they can also be used more simply to evaluate a *single* model or algorithm. For example, if you have implemented some learning algorithm and want to estimate how well it performs for your application (or if you have invented a novel learning algorithm and want to report in a technical paper how well it performs on various test sets), cross validation would give a reasonable way of doing so.

9.4 Bayesian statistics and regularization

In this section, we will talk about one more tool in our arsenal for our battle against overfitting.

At the beginning of the quarter, we talked about parameter fitting using maximum likelihood estimation (MLE), and chose our parameters according to

$$\theta_{\text{MLE}} = \arg\max_{\theta} \prod_{i=1}^{n} p(y^{(i)}|x^{(i)};\theta).$$

Throughout our subsequent discussions, we viewed θ as an unknown parameter of the world. This view of the θ as being *constant-valued but unknown* is taken in **frequentist** statistics. In the frequentist this view of the world, θ is not random—it just happens to be unknown—and it's our job to come up with statistical procedures (such as maximum likelihood) to try to estimate this parameter.

An alternative way to approach our parameter estimation problems is to take the **Bayesian** view of the world, and think of θ as being a *random variable* whose value is unknown. In this approach, we would specify a **prior distribution** $p(\theta)$ on θ that expresses our "prior beliefs" about the parameters. Given a training set $S = \{(x^{(i)}, y^{(i)})\}_{i=1}^{n}$, when we are asked to make a prediction on a new value of x, we can then compute the posterior distribution on the parameters

$$\begin{aligned} p(\theta|S) &= \frac{p(S|\theta)p(\theta)}{p(S)} \\ &= \frac{\left(\prod_{i=1}^{n} p(y^{(i)}|x^{(i)},\theta)\right) p(\theta)}{\int_{\theta} \left(\prod_{i=1}^{n} p(y^{(i)}|x^{(i)},\theta)p(\theta)\right) d\theta} \end{aligned} \tag{9.3}$$

In the equation above, $p(y^{(i)}|x^{(i)},\theta)$ comes from whatever model you're using for your learning problem. For example, if you are using Bayesian logistic regression, then you might choose $p(y^{(i)}|x^{(i)}, \theta) = h_\theta(x^{(i)})^{y^{(i)}}(1-h_\theta(x^{(i)}))^{(1-y^{(i)})}$, where $h_\theta(x^{(i)}) = 1/(1 + \exp(-\theta^T x^{(i)}))$.[7]

When we are given a new test example x and asked to make it prediction on it, we can compute our posterior distribution on the class label using the posterior distribution on θ:

$$p(y|x, S) = \int_\theta p(y|x, \theta)p(\theta|S)d\theta \tag{9.4}$$

In the equation above, $p(\theta|S)$ comes from Equation (9.3). Thus, for example, if the goal is to the predict the expected value of y given x, then we would output[8]

$$\mathrm{E}[y|x, S] = \int_y yp(y|x, S)dy$$

The procedure that we've outlined here can be thought of as doing "fully Bayesian" prediction, where our prediction is computed by taking an average with respect to the posterior $p(\theta|S)$ over θ. Unfortunately, in general it is computationally very difficult to compute this posterior distribution. This is because it requires taking integrals over the (usually high-dimensional) θ as in Equation (9.3), and this typically cannot be done in closed-form.

Thus, in practice we will instead approximate the posterior distribution for θ. One common approximation is to replace our posterior distribution for θ (as in Equation 9.4) with a single point estimate. The **MAP (maximum a posteriori)** estimate for θ is given by

$$\theta_{\mathrm{MAP}} = \arg\max_\theta \prod_{i=1}^n p(y^{(i)}|x^{(i)}, \theta)p(\theta). \tag{9.5}$$

Note that this is the same formulas as for the MLE (maximum likelihood) estimate for θ, except for the prior $p(\theta)$ term at the end.

In practical applications, a common choice for the prior $p(\theta)$ is to assume that $\theta \sim \mathcal{N}(0, \tau^2 I)$. Using this choice of prior, the fitted parameters θ_{MAP} will have smaller norm than that selected by maximum likelihood. In practice, this causes the Bayesian MAP estimate to be less susceptible to overfitting than the ML estimate of the parameters. For example, Bayesian logistic regression turns out to be an effective algorithm for text classification, even though in text classification we usually have $d \gg n$.

[7]Since we are now viewing θ as a random variable, it is okay to condition on it value, and write "$p(y|x, \theta)$" instead of "$p(y|x; \theta)$."

[8]The integral below would be replaced by a summation if y is discrete-valued.

Part IV

Unsupervised learning

Chapter 10

Clustering and the k-means algorithm

In the clustering problem, we are given a training set $\{x^{(1)}, \ldots, x^{(n)}\}$, and want to group the data into a few cohesive "clusters." Here, $x^{(i)} \in \mathbb{R}^d$ as usual; but no labels $y^{(i)}$ are given. So, this is an unsupervised learning problem.

The k-means clustering algorithm is as follows:

1. Initialize **cluster centroids** $\mu_1, \mu_2, \ldots, \mu_k \in \mathbb{R}^d$ randomly.

2. Repeat until convergence: {

   For every i, set
$$c^{(i)} := \arg\min_j ||x^{(i)} - \mu_j||^2.$$

   For each j, set
$$\mu_j := \frac{\sum_{i=1}^n 1\{c^{(i)} = j\}x^{(i)}}{\sum_{i=1}^n 1\{c^{(i)} = j\}}.$$

   }

In the algorithm above, k (a parameter of the algorithm) is the number of clusters we want to find; and the cluster centroids μ_j represent our current guesses for the positions of the centers of the clusters. To initialize the cluster centroids (in step 1 of the algorithm above), we could choose k training examples randomly, and set the cluster centroids to be equal to the values of these k examples. (Other initialization methods are also possible.)

The inner-loop of the algorithm repeatedly carries out two steps: (i) "Assigning" each training example $x^{(i)}$ to the closest cluster centroid μ_j, and

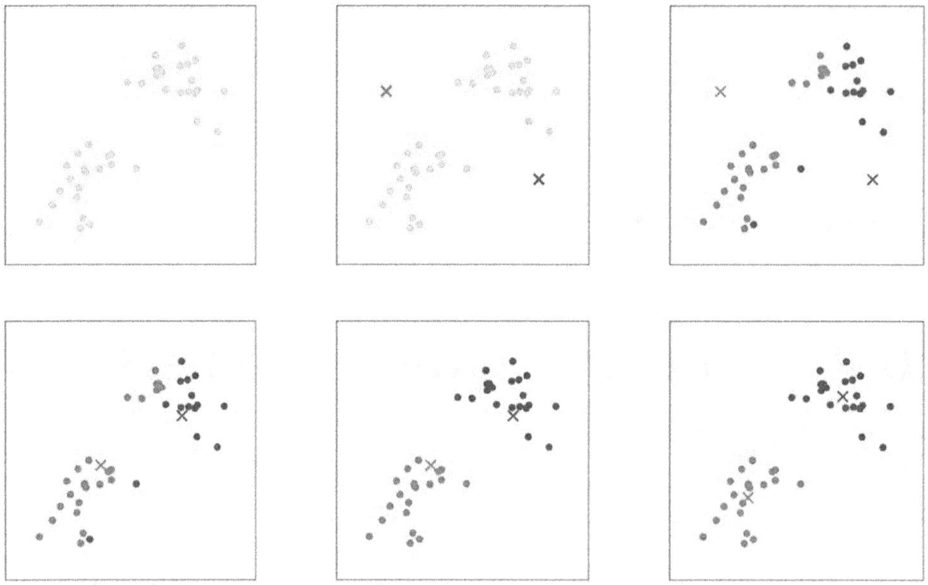

Figure 10.1: K-means algorithm. Training examples are shown as dots, and cluster centroids are shown as crosses. (a) Original dataset. (b) Random initial cluster centroids (in this instance, not chosen to be equal to two training examples). (c-f) Illustration of running two iterations of k-means. In each iteration, we assign each training example to the closest cluster centroid (shown by "painting" the training examples the same color as the cluster centroid to which is assigned); then we move each cluster centroid to the mean of the points assigned to it. (Best viewed in color.) Images courtesy Michael Jordan.

(ii) Moving each cluster centroid μ_j to the mean of the points assigned to it. Figure 10.1 shows an illustration of running k-means.

Is the k-means algorithm guaranteed to converge? Yes it is, in a certain sense. In particular, let us define the **distortion function** to be:

$$J(c, \mu) = \sum_{i=1}^{n} ||x^{(i)} - \mu_{c^{(i)}}||^2$$

Thus, J measures the sum of squared distances between each training example $x^{(i)}$ and the cluster centroid $\mu_{c^{(i)}}$ to which it has been assigned. It can be shown that k-means is exactly coordinate descent on J. Specifically, the inner-loop of k-means repeatedly minimizes J with respect to c while holding μ fixed, and then minimizes J with respect to μ while holding c fixed. Thus,

J must monotonically decrease, and the value of J must converge. (Usually, this implies that c and μ will converge too. In theory, it is possible for k-means to oscillate between a few different clusterings—i.e., a few different values for c and/or μ—that have exactly the same value of J, but this almost never happens in practice.)

The distortion function J is a non-convex function, and so coordinate descent on J is not guaranteed to converge to the global minimum. In other words, k-means can be susceptible to local optima. Very often k-means will work fine and come up with very good clusterings despite this. But if you are worried about getting stuck in bad local minima, one common thing to do is run k-means many times (using different random initial values for the cluster centroids μ_j). Then, out of all the different clusterings found, pick the one that gives the lowest distortion $J(c, \mu)$.

Chapter 11

EM algorithms

In this set of notes, we discuss the EM (Expectation-Maximization) algorithm for density estimation.

11.1 EM for mixture of Gaussians

Suppose that we are given a training set $\{x^{(1)}, \ldots, x^{(n)}\}$ as usual. Since we are in the unsupervised learning setting, these points do not come with any labels.

We wish to model the data by specifying a joint distribution $p(x^{(i)}, z^{(i)}) = p(x^{(i)}|z^{(i)})p(z^{(i)})$. Here, $z^{(i)} \sim \text{Multinomial}(\phi)$ (where $\phi_j \geq 0$, $\sum_{j=1}^{k} \phi_j = 1$, and the parameter ϕ_j gives $p(z^{(i)} = j)$), and $x^{(i)}|z^{(i)} = j \sim \mathcal{N}(\mu_j, \Sigma_j)$. We let k denote the number of values that the $z^{(i)}$'s can take on. Thus, our model posits that each $x^{(i)}$ was generated by randomly choosing $z^{(i)}$ from $\{1, \ldots, k\}$, and then $x^{(i)}$ was drawn from one of k Gaussians depending on $z^{(i)}$. This is called the **mixture of Gaussians** model. Also, note that the $z^{(i)}$'s are **latent** random variables, meaning that they're hidden/unobserved. This is what will make our estimation problem difficult.

The parameters of our model are thus ϕ, μ and Σ. To estimate them, we can write down the likelihood of our data:

$$
\begin{aligned}
\ell(\phi, \mu, \Sigma) &= \sum_{i=1}^{n} \log p(x^{(i)}; \phi, \mu, \Sigma) \\
&= \sum_{i=1}^{n} \log \sum_{z^{(i)}=1}^{k} p(x^{(i)}|z^{(i)}; \mu, \Sigma)p(z^{(i)}; \phi).
\end{aligned}
$$

However, if we set to zero the derivatives of this formula with respect to the parameters and try to solve, we'll find that it is not possible to find the maximum likelihood estimates of the parameters in closed form. (Try this yourself at home.)

The random variables $z^{(i)}$ indicate which of the k Gaussians each $x^{(i)}$ had come from. Note that if we knew what the $z^{(i)}$'s were, the maximum likelihood problem would have been easy. Specifically, we could then write down the likelihood as

$$\ell(\phi, \mu, \Sigma) = \sum_{i=1}^{n} \log p(x^{(i)}|z^{(i)}; \mu, \Sigma) + \log p(z^{(i)}; \phi).$$

Maximizing this with respect to ϕ, μ and Σ gives the parameters:

$$\begin{aligned} \phi_j &= \frac{1}{n}\sum_{i=1}^{n} 1\{z^{(i)} = j\}, \\ \mu_j &= \frac{\sum_{i=1}^{n} 1\{z^{(i)} = j\}x^{(i)}}{\sum_{i=1}^{n} 1\{z^{(i)} = j\}}, \\ \Sigma_j &= \frac{\sum_{i=1}^{n} 1\{z^{(i)} = j\}(x^{(i)} - \mu_j)(x^{(i)} - \mu_j)^T}{\sum_{i=1}^{n} 1\{z^{(i)} = j\}}. \end{aligned}$$

Indeed, we see that if the $z^{(i)}$'s were known, then maximum likelihood estimation becomes nearly identical to what we had when estimating the parameters of the Gaussian discriminant analysis model, except that here the $z^{(i)}$'s playing the role of the class labels.[1]

However, in our density estimation problem, the $z^{(i)}$'s are *not* known. What can we do?

The EM algorithm is an iterative algorithm that has two main steps. Applied to our problem, in the E-step, it tries to "guess" the values of the $z^{(i)}$'s. In the M-step, it updates the parameters of our model based on our guesses. Since in the M-step we are pretending that the guesses in the first part were correct, the maximization becomes easy. Here's the algorithm:

Repeat until convergence: {

(E-step) For each i, j, set

$$w_j^{(i)} := p(z^{(i)} = j|x^{(i)}; \phi, \mu, \Sigma)$$

[1]There are other minor differences in the formulas here from what we'd obtained in PS1 with Gaussian discriminant analysis, first because we've generalized the $z^{(i)}$'s to be multinomial rather than Bernoulli, and second because here we are using a different Σ_j for each Gaussian.

(M-step) Update the parameters:

$$\phi_j := \frac{1}{n}\sum_{i=1}^{n} w_j^{(i)},$$

$$\mu_j := \frac{\sum_{i=1}^{n} w_j^{(i)} x^{(i)}}{\sum_{i=1}^{n} w_j^{(i)}},$$

$$\Sigma_j := \frac{\sum_{i=1}^{n} w_j^{(i)} (x^{(i)} - \mu_j)(x^{(i)} - \mu_j)^T}{\sum_{i=1}^{n} w_j^{(i)}}$$

}

In the E-step, we calculate the posterior probability of our parameters the $z^{(i)}$'s, given the $x^{(i)}$ and using the current setting of our parameters. I.e., using Bayes rule, we obtain:

$$p(z^{(i)} = j | x^{(i)}; \phi, \mu, \Sigma) = \frac{p(x^{(i)}|z^{(i)} = j; \mu, \Sigma) p(z^{(i)} = j; \phi)}{\sum_{l=1}^{k} p(x^{(i)}|z^{(i)} = l; \mu, \Sigma) p(z^{(i)} = l; \phi)}$$

Here, $p(x^{(i)}|z^{(i)} = j; \mu, \Sigma)$ is given by evaluating the density of a Gaussian with mean μ_j and covariance Σ_j at $x^{(i)}$; $p(z^{(i)} = j; \phi)$ is given by ϕ_j, and so on. The values $w_j^{(i)}$ calculated in the E-step represent our "soft" guesses[2] for the values of $z^{(i)}$.

Also, you should contrast the updates in the M-step with the formulas we had when the $z^{(i)}$'s were known exactly. They are identical, except that instead of the indicator functions "$1\{z^{(i)} = j\}$" indicating from which Gaussian each datapoint had come, we now instead have the $w_j^{(i)}$'s.

The EM-algorithm is also reminiscent of the K-means clustering algorithm, except that instead of the "hard" cluster assignments $c(i)$, we instead have the "soft" assignments $w_j^{(i)}$. Similar to K-means, it is also susceptible to local optima, so reinitializing at several different initial parameters may be a good idea.

It's clear that the EM algorithm has a very natural interpretation of repeatedly trying to guess the unknown $z^{(i)}$'s; but how did it come about, and can we make any guarantees about it, such as regarding its convergence? In the next set of notes, we will describe a more general view of EM, one

[2]The term "soft" refers to our guesses being probabilities and taking values in $[0, 1]$; in contrast, a "hard" guess is one that represents a single best guess (such as taking values in $\{0, 1\}$ or $\{1, \ldots, k\}$).

that will allow us to easily apply it to other estimation problems in which there are also latent variables, and which will allow us to give a convergence guarantee.

11.2 Jensen's inequality

We begin our discussion with a very useful result called **Jensen's inequality**

Let f be a function whose domain is the set of real numbers. Recall that f is a convex function if $f''(x) \geq 0$ (for all $x \in \mathbb{R}$). In the case of f taking vector-valued inputs, this is generalized to the condition that its hessian H is positive semi-definite ($H \geq 0$). If $f''(x) > 0$ for all x, then we say f is **strictly** convex (in the vector-valued case, the corresponding statement is that H must be positive definite, written $H > 0$). Jensen's inequality can then be stated as follows:

Theorem. Let f be a convex function, and let X be a random variable. Then:

$$\mathrm{E}[f(X)] \geq f(\mathrm{E}X).$$

Moreover, if f is strictly convex, then $\mathrm{E}[f(X)] = f(\mathrm{E}X)$ holds true if and only if $X = \mathrm{E}[X]$ with probability 1 (i.e., if X is a constant).

Recall our convention of occasionally dropping the parentheses when writing expectations, so in the theorem above, $f(\mathrm{E}X) = f(\mathrm{E}[X])$.

For an interpretation of the theorem, consider the figure below.

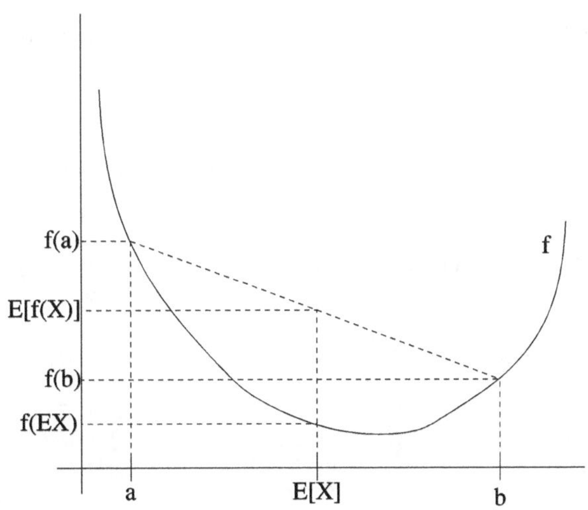

Here, f is a convex function shown by the solid line. Also, X is a random variable that has a 0.5 chance of taking the value a, and a 0.5 chance of taking the value b (indicated on the x-axis). Thus, the expected value of X is given by the midpoint between a and b.

We also see the values $f(a)$, $f(b)$ and $f(\mathrm{E}[X])$ indicated on the y-axis. Moreover, the value $\mathrm{E}[f(X)]$ is now the midpoint on the y-axis between $f(a)$ and $f(b)$. From our example, we see that because f is convex, it must be the case that $\mathrm{E}[f(X)] \geq f(\mathrm{E}X)$.

Incidentally, quite a lot of people have trouble remembering which way the inequality goes, and remembering a picture like this is a good way to quickly figure out the answer.

Remark. Recall that f is [strictly] concave if and only if $-f$ is [strictly] convex (i.e., $f''(x) \leq 0$ or $H \leq 0$). Jensen's inequality also holds for concave functions f, but with the direction of all the inequalities reversed ($\mathrm{E}[f(X)] \leq f(\mathrm{E}X)$, etc.).

11.3 General EM algorithms

Suppose we have an estimation problem in which we have a training set $\{x^{(1)}, \ldots, x^{(n)}\}$ consisting of n independent examples. We have a latent variable model $p(x, z; \theta)$ with z being the latent variable (which for simplicity is assumed to take finite number of values). The density for x can be obtained by marginalized over the latent variable z:

$$p(x;\theta) = \sum_z p(x, z; \theta) \tag{11.1}$$

We wish to fit the parameters θ by maximizing the log-likelihood of the data, defined by

$$\ell(\theta) = \sum_{i=1}^{n} \log p(x^{(i)}; \theta) \tag{11.2}$$

We can rewrite the objective in terms of the joint density $p(x, z; \theta)$ by

$$\begin{aligned} \ell(\theta) &= \sum_{i=1}^{n} \log p(x^{(i)}; \theta) && (11.3) \\ &= \sum_{i=1}^{n} \log \sum_{z^{(i)}} p(x^{(i)}, z^{(i)}; \theta). && (11.4) \end{aligned}$$

But, explicitly finding the maximum likelihood estimates of the parameters θ may be hard since it will result in difficult non-convex optimization problems.[3] Here, the $z^{(i)}$'s are the latent random variables; and it is often the case that if the $z^{(i)}$'s were observed, then maximum likelihood estimation would be easy.

In such a setting, the EM algorithm gives an efficient method for maximum likelihood estimation. Maximizing $\ell(\theta)$ explicitly might be difficult, and our strategy will be to instead repeatedly construct a lower-bound on ℓ (E-step), and then optimize that lower-bound (M-step).[4]

It turns out that the summation $\sum_{i=1}^{n}$ is not essential here, and towards a simpler exposition of the EM algorithm, we will first consider optimizing the the likelihood $\log p(x)$ for **a single example** x. After we derive the algorithm for optimizing $\log p(x)$, we will convert it to an algorithm that works for n examples by adding back the sum to each of the relevant equations. Thus, now we aim to optimize $\log p(x;\theta)$ which can be rewritten as

$$\log p(x;\theta) = \log \sum_z p(x,z;\theta) \tag{11.5}$$

Let Q be a distribution over the possible values of z. That is, $\sum_z Q(z) = 1$, $Q(z) \geq 0$).

Consider the following:[5]

$$\begin{aligned}
\log p(x;\theta) &= \log \sum_z p(x,z;\theta) \\
&= \log \sum_z Q(z) \frac{p(x,z;\theta)}{Q(z)} && (11.6) \\
&\geq \sum_z Q(z) \log \frac{p(x,z;\theta)}{Q(z)} && (11.7)
\end{aligned}$$

The last step of this derivation used Jensen's inequality. Specifically, $f(x) = \log x$ is a concave function, since $f''(x) = -1/x^2 < 0$ over its domain

[3]It's mostly an empirical observation that the optimization problem is difficult to optimize.

[4]Empirically, the E-step and M-step can often be computed more efficiently than optimizing the function $\ell(\cdot)$ directly. However, it doesn't necessarily mean that alternating the two steps can always converge to the global optimum of $\ell(\cdot)$. Even for mixture of Gaussians, the EM algorithm can either converge to a global optimum or get stuck, depending on the properties of the training data. Empirically, for real-world data, often EM can converge to a solution with relatively high likelihood (if not the optimum), and the theory behind it is still largely not understood.

[5]If z were continuous, then Q would be a density, and the summations over z in our discussion are replaced with integrals over z.

$x \in \mathbb{R}^+$. Also, the term

$$\sum_z Q(z) \left[\frac{p(x,z;\theta)}{Q(z)}\right]$$

in the summation is just an expectation of the quantity $[p(x,z;\theta)/Q(z)]$ with respect to z drawn according to the distribution given by Q.[6] By Jensen's inequality, we have

$$f\left(\mathrm{E}_{z\sim Q}\left[\frac{p(x,z;\theta)}{Q(z)}\right]\right) \geq \mathrm{E}_{z\sim Q}\left[f\left(\frac{p(x,z;\theta)}{Q(z)}\right)\right],$$

where the "$z \sim Q$" subscripts above indicate that the expectations are with respect to z drawn from Q. This allowed us to go from Equation (11.6) to Equation (11.7).

Now, for **any** distribution Q, the formula (11.7) gives a lower-bound on $\log p(x;\theta)$. There are many possible choices for the Q's. Which should we choose? Well, if we have some current guess θ of the parameters, it seems natural to try to make the lower-bound tight at that value of θ. I.e., we will make the inequality above hold with equality at our particular value of θ.

To make the bound tight for a particular value of θ, we need for the step involving Jensen's inequality in our derivation above to hold with equality. For this to be true, we know it is sufficient that the expectation be taken over a "constant"-valued random variable. I.e., we require that

$$\frac{p(x,z;\theta)}{Q(z)} = c$$

for some constant c that does not depend on z. This is easily accomplished by choosing

$$Q(z) \propto p(x,z;\theta).$$

Actually, since we know $\sum_z Q(z) = 1$ (because it is a distribution), this further tells us that

$$\begin{aligned} Q(z) &= \frac{p(x,z;\theta)}{\sum_z p(x,z;\theta)} \\ &= \frac{p(x,z;\theta)}{p(x;\theta)} \\ &= p(z|x;\theta) \end{aligned} \tag{11.8}$$

[6]We note that the notion $\frac{p(x,z;\theta)}{Q(z)}$ only makes sense if $Q(z) \neq 0$ whenever $p(x,z;\theta) \neq 0$. Here we implicitly assume that we only consider those Q with such a property.

Thus, we simply set the Q's to be the posterior distribution of the z's given x and the setting of the parameters θ.

Indeed, we can directly verify that when $Q(z) = p(z|x;\theta)$, then equation (11.7) is an equality because

$$\begin{aligned}
\sum_z Q(z) \log \frac{p(x,z;\theta)}{Q(z)} &= \sum_z p(z|x;\theta) \log \frac{p(x,z;\theta)}{p(z|x;\theta)} \\
&= \sum_z p(z|x;\theta) \log \frac{p(z|x;\theta)p(x;\theta)}{p(z|x;\theta)} \\
&= \sum_z p(z|x;\theta) \log p(x;\theta) \\
&= \log p(x;\theta) \sum_z p(z|x;\theta) \\
&= \log p(x;\theta) \qquad \text{(because } \textstyle\sum_z p(z|x;\theta) = 1\text{)}
\end{aligned}$$

For convenience, we call the expression in Equation (11.7) the **evidence lower bound** (ELBO) and we denote it by

$$\text{ELBO}(x;Q,\theta) = \sum_z Q(z) \log \frac{p(x,z;\theta)}{Q(z)} \tag{11.9}$$

With this equation, we can re-write equation (11.7) as

$$\forall Q,\theta,x, \quad \log p(x;\theta) \geq \text{ELBO}(x;Q,\theta) \tag{11.10}$$

Intuitively, the EM algorithm alternatively updates Q and θ by a) setting $Q(z) = p(z|x;\theta)$ following Equation (11.8) so that $\text{ELBO}(x;Q,\theta) = \log p(x;\theta)$ for x and the current θ, and b) maximizing $\text{ELBO}(x;Q,\theta)$ w.r.t θ while fixing the choice of Q.

Recall that all the discussion above was under the assumption that we aim to optimize the log-likelihood $\log p(x;\theta)$ for a single example x. It turns out that with multiple training examples, the basic idea is the same and we only needs to take a sum over examples at relevant places. Next, we will build the evidence lower bound for multiple training examples and make the EM algorithm formal.

Recall we have a training set $\{x^{(1)},\ldots,x^{(n)}\}$. Note that the optimal choice of Q is $p(z|x;\theta)$, and it depends on the particular example x. Therefore here we will introduce n distributions $Q_1,\ldots,Q_n$, one for each example $x^{(i)}$. For each example $x^{(i)}$, we can build the evidence lower bound

$$\log p(x^{(i)};\theta) \geq \text{ELBO}(x^{(i)};Q_i,\theta) = \sum_{z^{(i)}} Q_i(z^{(i)}) \log \frac{p(x^{(i)},z^{(i)};\theta)}{Q_i(z^{(i)})}$$

Taking sum over all the examples, we obtain a lower bound for the log-likelihood

$$\begin{aligned} \ell(\theta) &\geq \sum_i \text{ELBO}(x^{(i)}; Q_i, \theta) \qquad (11.11) \\ &= \sum_i \sum_{z^{(i)}} Q_i(z^{(i)}) \log \frac{p(x^{(i)}, z^{(i)}; \theta)}{Q_i(z^{(i)})} \end{aligned}$$

For *any* set of distributions $Q_1, \ldots, Q_n$, the formula (11.11) gives a lower-bound on $\ell(\theta)$, and analogous to the argument around equation (11.8), the Q_i that attains equality satisfies

$$Q_i(z^{(i)}) \quad = \quad p(z^{(i)}|x^{(i)}; \theta)$$

Thus, we simply set the Q_i's to be the posterior distribution of the $z^{(i)}$'s given $x^{(i)}$ with the current setting of the parameters θ.

Now, for this choice of the Q_i's, Equation (11.11) gives a lower-bound on the loglikelihood ℓ that we're trying to maximize. This is the E-step. In the M-step of the algorithm, we then maximize our formula in Equation (11.11) with respect to the parameters to obtain a new setting of the θ's. Repeatedly carrying out these two steps gives us the EM algorithm, which is as follows:

Repeat until convergence {

(E-step) For each i, set

$$Q_i(z^{(i)}) := p(z^{(i)}|x^{(i)}; \theta).$$

(M-step) Set

$$\begin{aligned} \theta &:= \arg\max_\theta \sum_{i=1}^{n} \text{ELBO}(x^{(i)}; Q_i, \theta) \\ &= \arg\max_\theta \sum_i \sum_{z^{(i)}} Q_i(z^{(i)}) \log \frac{p(x^{(i)}, z^{(i)}; \theta)}{Q_i(z^{(i)})}. \qquad (11.12) \end{aligned}$$

}

How do we know if this algorithm will converge? Well, suppose $\theta^{(t)}$ and $\theta^{(t+1)}$ are the parameters from two successive iterations of EM. We will now prove that $\ell(\theta^{(t)}) \leq \ell(\theta^{(t+1)})$, which shows EM always monotonically improves the log-likelihood. The key to showing this result lies in our choice of the Q_i's. Specifically, on the iteration of EM in which the parameters had started out as $\theta^{(t)}$, we would have chosen $Q_i^{(t)}(z^{(i)}) := p(z^{(i)}|x^{(i)};\theta^{(t)})$. We saw earlier that this choice ensures that Jensen's inequality, as applied to get Equation (11.11), holds with equality, and hence

$$\ell(\theta^{(t)}) = \sum_{i=1}^{n} \mathrm{ELBO}(x^{(i)}; Q_i^{(t)}, \theta^{(t)}) \tag{11.13}$$

The parameters $\theta^{(t+1)}$ are then obtained by maximizing the right hand side of the equation above. Thus,

$$\begin{aligned}
\ell(\theta^{(t+1)}) &\geq \sum_{i=1}^{n} \mathrm{ELBO}(x^{(i)}; Q_i^{(t)}, \theta^{(t+1)}) \\
&\qquad \text{(because ineqaulity (11.11) holds for all } Q \text{ and } \theta) \\
&\geq \sum_{i=1}^{n} \mathrm{ELBO}(x^{(i)}; Q_i^{(t)}, \theta^{(t)}) && \text{(see reason below)} \\
&= \ell(\theta^{(t)}) && \text{(by equation (11.13))}
\end{aligned}$$

where the last inequality follows from that $\theta^{(t+1)}$ is chosen explicitly to be

$$\arg\max_{\theta} \sum_{i=1}^{n} \mathrm{ELBO}(x^{(i)}; Q_i^{(t)}, \theta)$$

Hence, EM causes the likelihood to converge monotonically. In our description of the EM algorithm, we said we'd run it until convergence. Given the result that we just showed, one reasonable convergence test would be to check if the increase in $\ell(\theta)$ between successive iterations is smaller than some tolerance parameter, and to declare convergence if EM is improving $\ell(\theta)$ too slowly.

Remark. If we define (by overloading $\mathrm{ELBO}(\cdot)$)

$$\mathrm{ELBO}(Q, \theta) = \sum_{i=1}^{n} \mathrm{ELBO}(x^{(i)}; Q_i, \theta) = \sum_i \sum_{z^{(i)}} Q_i(z^{(i)}) \log \frac{p(x^{(i)}, z^{(i)}; \theta)}{Q_i(z^{(i)})} \tag{11.14}$$

then we know $\ell(\theta) \geq \mathrm{ELBO}(Q, \theta)$ from our previous derivation. The EM can also be viewed an alternating maximization algorithm on $\mathrm{ELBO}(Q, \theta)$, in which the E-step maximizes it with respect to Q (check this yourself), and the M-step maximizes it with respect to θ.

11.3.1 Other interpretation of ELBO

Let $\text{ELBO}(x; Q, \theta) = \sum_z Q(z) \log \frac{p(x,z;\theta)}{Q(z)}$ be defined as in equation (11.9). There are several other forms of ELBO. First, we can rewrite

$$\begin{aligned}\text{ELBO}(x; Q, \theta) &= \mathrm{E}_{z\sim Q}[\log p(x, z; \theta)] - \mathrm{E}_{z\sim Q}[\log Q(z)] \\ &= \mathrm{E}_{z\sim Q}[\log p(x|z; \theta)] - D_{KL}(Q\|p_z) \end{aligned} \tag{11.15}$$

where we use p_z to denote the marginal distribution of z (under the distribution $p(x, z; \theta)$), and $D_{KL}()$ denotes the KL divergence

$$D_{KL}(Q\|p_z) = \sum_z Q(z) \log \frac{Q(z)}{p(z)} \tag{11.16}$$

In many cases, the marginal distribution of z does not depend on the parameter θ. In this case, we can see that maximizing ELBO over θ is equivalent to maximizing the first term in (11.15). This corresponds to maximizing the conditional likelihood of x conditioned on z, which is often a simpler question than the original question.

Another form of ELBO$(\cdot)$ is (please verify yourself)

$$\text{ELBO}(x; Q, \theta) = \log p(x) - D_{KL}(Q\|p_{z|x}) \tag{11.17}$$

where $p_{z|x}$ is the conditional distribution of z given x under the parameter θ. This forms shows that the maximizer of ELBO(Q, θ) over Q is obtained when $Q = p_{z|x}$, which was shown in equation (11.8) before.

11.4 Mixture of Gaussians revisited

Armed with our general definition of the EM algorithm, let's go back to our old example of fitting the parameters ϕ, μ and Σ in a mixture of Gaussians. For the sake of brevity, we carry out the derivations for the M-step updates only for ϕ and μ_j, and leave the updates for Σ_j as an exercise for the reader.

The E-step is easy. Following our algorithm derivation above, we simply calculate

$$w_j^{(i)} = Q_i(z^{(i)} = j) = P(z^{(i)} = j|x^{(i)}; \phi, \mu, \Sigma).$$

Here, "$Q_i(z^{(i)} = j)$" denotes the probability of $z^{(i)}$ taking the value j under the distribution Q_i.

Next, in the M-step, we need to maximize, with respect to our parameters ϕ, μ, Σ, the quantity

$$\begin{aligned}
&\sum_{i=1}^{n} \sum_{z^{(i)}} Q_i(z^{(i)}) \log \frac{p(x^{(i)}, z^{(i)}; \phi, \mu, \Sigma)}{Q_i(z^{(i)})} \\
&\quad = \sum_{i=1}^{n} \sum_{j=1}^{k} Q_i(z^{(i)} = j) \log \frac{p(x^{(i)}|z^{(i)} = j; \mu, \Sigma) p(z^{(i)} = j; \phi)}{Q_i(z^{(i)} = j)} \\
&\quad = \sum_{i=1}^{n} \sum_{j=1}^{k} w_j^{(i)} \log \frac{\frac{1}{(2\pi)^{d/2}|\Sigma_j|^{1/2}} \exp\left(-\frac{1}{2}(x^{(i)} - \mu_j)^T \Sigma_j^{-1} (x^{(i)} - \mu_j)\right) \cdot \phi_j}{w_j^{(i)}}
\end{aligned}$$

Let's maximize this with respect to μ_l. If we take the derivative with respect to μ_l, we find

$$\begin{aligned}
&\nabla_{\mu_l} \sum_{i=1}^{n} \sum_{j=1}^{k} w_j^{(i)} \log \frac{\frac{1}{(2\pi)^{d/2}|\Sigma_j|^{1/2}} \exp\left(-\frac{1}{2}(x^{(i)} - \mu_j)^T \Sigma_j^{-1} (x^{(i)} - \mu_j)\right) \cdot \phi_j}{w_j^{(i)}} \\
&\quad = -\nabla_{\mu_l} \sum_{i=1}^{n} \sum_{j=1}^{k} w_j^{(i)} \frac{1}{2} (x^{(i)} - \mu_j)^T \Sigma_j^{-1} (x^{(i)} - \mu_j) \\
&\quad = \frac{1}{2} \sum_{i=1}^{n} w_l^{(i)} \nabla_{\mu_l} 2\mu_l^T \Sigma_l^{-1} x^{(i)} - \mu_l^T \Sigma_l^{-1} \mu_l \\
&\quad = \sum_{i=1}^{n} w_l^{(i)} \left(\Sigma_l^{-1} x^{(i)} - \Sigma_l^{-1} \mu_l\right)
\end{aligned}$$

Setting this to zero and solving for μ_l therefore yields the update rule

$$\mu_l := \frac{\sum_{i=1}^{n} w_l^{(i)} x^{(i)}}{\sum_{i=1}^{n} w_l^{(i)}},$$

which was what we had in the previous set of notes.

Let's do one more example, and derive the M-step update for the parameters ϕ_j. Grouping together only the terms that depend on ϕ_j, we find that we need to maximize

$$\sum_{i=1}^{n} \sum_{j=1}^{k} w_j^{(i)} \log \phi_j.$$

However, there is an additional constraint that the ϕ_j's sum to 1, since they represent the probabilities $\phi_j = p(z^{(i)} = j; \phi)$. To deal with the constraint that $\sum_{j=1}^k \phi_j = 1$, we construct the Lagrangian

$$\mathcal{L}(\phi) = \sum_{i=1}^{n}\sum_{j=1}^{k} w_j^{(i)} \log \phi_j + \beta(\sum_{j=1}^{k} \phi_j - 1),$$

where β is the Lagrange multiplier.[7] Taking derivatives, we find

$$\frac{\partial}{\partial \phi_j}\mathcal{L}(\phi) = \sum_{i=1}^{n} \frac{w_j^{(i)}}{\phi_j} + \beta$$

Setting this to zero and solving, we get

$$\phi_j = \frac{\sum_{i=1}^n w_j^{(i)}}{-\beta}$$

I.e., $\phi_j \propto \sum_{i=1}^n w_j^{(i)}$. Using the constraint that $\sum_j \phi_j = 1$, we easily find that $-\beta = \sum_{i=1}^n \sum_{j=1}^k w_j^{(i)} = \sum_{i=1}^n 1 = n$. (This used the fact that $w_j^{(i)} = Q_i(z^{(i)} = j)$, and since probabilities sum to 1, $\sum_j w_j^{(i)} = 1$.) We therefore have our M-step updates for the parameters ϕ_j:

$$\phi_j := \frac{1}{n}\sum_{i=1}^{n} w_j^{(i)}.$$

The derivation for the M-step updates to Σ_j are also entirely straightforward.

11.5 Variational inference and variational auto-encoder (optional reading)

Loosely speaking, variational auto-encoder Kingma and Welling [2013] generally refers to a family of algorithms that extend the EM algorithms to more complex models parameterized by neural networks. It extends the technique of variational inference with the additional "re-parametrization trick" which will be introduced below. Variational auto-encoder may not give the best performance for many datasets, but it contains several central ideas about how to extend EM algorithms to high-dimensional continuous latent variables

[7]We don't need to worry about the constraint that $\phi_j \geq 0$, because as we'll shortly see, the solution we'll find from this derivation will automatically satisfy that anyway.

with non-linear models. Understanding it will likely give you the language and backgrounds to understand various recent papers related to it.

As a running example, we will consider the following parameterization of $p(x, z; \theta)$ by a neural network. Let θ be the collection of the weights of a neural network $g(z; \theta)$ that maps $z \in \mathbb{R}^k$ to $\mathbb{R}^d$. Let

$$z \sim \mathcal{N}(0, I_{k\times k}) \tag{11.18}$$

$$x|z \sim \mathcal{N}(g(z;\theta), \sigma^2 I_{d\times d}) \tag{11.19}$$

Here $I_{k\times k}$ denotes identity matrix of dimension k by k, and σ is a scalar that we assume to be known for simplicity.

For the Gaussian mixture models in Section 11.4, the optimal choice of $Q(z) = p(z|x;\theta)$ for each fixed θ, that is the posterior distribution of z, can be analytically computed. In many more complex models such as the model (11.19), it's intractable to compute the exact the posterior distribution $p(z|x;\theta)$.

Recall that from equation (11.10), ELBO is always a lower bound for any choice of Q, and therefore, we can also aim for finding an **approximation** of the true posterior distribution. Often, one has to use some particular form to approximate the true posterior distribution. Let $\mathcal{Q}$ be a family of Q's that we are considering, and we will aim to find a Q within the family of $\mathcal{Q}$ that is closest to the true posterior distribution. To formalize, recall the definition of the ELBO lower bound as a function of Q and θ defined in equation (11.14)

$$\text{ELBO}(Q, \theta) = \sum_{i=1}^{n} \text{ELBO}(x^{(i)}; Q_i, \theta) = \sum_i \sum_{z^{(i)}} Q_i(z^{(i)}) \log \frac{p(x^{(i)}, z^{(i)}; \theta)}{Q_i(z^{(i)})}$$

Recall that EM can be viewed as alternating maximization of $\text{ELBO}(Q, \theta)$. Here instead, we optimize the EBLO over $Q \in \mathcal{Q}$

$$\max_{Q\in\mathcal{Q}} \max_{\theta} \text{ELBO}(Q, \theta) \tag{11.20}$$

Now the next question is what form of Q (or what structural assumptions to make about Q) allows us to efficiently maximize the objective above. When the latent variable z are high-dimensional discrete variables, one popular assumption is the **mean field assumption**, which assumes that $Q_i(z)$ gives a distribution with independent coordinates, or in other words, Q_i can be decomposed into $Q_i(z) = Q_i^1(z_1) \cdots Q_i^k(z_k)$. There are tremendous applications of mean field assumptions to learning generative models with discrete latent variables, and we refer to Blei et al. [2017] for a survey of these models and their impact to a wide range of applications including computational biology, computational neuroscience, social sciences. We will not get into the details about the discrete latent variable cases, and our main focus is to deal with continuous latent variables, which requires not only mean field assumptions, but additional techniques.

When $z \in \mathbb{R}^k$ is a continuous latent variable, there are several decisions to make towards successfully optimizing (11.20). First we need to give a succinct representation of the distribution Q_i because it is over an infinite number of points. A natural choice is to assume Q_i is a Gaussian distribution with some mean and variance. We would also like to have more succinct representation of the means of Q_i of all the examples. Note that $Q_i(z^{(i)})$ is supposed to approximate $p(z^{(i)}|x^{(i)};\theta)$. It would make sense let all the means of the Q_i's be some function of $x^{(i)}$. Concretely, let $q(\cdot;\phi), v(\cdot;\phi)$ be two functions that map from dimension d to k, which are parameterized by ϕ and ψ, we assume that

$$Q_i = \mathcal{N}(q(x^{(i)};\phi), \operatorname{diag}(v(x^{(i)};\psi))^2) \tag{11.21}$$

Here $\operatorname{diag}(w)$ means the $k \times k$ matrix with the entries of $w \in \mathbb{R}^k$ on the diagonal. In other words, the distribution Q_i is assumed to be a Gaussian distribution with independent coordinates, and the mean and standard deviations are governed by q and v. Often in variational auto-encoder, q and v are chosen to be neural networks.[8] In recent deep learning literature, often q, v are called **encoder** (in the sense of encoding the data into latent code), whereas $g(z;\theta)$ if often referred to as the **decoder.**

We remark that Q_i of such form in many cases are very far from a good approximation of the true posterior distribution. However, some approximation is necessary for feasible optimization. In fact, the form of Q_i needs to satisfy other requirements (which happened to be satisfied by the form (11.21))

Before optimizing the ELBO, let's first verify whether we can efficiently evaluate the value of the ELBO for fixed Q of the form (11.21) and θ. We rewrite the ELBO as a function of ϕ, ψ, θ by

$$\text{ELBO}(\phi,\psi,\theta) = \sum_{i=1}^{n} \mathrm{E}_{z^{(i)}\sim Q_i}\left[\log \frac{p(x^{(i)}, z^{(i)};\theta)}{Q_i(z^{(i)})}\right], \tag{11.22}$$
$$\text{where } Q_i = \mathcal{N}(q(x^{(i)};\phi), \operatorname{diag}(v(x^{(i)};\psi))^2)$$

Note that to evaluate $Q_i(z^{(i)})$ inside the expectation, we should be able **to compute the density of** Q_i. To estimate the expectation $\mathrm{E}_{z^{(i)}\sim Q_i}$, we

[8] q and v can also share parameters. We sweep this level of details under the rug in this note.

should be able **to sample from distribution** Q_i so that we can build an empirical estimator with samples. It happens that for Gaussian distribution $Q_i = \mathcal{N}(q(x^{(i)};\phi), \text{diag}(v(x^{(i)};\psi))^2)$, we are able to be both efficiently.

Now let's optimize the ELBO. It turns out that we can run gradient ascent over ϕ, ψ, θ instead of alternating maximization. There is no strong need to compute the maximum over each variable at a much greater cost. (For Gaussian mixture model in Section 11.4, computing the maximum is analytically feasible and relatively cheap, and therefore we did alternating maximization.) Mathematically, let η be the learning rate, the gradient ascent step is

$$\begin{aligned}
\theta &:= \theta + \eta \nabla_\theta \text{ELBO}(\phi, \psi, \theta) \\
\phi &:= \phi + \eta \nabla_\phi \text{ELBO}(\phi, \psi, \theta) \\
\psi &:= \psi + \eta \nabla_\psi \text{ELBO}(\phi, \psi, \theta)
\end{aligned}$$

Computing the gradient over θ is simple because

$$\begin{aligned}
\nabla_\theta \text{ELBO}(\phi, \psi, \theta) &= \nabla_\theta \sum_{i=1}^{n} \text{E}_{z^{(i)} \sim Q_i} \left[\log \frac{p(x^{(i)}, z^{(i)}; \theta)}{Q_i(z^{(i)})} \right] \\
&= \nabla_\theta \sum_{i=1}^{n} \text{E}_{z^{(i)} \sim Q_i} \left[\log p(x^{(i)}, z^{(i)}; \theta) \right] \\
&= \sum_{i=1}^{n} \text{E}_{z^{(i)} \sim Q_i} \left[\nabla_\theta \log p(x^{(i)}, z^{(i)}; \theta) \right], \qquad (11.23)
\end{aligned}$$

But computing the gradient over ϕ and ψ is tricky because the sampling distribution Q_i depends on ϕ and ψ. (Abstractly speaking, the issue we face can be simplified as the problem of computing the gradient $\text{E}_{z\sim Q_\phi}[f(\phi)]$ with respect to variable ϕ. We know that in general, $\nabla \text{E}_{z\sim Q_\phi}[f(\phi)] \neq \text{E}_{z\sim Q_\phi}[\nabla f(\phi)]$ because the dependency of Q_ϕ on ϕ has to be taken into account as well.)

The idea that comes to rescue is the so-called **re-parameterization trick**: we rewrite $z^{(i)} \sim Q_i = \mathcal{N}(q(x^{(i)};\phi), \text{diag}(v(x^{(i)};\psi))^2)$ in an equivalent way:

$$z^{(i)} = q(x^{(i)};\phi) + v(x^{(i)};\psi) \odot \xi^{(i)} \text{ where } \xi^{(i)} \sim \mathcal{N}(0, I_{k\times k}) \qquad (11.24)$$

Here $x \odot y$ denotes the entry-wise product of two vectors of the same dimension. Here we used the fact that $x \sim N(\mu, \sigma^2)$ is equivalent to that $x = \mu + \xi\sigma$ with $\xi \sim N(0,1)$. We mostly just used this fact in every dimension simultaneously for the random variable $z^{(i)} \sim Q_i$.

With this re-parameterization, we have that

$$\begin{aligned}
&\mathrm{E}_{z^{(i)}\sim Q_i}\left[\log \frac{p(x^{(i)}, z^{(i)}; \theta)}{Q_i(z^{(i)})}\right] \\
&= \mathrm{E}_{\xi^{(i)}\sim \mathcal{N}(0,1)}\left[\log \frac{p(x^{(i)}, q(x^{(i)}; \phi) + v(x^{(i)}; \psi) \odot \xi^{(i)}; \theta)}{Q_i(q(x^{(i)}; \phi) + v(x^{(i)}; \psi) \odot \xi^{(i)})}\right]
\end{aligned} \tag{11.25}$$

It follows that

$$\begin{aligned}
&\nabla_\phi \mathrm{E}_{z^{(i)}\sim Q_i}\left[\log \frac{p(x^{(i)}, z^{(i)}; \theta)}{Q_i(z^{(i)})}\right] \\
&= \nabla_\phi \mathrm{E}_{\xi^{(i)}\sim \mathcal{N}(0,1)}\left[\log \frac{p(x^{(i)}, q(x^{(i)}; \phi) + v(x^{(i)}; \psi) \odot \xi^{(i)}; \theta)}{Q_i(q(x^{(i)}; \phi) + v(x^{(i)}; \psi) \odot \xi^{(i)})}\right] \\
&= \mathrm{E}_{\xi^{(i)}\sim \mathcal{N}(0,1)}\left[\nabla_\phi \log \frac{p(x^{(i)}, q(x^{(i)}; \phi) + v(x^{(i)}; \psi) \odot \xi^{(i)}; \theta)}{Q_i(q(x^{(i)}; \phi) + v(x^{(i)}; \psi) \odot \xi^{(i)})}\right]
\end{aligned}$$

We can now sample multiple copies of $\xi^{(i)}$'s to estimate the the expectation in the RHS of the equation above.[9] We can estimate the gradient with respect to ψ similarly, and with these, we can implement the gradient ascent algorithm to optimize the ELBO over ϕ, ψ, θ.

There are not many high-dimensional distributions with analytically computable density function are known to be re-parameterizable. We refer to Kingma and Welling [2013] for a few other choices that can replace Gaussian distribution.

[9]Empirically people sometimes just use one sample to estimate it for maximum computational efficiency.

Chapter 12

Principal components analysis

In this set of notes, we will develop a method, Principal Components Analysis (PCA), that tries to identify the subspace in which the data approximately lies. PCA is computationally efficient: it will require only an eigenvector calculation (easily done with the `eig` function in Matlab).

Suppose we are given a dataset $\{x^{(i)}; i = 1, \ldots, n\}$ of attributes of n different types of automobiles, such as their maximum speed, turn radius, and so on. Let $x^{(i)} \in \mathbb{R}^d$ for each i ($d \ll n$). But unknown to us, two different attributes—some x_i and x_j—respectively give a car's maximum speed measured in miles per hour, and the maximum speed measured in kilometers per hour. These two attributes are therefore almost linearly dependent, up to only small differences introduced by rounding off to the nearest mph or kph. Thus, the data really lies approximately on an $n - 1$ dimensional subspace. How can we automatically detect, and perhaps remove, this redundancy?

For a less contrived example, consider a dataset resulting from a survey of pilots for radio-controlled helicopters, where $x_1^{(i)}$ is a measure of the piloting skill of pilot i, and $x_2^{(i)}$ captures how much he/she enjoys flying. Because RC helicopters are very difficult to fly, only the most committed students, ones that truly enjoy flying, become good pilots. So, the two attributes x_1 and x_2 are strongly correlated. Indeed, we might posit that that the data actually likes along some diagonal axis (the u_1 direction) capturing the intrinsic piloting "karma" of a person, with only a small amount of noise lying off this axis. (See figure.) How can we automatically compute this u_1 direction?

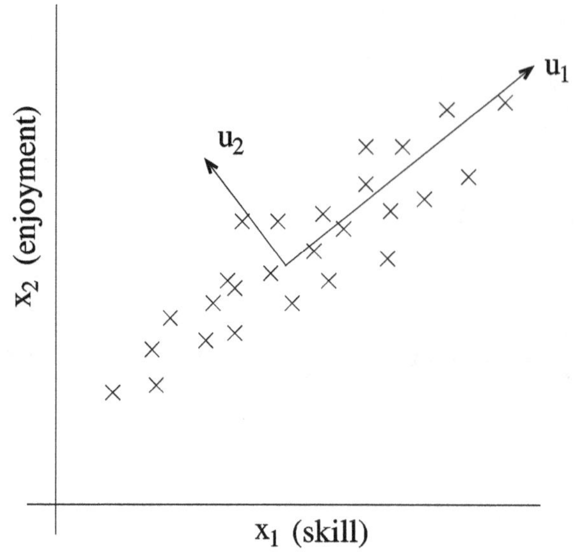

We will shortly develop the PCA algorithm. But prior to running PCA per se, typically we first preprocess the data by normalizing each feature to have mean 0 and variance 1. We do this by subtracting the mean and dividing by the empirical standard deviation:

$$x_j^{(i)} \leftarrow \frac{x_j^{(i)} - \mu_j}{\sigma_j}$$

where $\mu_j = \frac{1}{n}\sum_{i=1}^n x_j^{(i)}$ and $\sigma_j^2 = \frac{1}{n}\sum_{i=1}^n (x_j^{(i)} - \mu_j)^2$ are the mean variance of feature j, respectively.

Subtracting μ_j zeros out the mean and may be omitted for data known to have zero mean (for instance, time series corresponding to speech or other acoustic signals). Dividing by the standard deviation σ_j rescales each coordinate to have unit variance, which ensures that different attributes are all treated on the same "scale." For instance, if x_1 was cars' maximum speed in mph (taking values in the high tens or low hundreds) and x_2 were the number of seats (taking values around 2-4), then this renormalization rescales the different attributes to make them more comparable. This rescaling may be omitted if we had a priori knowledge that the different attributes are all on the same scale. One example of this is if each data point represented a grayscale image, and each $x_j^{(i)}$ took a value in $\{0, 1, \ldots, 255\}$ corresponding to the intensity value of pixel j in image i.

Now, having normalized our data, how do we compute the "major axis of variation" u—that is, the direction on which the data approximately lies? One way is to pose this problem as finding the unit vector u so that when the data is projected onto the direction corresponding to u, the variance of the projected data is maximized. Intuitively, the data starts off with some amount of variance/information in it. We would like to choose a direction u so that if we were to approximate the data as lying in the direction/subspace corresponding to u, as much as possible of this variance is still retained.

Consider the following dataset, on which we have already carried out the normalization steps:

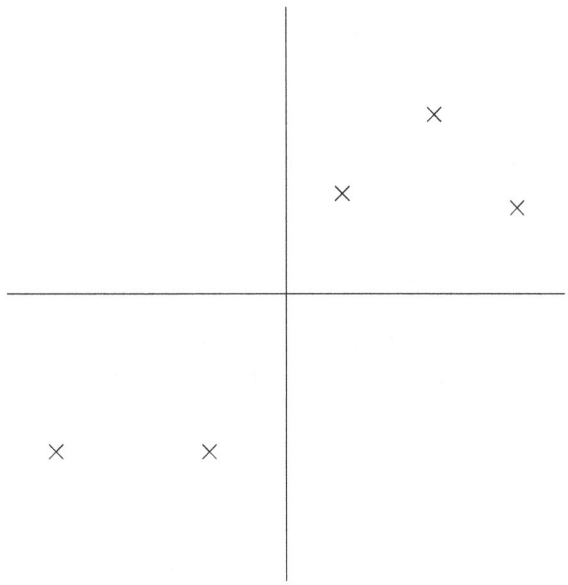

Now, suppose we pick u to correspond the the direction shown in the figure below. The circles denote the projections of the original data onto this line.

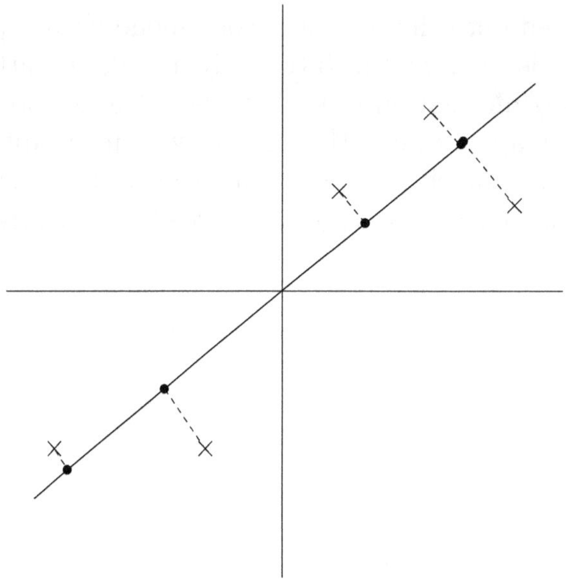

We see that the projected data still has a fairly large variance, and the points tend to be far from zero. In contrast, suppose had instead picked the following direction:

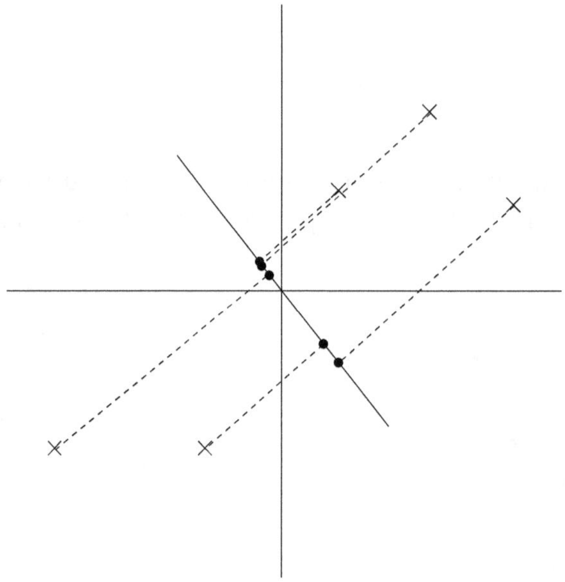

Here, the projections have a significantly smaller variance, and are much closer to the origin.

We would like to automatically select the direction u corresponding to the first of the two figures shown above. To formalize this, note that given a unit vector u and a point x, the length of the projection of x onto u is given by $x^T u$. I.e., if $x^{(i)}$ is a point in our dataset (one of the crosses in the plot), then its projection onto u (the corresponding circle in the figure) is distance $x^T u$ from the origin. Hence, to maximize the variance of the projections, we would like to choose a unit-length u so as to maximize:

$$\begin{aligned}\frac{1}{n}\sum_{i=1}^{n}(x^{(i)^T}u)^2 &= \frac{1}{n}\sum_{i=1}^{n}u^T x^{(i)} x^{(i)^T} u \\ &= u^T\left(\frac{1}{n}\sum_{i=1}^{n}x^{(i)}x^{(i)^T}\right)u.\end{aligned}$$

We easily recognize that the maximizing this subject to $\|u\|_2 = 1$ gives the principal eigenvector of $\Sigma = \frac{1}{n}\sum_{i=1}^{n}x^{(i)}x^{(i)^T}$, which is just the empirical covariance matrix of the data (assuming it has zero mean).[1]

To summarize, we have found that if we wish to find a 1-dimensional subspace with with to approximate the data, we should choose u to be the principal eigenvector of Σ. More generally, if we wish to project our data into a k-dimensional subspace ($k < d$), we should choose $u_1, \ldots, u_k$ to be the top k eigenvectors of Σ. The u_i's now form a new, orthogonal basis for the data.[2]

Then, to represent $x^{(i)}$ in this basis, we need only compute the corresponding vector

$$y^{(i)} = \begin{bmatrix} u_1^T x^{(i)} \\ u_2^T x^{(i)} \\ \vdots \\ u_k^T x^{(i)} \end{bmatrix} \in \mathbb{R}^k.$$

Thus, whereas $x^{(i)} \in \mathbb{R}^d$, the vector $y^{(i)}$ now gives a lower, k-dimensional, approximation/representation for $x^{(i)}$. PCA is therefore also referred to as a **dimensionality reduction** algorithm. The vectors $u_1, \ldots, u_k$ are called the first k **principal components** of the data.

Remark. Although we have shown it formally only for the case of $k = 1$, using well-known properties of eigenvectors it is straightforward to show that

[1]If you haven't seen this before, try using the method of Lagrange multipliers to maximize $u^T\Sigma u$ subject to that $u^T u = 1$. You should be able to show that $\Sigma u = \lambda u$, for some λ, which implies u is an eigenvector of Σ, with eigenvalue λ.

[2]Because Σ is symmetric, the u_i's will (or always can be chosen to be) orthogonal to each other.

of all possible orthogonal bases $u_1, \ldots, u_k$, the one that we have chosen maximizes $\sum_i \|y^{(i)}\|_2^2$. Thus, our choice of a basis preserves as much variability as possible in the original data.

PCA can also be derived by picking the basis that minimizes the approximation error arising from projecting the data onto the k-dimensional subspace spanned by them. (See more in homework.)

PCA has many applications; we will close our discussion with a few examples. First, compression—representing $x^{(i)}$'s with lower dimension $y^{(i)}$'s—is an obvious application. If we reduce high dimensional data to $k = 2$ or 3 dimensions, then we can also plot the $y^{(i)}$'s to visualize the data. For instance, if we were to reduce our automobiles data to 2 dimensions, then we can plot it (one point in our plot would correspond to one car type, say) to see what cars are similar to each other and what groups of cars may cluster together.

Another standard application is to preprocess a dataset to reduce its dimension before running a supervised learning learning algorithm with the $x^{(i)}$'s as inputs. Apart from computational benefits, reducing the data's dimension can also reduce the complexity of the hypothesis class considered and help avoid overfitting (e.g., linear classifiers over lower dimensional input spaces will have smaller VC dimension).

Lastly, as in our RC pilot example, we can also view PCA as a noise reduction algorithm. In our example it, estimates the intrinsic "piloting karma" from the noisy measures of piloting skill and enjoyment. In class, we also saw the application of this idea to face images, resulting in **eigenfaces** method. Here, each point $x^{(i)} \in \mathbb{R}^{100\times 100}$ was a 10000 dimensional vector, with each coordinate corresponding to a pixel intensity value in a 100x100 image of a face. Using PCA, we represent each image $x^{(i)}$ with a much lower-dimensional $y^{(i)}$. In doing so, we hope that the principal components we found retain the interesting, systematic variations between faces that capture what a person really looks like, but not the "noise" in the images introduced by minor lighting variations, slightly different imaging conditions, and so on. We then measure distances between faces i and j by working in the reduced dimension, and computing $\|y^{(i)} - y^{(j)}\|_2$. This resulted in a surprisingly good face-matching and retrieval algorithm.

Chapter 13

Independent components analysis

Our next topic is Independent Components Analysis (ICA). Similar to PCA, this will find a new basis in which to represent our data. However, the goal is very different.

As a motivating example, consider the "cocktail party problem." Here, d speakers are speaking simultaneously at a party, and any microphone placed in the room records only an overlapping combination of the d speakers' voices. But lets say we have d different microphones placed in the room, and because each microphone is a different distance from each of the speakers, it records a different combination of the speakers' voices. Using these microphone recordings, can we separate out the original d speakers' speech signals?

To formalize this problem, we imagine that there is some data $s \in \mathbb{R}^d$ that is generated via d independent sources. What we observe is

$$x = As,$$

where A is an unknown square matrix called the **mixing matrix**. Repeated observations gives us a dataset $\{x^{(i)}; i = 1, \ldots, n\}$, and our goal is to recover the sources $s^{(i)}$ that had generated our data ($x^{(i)} = As^{(i)}$).

In our cocktail party problem, $s^{(i)}$ is an d-dimensional vector, and $s_j^{(i)}$ is the sound that speaker j was uttering at time i. Also, $x^{(i)}$ in an d-dimensional vector, and $x_j^{(i)}$ is the acoustic reading recorded by microphone j at time i.

Let $W = A^{-1}$ be the **unmixing matrix.** Our goal is to find W, so that given our microphone recordings $x^{(i)}$, we can recover the sources by computing $s^{(i)} = Wx^{(i)}$. For notational convenience, we also let w_i^T denote the i-th row of W, so that

$$W = \begin{bmatrix} — w_1^T — \\ \vdots \\ — w_d^T — \end{bmatrix}.$$

Thus, $w_i \in \mathbb{R}^d$, and the j-th source can be recovered as $s_j^{(i)} = w_j^T x^{(i)}$.

13.1 ICA ambiguities

To what degree can $W = A^{-1}$ be recovered? If we have no prior knowledge about the sources and the mixing matrix, it is easy to see that there are some inherent ambiguities in A that are impossible to recover, given only the $x^{(i)}$'s.

Specifically, let P be any d-by-d permutation matrix. This means that each row and each column of P has exactly one "1." Here are some examples of permutation matrices:

$$P = \begin{bmatrix} 0 & 1 & 0 \\ 1 & 0 & 0 \\ 0 & 0 & 1 \end{bmatrix}; \quad P = \begin{bmatrix} 0 & 1 \\ 1 & 0 \end{bmatrix}; \quad P = \begin{bmatrix} 1 & 0 \\ 0 & 1 \end{bmatrix}.$$

If z is a vector, then Pz is another vector that contains a permuted version of z's coordinates. Given only the $x^{(i)}$'s, there will be no way to distinguish between W and PW. Specifically, the permutation of the original sources is ambiguous, which should be no surprise. Fortunately, this does not matter for most applications.

Further, there is no way to recover the correct scaling of the w_i's. For instance, if A were replaced with $2A$, and every $s^{(i)}$ were replaced with $(0.5)s^{(i)}$, then our observed $x^{(i)} = 2A \cdot (0.5)s^{(i)}$ would still be the same. More broadly, if a single column of A were scaled by a factor of α, and the corresponding source were scaled by a factor of $1/\alpha$, then there is again no way to determine that this had happened given only the $x^{(i)}$'s. Thus, we cannot recover the "correct" scaling of the sources. However, for the applications that we are concerned with—including the cocktail party problem—this ambiguity also does not matter. Specifically, scaling a speaker's speech signal $s_j^{(i)}$ by some positive factor α affects only the volume of that speaker's speech. Also, sign changes do not matter, and $s_j^{(i)}$ and $-s_j^{(i)}$ sound identical when played on a speaker. Thus, if the w_i found by an algorithm is scaled by any non-zero real number, the corresponding recovered source $s_i = w_i^T x$ will be scaled by the same factor; but this usually does not matter. (These comments also apply to ICA for the brain/MEG data that we talked about in class.)

Are these the only sources of ambiguity in ICA? It turns out that they are, so long as the sources s_i are *non-Gaussian*. To see what the difficulty is with Gaussian data, consider an example in which $n = 2$, and $s \sim \mathcal{N}(0, I)$. Here, I is the 2x2 identity matrix. Note that the contours of the density of the standard normal distribution $\mathcal{N}(0, I)$ are circles centered on the origin, and the density is rotationally symmetric.

Now, suppose we observe some $x = As$, where A is our mixing matrix. Then, the distribution of x will be Gaussian, $x \sim \mathcal{N}(0, AA^T)$, since

$$\mathrm{E}_{s\sim\mathcal{N}(0,I)}[x] = \mathrm{E}[As] = A\mathrm{E}[s] = 0$$
$$\mathrm{Cov}[x] = \mathrm{E}_{s\sim\mathcal{N}(0,I)}[xx^T] = \mathrm{E}[Ass^TA^T] = A\mathrm{E}[ss^T]A^T = A \cdot \mathrm{Cov}[s] \cdot A^T = AA^T$$

Now, let R be an arbitrary orthogonal (less formally, a rotation/reflection) matrix, so that $RR^T = R^TR = I$, and let $A' = AR$. Then if the data had been mixed according to A' instead of A, we would have instead observed $x' = A's$. The distribution of x' is also Gaussian, $x' \sim \mathcal{N}(0, AA^T)$, since $\mathrm{E}_{s\sim\mathcal{N}(0,I)}[x'(x')^T] = \mathrm{E}[A'ss^T(A')^T] = \mathrm{E}[ARss^T(AR)^T] = ARR^TA^T = AA^T$. Hence, whether the mixing matrix is A or A', we would observe data from a $\mathcal{N}(0, AA^T)$ distribution. Thus, there is no way to tell if the sources were mixed using A and A'. There is an arbitrary rotational component in the mixing matrix that cannot be determined from the data, and we cannot recover the original sources.

Our argument above was based on the fact that the multivariate standard normal distribution is rotationally symmetric. Despite the bleak picture that this paints for ICA on Gaussian data, it turns out that, so long as the data is *not* Gaussian, it is possible, given enough data, to recover the d independent sources.

13.2 Densities and linear transformations

Before moving on to derive the ICA algorithm proper, we first digress briefly to talk about the effect of linear transformations on densities.

Suppose a random variable s is drawn according to some density $p_s(s)$. For simplicity, assume for now that $s \in \mathbb{R}$ is a real number. Now, let the random variable x be defined according to $x = As$ (here, $x \in \mathbb{R}, A \in \mathbb{R}$). Let p_x be the density of x. What is p_x?

Let $W = A^{-1}$. To calculate the "probability" of a particular value of x, it is tempting to compute $s = Wx$, then then evaluate p_s at that point, and conclude that "$p_x(x) = p_s(Wx)$." However, *this is incorrect.* For example, let $s \sim \text{Uniform}[0,1]$, so $p_s(s) = 1\{0 \le s \le 1\}$. Now, let $A = 2$, so $x = 2s$. Clearly, x is distributed uniformly in the interval $[0,2]$. Thus, its density is given by $p_x(x) = (0.5)1\{0 \le x \le 2\}$. This does not equal $p_s(Wx)$, where $W = 0.5 = A^{-1}$. Instead, the correct formula is $p_x(x) = p_s(Wx)|W|$.

More generally, if s is a vector-valued distribution with density p_s, and $x = As$ for a square, invertible matrix A, then the density of x is given by

$$p_x(x) = p_s(Wx) \cdot |W|,$$

where $W = A^{-1}$.

Remark. If you're seen the result that A maps $[0,1]^d$ to a set of volume $|A|$, then here's another way to remember the formula for p_x given above, that also generalizes our previous 1-dimensional example. Specifically, let $A \in \mathbb{R}^{d\times d}$ be given, and let $W = A^{-1}$ as usual. Also let $C_1 = [0,1]^d$ be the d-dimensional hypercube, and define $C_2 = \{As : s \in C_1\} \subseteq \mathbb{R}^d$ to be the image of C_1 under the mapping given by A. Then it is a standard result in linear algebra (and, indeed, one of the ways of defining determinants) that the volume of C_2 is given by $|A|$. Now, suppose s is uniformly distributed in $[0,1]^d$, so its density is $p_s(s) = 1\{s \in C_1\}$. Then clearly x will be uniformly distributed in C_2. Its density is therefore found to be $p_x(x) = 1\{x \in C_2\}/\text{vol}(C_2)$ (since it must integrate over C_2 to 1). But using the fact that the determinant of the inverse of a matrix is just the inverse of the determinant, we have $1/\text{vol}(C_2) = 1/|A| = |A^{-1}| = |W|$. Thus, $p_x(x) = 1\{x \in C_2\}|W| = 1\{Wx \in C_1\}|W| = p_s(Wx)|W|$.

13.3 ICA algorithm

We are now ready to derive an ICA algorithm. We describe an algorithm by Bell and Sejnowski, and we give an interpretation of their algorithm as a method for maximum likelihood estimation. (This is different from their original interpretation involving a complicated idea called the infomax principal which is no longer necessary given the modern understanding of ICA.)

We suppose that the distribution of each source s_j is given by a density p_s, and that the joint distribution of the sources s is given by

$$p(s) = \prod_{j=1}^{d} p_s(s_j).$$

Note that by modeling the joint distribution as a product of marginals, we capture the assumption that the sources are independent. Using our formulas from the previous section, this implies the following density on $x = As = W^{-1}s$:

$$p(x) = \prod_{j=1}^{d} p_s(w_j^T x) \cdot |W|.$$

All that remains is to specify a density for the individual sources p_s.

Recall that, given a real-valued random variable z, its cumulative distribution function (cdf) F is defined by $F(z_0) = P(z \le z_0) = \int_{-\infty}^{z_0} p_z(z)dz$ and the density is the derivative of the cdf: $p_z(z) = F'(z)$.

Thus, to specify a density for the s_i's, all we need to do is to specify some cdf for it. A cdf has to be a monotonic function that increases from zero to one. Following our previous discussion, we cannot choose the Gaussian cdf, as ICA doesn't work on Gaussian data. What we'll choose instead as a reasonable "default" cdf that slowly increases from 0 to 1, is the sigmoid function $g(s) = 1/(1 + e^{-s})$. Hence, $p_s(s) = g'(s)$.[1]

The square matrix W is the parameter in our model. Given a training set $\{x^{(i)}; i = 1, \ldots, n\}$, the log likelihood is given by

$$\ell(W) = \sum_{i=1}^{n} \left(\sum_{j=1}^{d} \log g'(w_j^T x^{(i)}) + \log |W| \right).$$

We would like to maximize this in terms W. By taking derivatives and using the fact (from the first set of notes) that $\nabla_W |W| = |W|(W^{-1})^T$, we easily derive a stochastic gradient ascent learning rule. For a training example $x^{(i)}$, the update rule is:

$$W := W + \alpha \left(\begin{bmatrix} 1 - 2g(w_1^T x^{(i)}) \\ 1 - 2g(w_2^T x^{(i)}) \\ \vdots \\ 1 - 2g(w_d^T x^{(i)}) \end{bmatrix} x^{(i)T} + (W^T)^{-1} \right),$$

[1]If you have prior knowledge that the sources' densities take a certain form, then it is a good idea to substitute that in here. But in the absence of such knowledge, the sigmoid function can be thought of as a reasonable default that seems to work well for many problems. Also, the presentation here assumes that either the data $x^{(i)}$ has been preprocessed to have zero mean, or that it can naturally be expected to have zero mean (such as acoustic signals). This is necessary because our assumption that $p_s(s) = g'(s)$ implies $\mathrm{E}[s] = 0$ (the derivative of the logistic function is a symmetric function, and hence gives a density corresponding to a random variable with zero mean), which implies $\mathrm{E}[x] = \mathrm{E}[As] = 0$.

where α is the learning rate.

After the algorithm converges, we then compute $s^{(i)} = Wx^{(i)}$ to recover the original sources.

Remark. When writing down the likelihood of the data, we implicitly assumed that the $x^{(i)}$'s were independent of each other (for different values of i; note this issue is different from whether the different coordinates of $x^{(i)}$ are independent), so that the likelihood of the training set was given by $\prod_i p(x^{(i)}; W)$. This assumption is clearly incorrect for speech data and other time series where the $x^{(i)}$'s are dependent, but it can be shown that having correlated training examples will not hurt the performance of the algorithm if we have sufficient data. However, for problems where successive training examples are correlated, when implementing stochastic gradient ascent, it sometimes helps accelerate convergence if we visit training examples in a randomly permuted order. (I.e., run stochastic gradient ascent on a randomly shuffled copy of the training set.)

Chapter 14

Self-supervised learning and foundation models

Despite its huge success, supervised learning with neural networks typically relies on the availability of a labeled dataset of decent size, which is sometimes costly to collect. Recently, AI and machine learning are undergoing a paradigm shift with the rise of models (e.g., BERT [Devlin et al., 2019] and GPT-3 [Brown et al., 2020]) that are pre-trained on broad data at scale and are adaptable to a wide range of downstream tasks. These models, called foundation models by Bommasani et al. [2021], oftentimes leverage massive unlabeled data so that much fewer labeled data in the downstream tasks are needed. Moreover, though foundation models are based on standard deep learning and transfer learning, their scale results in new emergent capabilities. These models are typically (pre-)trained by self-supervised learning methods where the supervisions/labels come from parts of the inputs.

This chapter will introduce the paradigm of foundation models and basic related concepts.

14.1 Pretraining and adaptation

The foundation models paradigm consists of two phases: pretraining (or simply training) and adaptation. We first pretrain a large model on a massive unlabeled dataset (e.g., billions of unlabeled images).[1] Then, we adapt the pretrained model to a downstream task (e.g., detecting cancer from scan images). These downstream tasks are often prediction tasks with limited or

[1]Sometimes, pretraining can involve large-scale labeled datasets as well (e.g., the ImageNet dataset).

even no labeled data. The intuition is that the pretrained models learn good *representations* that capture intrinsic semantic structure/ information about the data, and the adaptation phase customizes the model to a particular downstream task by, e.g., retrieving the information specific to it. For example, a model pretrained on massive unlabeled image data may learn good general visual representations/features, and we adapt the representations to solve biomedical imagining tasks.

We formalize the two phases below.

Pretraining. Suppose we have an unlabeled pretraining dataset $\{x^{(1)}, x^{(2)} \cdots, x^{(n)}\}$ that consists of n examples in $\mathbb{R}^d$. Let ϕ_θ be a model that is parameterized by θ and maps the input x to some m-dimensional representation $\phi_\theta(x)$. (People also call $\phi_\theta(x) \in \mathbb{R}^m$ the embedding or features of the example x.) We pretrain the model θ with a pretraining loss, which is often an average of loss functions on all the examples: $L_{\text{pre}}(\theta) = \frac{1}{n}\sum_{i=1}^{n} \ell_{\text{pre}}(\theta, x^{(i)})$. Here ℓ_{pre} is a so-called self-supervised loss on a single datapoint $x^{(i)}$, because as shown later, e.g., in Section 14.3, the "supervision" comes from the data point $x^{(i)}$ itself. It is also possible that the pretraining loss is not a sum of losses on individual examples. We will discuss two pretraining losses in Section 14.2 and Section 14.3.

We use some optimizers (mostly likely SGD or ADAM [Kingma and Ba, 2014]) to minimize $L_{\text{pre}}(\theta)$. We denote the obtained pretrained model by $\hat{\theta}$.

Adaptation. For a downstream task, we usually have a labeled dataset $\{(x_{\text{task}}^{(1)}, y_{\text{task}}^{(1)}), \cdots, (x_{\text{task}}^{(n_{\text{task}})}, y_{\text{task}}^{(n_{\text{task}})})\}$ with n_{task} examples. The setting when $n_{\text{task}} = 0$ is called zero-shot learning—the downstream task doesn't have any labeled examples. When n_{task} is relatively small (say, between 1 and 50), the setting is called few-shot learning. It's also pretty common to have a larger n_{task} on the order of ranging from hundreds to tens of thousands.

An adaptation algorithm generally takes in a downstream dataset and the pretrained model $\hat{\theta}$, and outputs a variant of $\hat{\theta}$ that solves the downstream task. We will discuss below two popular and general adaptation methods, linear probe and finetuning. In addition, two other methods specific to language problems are introduced in 14.3.2.

The linear probe approach uses a linear head on top of the representation to predict the downstream labels. Mathematically, the adapted model outputs $w^\top \phi_{\hat{\theta}}(x)$, where $w \in \mathbb{R}^m$ is a parameter to be learned, and $\hat{\theta}$ is exactly the pretrained model (fixed). We can use SGD (or other optimizers) to train

w on the downstream task loss to predict the task label

$$\min_{w\in\mathbb{R}^m} \frac{1}{n_{\text{task}}} \sum_{i=1}^{n_{\text{task}}} \ell_{\text{task}}(y_{\text{task}}^{(i)}, w^\top \phi_{\hat{\theta}}(x_{\text{task}}^{(i)})) \tag{14.1}$$

E.g., if the downstream task is a regression problem, we will have $\ell_{\text{task}}(y_{\text{task}}, w^\top \phi_{\hat{\theta}}(x_{\text{task}})) = (y_{\text{task}} - w^\top \phi_{\hat{\theta}}(x_{\text{task}}))^2$.

The finetuning algorithm uses a similar structure for the downstream prediction model, but also further finetunes the pretrained model (instead of keeping it fixed). Concretely, the prediction model is $w^\top \phi_\theta(x)$ with parameters w and θ. We optimize both w and θ to fit the downstream data, but initialize θ with the pretrained model $\hat{\theta}$. The linear head w is usually initialized randomly.

$$\begin{aligned} &\underset{w,\theta}{\text{minimize}} && \frac{1}{n_{\text{task}}} \sum_{i=1}^{n_{\text{task}}} \ell_{\text{task}}(y_{\text{task}}^{(i)}, w^\top \phi_\theta(x_{\text{task}}^{(i)})) && (14.2) \\ &\text{with initialization} && w \leftarrow \text{random vector} && (14.3) \\ & && \theta \leftarrow \hat{\theta} && (14.4) \end{aligned}$$

Various other adaptation methods exists and are sometimes specialized to the particular pretraining methods. We will discuss one of them in Section 14.3.2.

14.2 Pretraining methods in computer vision

This section introduces two concrete pretraining methods for computer vision: supervised pretraining and contrastive learning.

Supervised pretraining. Here, the pretraining dataset is a large-scale *labeled* dataset (e.g., ImageNet), and the pretrained models are simply a neural network trained with vanilla supervised learning (with the last layer being removed). Concretely, suppose we write the learned neural network as $U\phi_{\hat{\theta}}(x)$, where U is the last (fully-connected) layer parameters, $\hat{\theta}$ corresponds to the parameters of all the other layers, and $\phi_{\hat{\theta}}(x)$ are the penultimate activations layer (which serves as the representation). We simply discard U and use $\phi_{\hat{\theta}}(x)$ as the pretrained model.

Contrastive learning. Contrastive learning is a self-supervised pretraining method that uses only unlabeled data. The main intuition is that a good representation function $\phi_\theta(\cdot)$ should map semantically similar images to similar representations, and that random pair of images should generally have distinct representations. E.g., we may want to map images of two huskies to similar representations, but a husky and an elephant should have different representations. One definition of similarity is that images from the same class are similar. Using this definition will result in the so-called supervised contrastive algorithms that work well when labeled pretraining datasets are available.

Without labeled data, we can use data augmentation to generate a pair of "similar" augmented images given an original image x. Data augmentation typically means that we apply *random* cropping, flipping, and/or color transformation on the original image x to generate a variant. We can take two random augmentations, denoted by $\hat{x}$ and $\tilde{x}$, of the same original image x, and call them a positive pair. We observe that positive pairs of images are often semantically related because they are augmentations of the same image. We will design a loss function for θ such that the representations of a positive pair, $\phi_\theta(\hat{x}), \phi_\theta(\tilde{x})$, as close to each other as possible.

On the other hand, we can also take another random image z from the pretraining dataset and generate an augmentation $\hat{z}$ from z. Note that $(\hat{x}, \hat{z})$ are from different images; therefore, with a good chance, they are not semantically related. We call $(\hat{x}, \hat{z})$ a negative or random pair.[2] We will design a loss to push the representation of random pairs, $\phi_\theta(\hat{x}), \phi_\theta(\hat{z})$, far away from each other.

There are many recent algorithms based on the contrastive learning principle, and here we introduce SIMCLR [Chen et al., 2020] as an concrete example. The loss function is defined on a batch of examples $(x^1, \cdots, x^{(B)})$ with batch size B. The algorithm computes two random augmentations for each example $x^{(i)}$ in the batch, denoted by $\hat{x}^{(i)}$ and $\tilde{x}^{(i)}$. As a result, we have the augmented batch of $2B$ examples: $\hat{x}^1, \cdots, \hat{x}^{(B)}$, $\tilde{x}^1, \cdots, \tilde{x}^{(B)}$. The SIMCLR loss is defined as[3]

$$L_{\text{pre}}(\theta) = -\sum_{i=1}^{B} \log \frac{\exp\left(\phi_\theta(\hat{x}^{(i)})^\top \phi_\theta(\tilde{x}^{(i)})\right)}{\exp\left(\phi_\theta(\hat{x}^{(i)})^\top \phi_\theta(\tilde{x}^{(i)})\right) + \sum_{j\neq i} \exp\left(\phi_\theta(\hat{x}^{(i)})^\top \phi_\theta(\tilde{x}^{(j)})\right)}.$$

The intuition is as follows. The loss is increasing in $\phi_\theta(\hat{x}^{(i)})^\top \phi_\theta(\tilde{x}^{(j)})$, and thus minimizing the loss encourages $\phi_\theta(\hat{x}^{(i)})^\top \phi_\theta(\tilde{x}^{(j)})$ to be small, making $\phi_\theta(\hat{x}^{(i)})$ far away from $\phi_\theta(\tilde{x}^{(j)})$. On the other hand, the loss is decreasing in

[2]Random pair may be a more accurate term because it's still possible (though not likely) that x and z are semantically related, so are $\hat{x}$ and $\hat{z}$. But in the literature, the term negative pair seems to be also common.

[3]This is a variant and simplification of the original loss that does not change the essence (but may change the efficiency slightly).

$\phi_\theta(\hat{x}^{(i)})^\top \phi_\theta(\tilde{x}^{(i)})$, and thus minimizing the loss encourages $\phi_\theta(\hat{x}^{(i)})^\top \phi_\theta(\tilde{x}^{(i)})$ to be large, resulting in $\phi_\theta(\hat{x}^{(i)})$ and $\phi_\theta(\tilde{x}^{(i)})$ to be close.[4]

14.3 Pretrained large language models

Natural language processing is another area where pretraining models are particularly successful. In language problems, an example typically corresponds to a document or generally a sequence/trunk of words,[5] denoted by $x = (x_1, \cdots, x_T)$ where T is the length of the document/sequence, $x_i \in \{1, \cdots, V\}$ are words in the document, and V is the vocabulary size.[6]

A language model is a probabilistic model representing the probability of a document, denoted by $p(x_1, \cdots, x_T)$. This probability distribution is very complex because its support size is V^T — exponential in the length of the document. Instead of modeling the distribution of a document itself, we can apply the chain rule of conditional probability to decompose it as follows:

$$p(x_1, \cdots, x_T) = p(x_1)p(x_2|x_1) \cdots p(x_T|x_1, \cdots, x_{T-1}). \tag{14.5}$$

Now the support size of each of the conditional probability $p(x_t|x_1, \cdots, x_{t-1})$ is V.

We will model the conditional probability $p(x_t|x_1, \cdots, x_{t-1})$ as a function of $x_1, \ldots, x_{t-1}$ parameterized by some parameter θ.

A parameterized model takes in numerical inputs and therefore we first introduce embeddings or representations fo the words. Let $e_i \in \mathbb{R}^d$ be the embedding of the word $i \in \{1, 2, \cdots, V\}$. We call $[e_1, \cdots, e_V] \in \mathbb{R}^{d \times V}$ the embedding matrix.

The most commonly used model is Transformer [Vaswani et al., 2017]. In this subsection, we will introduce the input-output interface of a Transformer, but treat the intermediate computation in the Transformer as a blackbox. We refer the students to the transformer paper or more advanced courses for more details. As shown in Figure 14.1, given a document $(x_1, \cdots, x_T)$, we first translate the sequence of discrete variables into a sequence of corresponding

[4]To see this, you can verify that the function $-\log \frac{p}{p+q}$ is decreasing in p, and increasing in q when $p, q > 0$.

[5]In the practical implementations, typically all the data are concatenated into a single sequence in some order, and each example typically corresponds a sub-sequence of consecutive words which may corresponds to a subset of a document or may span across multiple documents.

[6]Technically, words may be decomposed into tokens which could be words or sub-words (combinations of letters), but this note omits this technicality. In fact most commons words are a single token themselves.

word embeddings $(e_{x_1}, \cdots, e_{x_T})$. We also introduce a fixed special token $x_0 = \perp$ in the vocabulary with corresponding embedding e_{x_0} to mark the beginning of a document. Then, the word embeddings are passed into a Transformer model, which takes in a sequence of vectors $(e_{x_0}, e_{x_1}, \cdots, e_{x_T})$ and outputs a sequence of vectors $(u_1, u_2, \cdots, u_{T+1})$, where $u_t \in \mathbb{R}^V$ will be interpreted as the logits for the probability distribution of the next word. Here we use the autoregressive version of the Transformers which by design ensures u_t only depends on $x_1, \cdots, x_{t-1}$ (note that this property does not hold in masked language models [Devlin et al., 2019] where the losses are also different.) We view the whole mapping from x's to u's a blackbox in this subsection and call it a Transformer, denoted it by f_θ, where θ include both the parameters in the Transformer and the input embeddings. We write $u_t = f_\theta(x_0, x_1, \ldots, x_{t-1})$ where f_θ denotes the mapping from the input to the outputs.

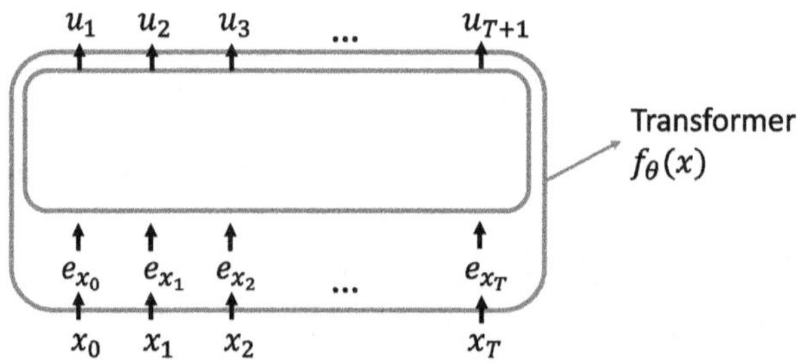

Figure 14.1: The inputs and outputs of a Transformer model.

The conditional probability $p(x_t|x_1, \cdots, x_{t-1})$ is the softtmax of the logits:

$$\begin{bmatrix} p(x_t = 1|x_1 \cdots, x_{t-1}) \\ p(x_t = 2|x_1 \cdots, x_{t-1}) \\ \vdots \\ p(x_t = V|x_1 \cdots, x_{t-1}) \end{bmatrix} = \text{softmax}(u_t) \in \mathbb{R}^V \tag{14.6}$$

$$= \text{softmax}(f_\theta(x_0, \ldots, x_{t-1})) \tag{14.7}$$

We train the Transformer parameter θ by minimizing the negative log-likelihood of seeing the data under the probabilistic model defined by θ, which is the cross-entropy loss on the logitis.

$$\begin{aligned}
\text{loss}(\theta) &= \frac{1}{T}\sum_{t=1}^{T} -\log(p_\theta(x_t|x_1,\dots,x_{t-1})) \qquad (14.8)\\
&= \frac{1}{T}\sum_{t=1}^{T} \ell_{\text{ce}}(f_\theta(x_0,x_1,\cdots,x_{t-1}),x_t)\\
&= \frac{1}{T}\sum_{t=1}^{T} -\log(\text{softmax}(f_\theta(x_0,x_1,\cdots,x_{t-1}))_{x_t})\,.
\end{aligned}$$

Autoregressive text decoding / generation. Given a autoregressive Transformer, we can simply sample text from it sequentially. Given a prefix $x_1, \dots x_t$, we generate text completion $x_{t+1}, \dots x_T$ sequentially using the conditional distribution.

$$x_{t+1} \sim \text{softmax}(f_\theta(x_0, x_1, \cdots, x_t)) \qquad (14.9)$$

$$x_{t+2} \sim \text{softmax}(f_\theta(x_0, x_1, \cdots, x_{t+1})) \qquad (14.10)$$

$$\dots \qquad (14.11)$$

$$x_T \sim \text{softmax}(f_\theta(x_0, x_1, \cdots, x_{T-1}))\,. \qquad (14.12)$$

Note that each generated token is used as the input to the model when generating the following tokens. In practice, people often introduce a parameter $\tau > 0$ named *temperature* to further adjust the entropy/sharpness of the generated distribution,

$$x_{t+1} \sim \text{softmax}(f_\theta(x_0, x_1, \cdots, x_t)/\tau) \qquad (14.13)$$

$$x_{t+2} \sim \text{softmax}(f_\theta(x_0, x_1, \cdots, x_{t+1})/\tau) \qquad (14.14)$$

$$\dots \qquad (14.15)$$

$$x_T \sim \text{softmax}(f_\theta(x_0, x_1, \cdots, x_{T-1})/\tau)\,. \qquad (14.16)$$

When $\tau = 1$, the text is sampled from the original conditional probability defined by the model. With a decreasing τ, the generated text gradually becomes more "deterministic". $\tau \to 0$ reduces to greedy decoding, where we generate the most probable next token from the conditional probability.

14.3.1 Zero-shot learning and in-context learning

For language models, there are many ways to adapt a pretrained model to downstream tasks. In this notes, we discuss three of them: finetuning, zero-shot learning, and in-context learning.

Finetuning is not very common for the autoregressive language models that we introduced in Section 14.3 but much more common for other variants such as masked language models which has similar input-output interfaces but are pretrained differently [Devlin et al., 2019]. The finetuning method is the same as introduced generally in Section 14.1—the only question is how we define the prediction task with an additional linear head. One option is to treat $c_{T+1} = \phi_\theta(x_1, \cdots, x_T)$ as the representation and use $w^\top c_{T+1} = w^\top \phi_\theta(x_1, \cdots, x_T)$ to predict task label. As described in Section 14.1, we initialize θ to the pretrained model $\hat{\theta}$ and then optimize both w and θ.

Zero-shot adaptation or zero-shot learning is the setting where there is no input-output pairs from the downstream tasks. For language problems tasks, typically the task is formatted as a question or a cloze test form via natural language. For example, we can format an example as a question:

$$x_{\text{task}} = (x_{\text{task},1}, \cdots, x_{\text{task},T}) = \text{“Is the speed of light a universal constant?”}$$

Then, we compute the most likely next word predicted by the language model given this question, that is, computing $\text{argmax}_{x_{T+1}} p(x_{T+1} \mid x_{\text{task},1}, \cdots, x_{\text{task},T})$. In this case, if the most likely next word x_{T+1} is “No”, then we solve the task. (The speed of light is only a constant in vacuum). We note that there are many ways to decode the answer from the language models, e.g., instead of computing the argmax, we may use the language model to generate a few words word. It is an active research question to find the best way to utilize the language models.

In-context learning is mostly used for few-shot settings where we have a few labeled examples $(x^{(1)}_{\text{task}}, y^{(1)}_{\text{task}}), \cdots, (x^{(n_{\text{task}})}_{\text{task}}, y^{(n_{\text{task}})}_{\text{task}})$. Given a test example x_{test}, we construct a document $(x_1, \cdots, x_T)$, which is more commonly called a “prompt” in this context, by concatenating the labeled examples and the text example in some format. For example, we may construct the prompt as follows

$$\begin{aligned}
x_1, \cdots, x_T \quad = \quad & \text{“Q: } 2 \sim 3 = \text{?} && x^{(1)}_{\text{task}} \\
& \text{A: } 5 && y^{(1)}_{\text{task}} \\
& \text{Q: } 6 \sim 7 = \text{?} && x^{(2)}_{\text{task}} \\
& \text{A: } 13 && y^{(2)}_{\text{task}} \\
& \cdots \\
& \text{Q: } 15 \sim 2 = \text{?”} && x_{\text{test}}
\end{aligned}$$

Then, we let the pretrained model generate the most likely $x_{T+1}, x_{T+2}, \cdots$. In this case, if the model can "learn" that the symbol $\sim$ means addition from the few examples, we will obtain the following which suggests the answer is 17.

$$x_{T+1}, x_{T+2}, \cdots = \text{"A: 17"}.$$

The area of foundation models is very new and quickly growing. The notes here only attempt to introduce these models on a conceptual level with a significant amount of simplification. We refer the readers to other materials, e.g., Bommasani et al. [2021], for more details.

Part V

Reinforcement Learning and Control

Chapter 15

Reinforcement learning

We now begin our study of reinforcement learning and adaptive control.

In supervised learning, we saw algorithms that tried to make their outputs mimic the labels y given in the training set. In that setting, the labels gave an unambiguous "right answer" for each of the inputs x. In contrast, for many sequential decision making and control problems, it is very difficult to provide this type of explicit supervision to a learning algorithm. For example, if we have just built a four-legged robot and are trying to program it to walk, then initially we have no idea what the "correct" actions to take are to make it walk, and so do not know how to provide explicit supervision for a learning algorithm to try to mimic.

In the reinforcement learning framework, we will instead provide our algorithms only a reward function, which indicates to the learning agent when it is doing well, and when it is doing poorly. In the four-legged walking example, the reward function might give the robot positive rewards for moving forwards, and negative rewards for either moving backwards or falling over. It will then be the learning algorithm's job to figure out how to choose actions over time so as to obtain large rewards.

Reinforcement learning has been successful in applications as diverse as autonomous helicopter flight, robot legged locomotion, cell-phone network routing, marketing strategy selection, factory control, and efficient web-page indexing. Our study of reinforcement learning will begin with a definition of the **Markov decision processes (MDP)**, which provides the formalism in which RL problems are usually posed.

15.1 Markov decision processes

A Markov decision process is a tuple $(S, A, \{P_{sa}\}, \gamma, R)$, where:

- S is a set of **states**. (For example, in autonomous helicopter flight, S might be the set of all possible positions and orientations of the helicopter.)

- A is a set of **actions**. (For example, the set of all possible directions in which you can push the helicopter's control sticks.)

- P_{sa} are the state transition probabilities. For each state $s \in S$ and action $a \in A$, P_{sa} is a distribution over the state space. We'll say more about this later, but briefly, P_{sa} gives the distribution over what states we will transition to if we take action a in state s.

- $\gamma \in [0, 1)$ is called the **discount factor**.

- $R : S \times A \mapsto \mathbb{R}$ is the **reward function**. (Rewards are sometimes also written as a function of a state S only, in which case we would have $R : S \mapsto \mathbb{R}$).

The dynamics of an MDP proceeds as follows: We start in some state s_0, and get to choose some action $a_0 \in A$ to take in the MDP. As a result of our choice, the state of the MDP randomly transitions to some successor state s_1, drawn according to $s_1 \sim P_{s_0 a_0}$. Then, we get to pick another action a_1. As a result of this action, the state transitions again, now to some $s_2 \sim P_{s_1 a_1}$. We then pick a_2, and so on.... Pictorially, we can represent this process as follows:

$$s_0 \xrightarrow{a_0} s_1 \xrightarrow{a_1} s_2 \xrightarrow{a_2} s_3 \xrightarrow{a_3} \dots$$

Upon visiting the sequence of states $s_0, s_1, \dots$ with actions $a_0, a_1, \dots$, our total payoff is given by

$$R(s_0, a_0) + \gamma R(s_1, a_1) + \gamma^2 R(s_2, a_2) + \cdots .$$

Or, when we are writing rewards as a function of the states only, this becomes

$$R(s_0) + \gamma R(s_1) + \gamma^2 R(s_2) + \cdots .$$

For most of our development, we will use the simpler state-rewards $R(s)$, though the generalization to state-action rewards $R(s, a)$ offers no special difficulties.

Our goal in reinforcement learning is to choose actions over time so as to maximize the expected value of the total payoff:

$$\mathrm{E}\left[R(s_0) + \gamma R(s_1) + \gamma^2 R(s_2) + \cdots\right]$$

Note that the reward at timestep t is **discounted** by a factor of γ^t. Thus, to make this expectation large, we would like to accrue positive rewards as soon as possible (and postpone negative rewards as long as possible). In economic applications where $R(\cdot)$ is the amount of money made, γ also has a natural interpretation in terms of the interest rate (where a dollar today is worth more than a dollar tomorrow).

A **policy** is any function $\pi : S \mapsto A$ mapping from the states to the actions. We say that we are **executing** some policy π if, whenever we are in state s, we take action $a = \pi(s)$. We also define the **value function** for a policy π according to

$$V^\pi(s) = \mathrm{E}\left[R(s_0) + \gamma R(s_1) + \gamma^2 R(s_2) + \cdots \,\middle|\, s_0 = s, \pi\right].$$

$V^\pi(s)$ is simply the expected sum of discounted rewards upon starting in state s, and taking actions according to π.[1]

Given a fixed policy π, its value function V^π satisfies the **Bellman equations**:

$$V^\pi(s) = R(s) + \gamma \sum_{s' \in S} P_{s\pi(s)}(s') V^\pi(s').$$

This says that the expected sum of discounted rewards $V^\pi(s)$ for starting in s consists of two terms: First, the **immediate reward** $R(s)$ that we get right away simply for starting in state s, and second, the expected sum of future discounted rewards. Examining the second term in more detail, we see that the summation term above can be rewritten $\mathrm{E}_{s' \sim P_{s\pi(s)}}[V^\pi(s')]$. This is the expected sum of discounted rewards for starting in state s', where s' is distributed according $P_{s\pi(s)}$, which is the distribution over where we will end up after taking the first action $\pi(s)$ in the MDP from state s. Thus, the second term above gives the expected sum of discounted rewards obtained *after* the first step in the MDP.

Bellman's equations can be used to efficiently solve for V^π. Specifically, in a finite-state MDP ($|S| < \infty$), we can write down one such equation for $V^\pi(s)$ for every state s. This gives us a set of $|S|$ linear equations in $|S|$ variables (the unknown $V^\pi(s)$'s, one for each state), which can be efficiently solved for the $V^\pi(s)$'s.

[1]This notation in which we condition on π isn't technically correct because π isn't a random variable, but this is quite standard in the literature.

We also define the **optimal value function** according to

$$V^*(s) = \max_\pi V^\pi(s). \tag{15.1}$$

In other words, this is the best possible expected sum of discounted rewards that can be attained using any policy. There is also a version of Bellman's equations for the optimal value function:

$$V^*(s) = R(s) + \max_{a \in A} \gamma \sum_{s' \in S} P_{sa}(s') V^*(s'). \tag{15.2}$$

The first term above is the immediate reward as before. The second term is the maximum over all actions a of the expected future sum of discounted rewards we'll get upon after action a. You should make sure you understand this equation and see why it makes sense.

We also define a policy $\pi^* : S \mapsto A$ as follows:

$$\pi^*(s) = \arg\max_{a \in A} \sum_{s' \in S} P_{sa}(s') V^*(s'). \tag{15.3}$$

Note that $\pi^*(s)$ gives the action a that attains the maximum in the "max" in Equation (15.2).

It is a fact that for every state s and every policy π, we have

$$V^*(s) = V^{\pi^*}(s) \geq V^\pi(s).$$

The first equality says that the V^{π^*}, the value function for π^*, is equal to the optimal value function V^* for every state s. Further, the inequality above says that π^*'s value is at least a large as the value of any other other policy. In other words, π^* as defined in Equation (15.3) is the optimal policy.

Note that π^* has the interesting property that it is the optimal policy for *all* states s. Specifically, it is not the case that if we were starting in some state s then there'd be some optimal policy for that state, and if we were starting in some other state s' then there'd be some other policy that's optimal policy for s'. The same policy π^* attains the maximum in Equation (15.1) for *all* states s. This means that we can use the same policy π^* no matter what the initial state of our MDP is.

15.2 Value iteration and policy iteration

We now describe two efficient algorithms for solving finite-state MDPs. For now, we will consider only MDPs with finite state and action spaces ($|S| <$

∞, $|A| < \infty$). In this section, we will also assume that we know the state transition probabilities $\{P_{sa}\}$ and the reward function R.

The first algorithm, **value iteration**, is as follows:

Algorithm 4 Value Iteration

For each state s, initialize $V(s) := 0$.
for until convergence **do**
    For every state, update

$$V(s) := R(s) + \max_{a \in A} \gamma \sum_{s'} P_{sa}(s')V(s'). \tag{15.4}$$

This algorithm can be thought of as repeatedly trying to update the estimated value function using Bellman Equations (15.2).

There are two possible ways of performing the updates in the inner loop of the algorithm. In the first, we can first compute the new values for $V(s)$ for every state s, and then overwrite all the old values with the new values. This is called a **synchronous** update. In this case, the algorithm can be viewed as implementing a "Bellman backup operator" that takes a current estimate of the value function, and maps it to a new estimate. (See homework problem for details.) Alternatively, we can also perform **asynchronous** updates. Here, we would loop over the states (in some order), updating the values one at a time.

Under either synchronous or asynchronous updates, it can be shown that value iteration will cause V to converge to V^*. Having found V^*, we can then use Equation (15.3) to find the optimal policy.

Apart from value iteration, there is a second standard algorithm for finding an optimal policy for an MDP. The **policy iteration** algorithm proceeds as follows:

Thus, the inner-loop repeatedly computes the value function for the current policy, and then updates the policy using the current value function. (The policy π found in step (b) is also called the policy that is **greedy with respect to** V.) Note that step (a) can be done via solving Bellman's equations as described earlier, which in the case of a fixed policy, is just a set of $|S|$ linear equations in $|S|$ variables.

After at most a *finite* number of iterations of this algorithm, V will converge to V^*, and π will converge to π^*.[2]

---

[2]Note that value iteration cannot reach the exact V^* in a finite number of iterations,

Algorithm 5 Policy Iteration

Initialize π randomly.
for until convergence **do**
  Let $V := V^{\pi}$. ▷ typically by linear system solver
  For each state s, let

$$\pi(s) := \arg\max_{a \in A} \sum_{s'} P_{sa}(s')V(s').$$

Both value iteration and policy iteration are standard algorithms for solving MDPs, and there isn't currently universal agreement over which algorithm is better. For small MDPs, policy iteration is often very fats and converges with very few iterations. However, for MDPs with large state spaces, solving for V^{π} explicitly would involve solving a large system of linear equations, and could be difficult (and note that one has to solve the linear system multiple times in policy iteration). In these problems, value iteration may be preferred. For this reason, in practice value iteration seems to be used more often than policy iteration. For some more discussions on the comparison and connection of value iteration and policy iteration, please see Section 15.5.

15.3 Learning a model for an MDP

So far, we have discussed MDPs and algorithms for MDPs assuming that the state transition probabilities and rewards are known. In many realistic problems, we are not given state transition probabilities and rewards explicitly, but must instead estimate them from data. (Usually, S, A and γ are known.)

For example, suppose that, for the inverted pendulum problem (see prob-

whereas policy iteration with an exact linear system solver, can. This is because when the actions space and policy space are discrete and finite, and once the policy reaches the optimal policy in policy iteration, then it will not change at all. On the other hand, even though value iteration will converge to the V^*, but there is always some non-zero error in the learned value function.

lem set 4), we had a number of trials in the MDP, that proceeded as follows:

$$s_0^{(1)} \xrightarrow{a_0^{(1)}} s_1^{(1)} \xrightarrow{a_1^{(1)}} s_2^{(1)} \xrightarrow{a_2^{(1)}} s_3^{(1)} \xrightarrow{a_3^{(1)}} \dots$$
$$s_0^{(2)} \xrightarrow{a_0^{(2)}} s_1^{(2)} \xrightarrow{a_1^{(2)}} s_2^{(2)} \xrightarrow{a_2^{(2)}} s_3^{(2)} \xrightarrow{a_3^{(2)}} \dots$$
$$\dots$$

Here, $s_i^{(j)}$ is the state we were at time i of trial j, and $a_i^{(j)}$ is the corresponding action that was taken from that state. In practice, each of the trials above might be run until the MDP terminates (such as if the pole falls over in the inverted pendulum problem), or it might be run for some large but finite number of timesteps.

Given this "experience" in the MDP consisting of a number of trials, we can then easily derive the maximum likelihood estimates for the state transition probabilities:

$$P_{sa}(s') = \frac{\#\text{times took we action } a \text{ in state } s \text{ and got to } s'}{\#\text{times we took action a in state } s} \tag{15.5}$$

Or, if the ratio above is "0/0"—corresponding to the case of never having taken action a in state s before—the we might simply estimate $P_{sa}(s')$ to be $1/|S|$. (I.e., estimate P_{sa} to be the uniform distribution over all states.)

Note that, if we gain more experience (observe more trials) in the MDP, there is an efficient way to update our estimated state transition probabilities using the new experience. Specifically, if we keep around the counts for both the numerator and denominator terms of (15.5), then as we observe more trials, we can simply keep accumulating those counts. Computing the ratio of these counts then given our estimate of P_{sa}.

Using a similar procedure, if R is unknown, we can also pick our estimate of the expected immediate reward $R(s)$ in state s to be the average reward observed in state s.

Having learned a model for the MDP, we can then use either value iteration or policy iteration to solve the MDP using the estimated transition probabilities and rewards. For example, putting together model learning and value iteration, here is one possible algorithm for learning in an MDP with unknown state transition probabilities:

1. Initialize π randomly.

2. Repeat {

   (a) Execute π in the MDP for some number of trials.

(b) Using the accumulated experience in the MDP, update our estimates for P_{sa} (and R, if applicable).

(c) Apply value iteration with the estimated state transition probabilities and rewards to get a new estimated value function V.

(d) Update π to be the greedy policy with respect to V.

}

We note that, for this particular algorithm, there is one simple optimization that can make it run much more quickly. Specifically, in the inner loop of the algorithm where we apply value iteration, if instead of initializing value iteration with $V = 0$, we initialize it with the solution found during the previous iteration of our algorithm, then that will provide value iteration with a much better initial starting point and make it converge more quickly.

15.4 Continuous state MDPs

So far, we've focused our attention on MDPs with a finite number of states. We now discuss algorithms for MDPs that may have an infinite number of states. For example, for a car, we might represent the state as $(x, y, \theta, \dot{x}, \dot{y}, \dot{\theta})$, comprising its position (x, y); orientation θ; velocity in the x and y directions $\dot{x}$ and $\dot{y}$; and angular velocity $\dot{\theta}$. Hence, $S = \mathbb{R}^6$ is an infinite set of states, because there is an infinite number of possible positions and orientations for the car.[3] Similarly, the inverted pendulum you saw in PS4 has states $(x, \theta, \dot{x}, \dot{\theta})$, where θ is the angle of the pole. And, a helicopter flying in 3d space has states of the form $(x, y, z, \phi, \theta, \psi, \dot{x}, \dot{y}, \dot{z}, \dot{\phi}, \dot{\theta}, \dot{\psi})$, where here the roll ϕ, pitch θ, and yaw ψ angles specify the 3d orientation of the helicopter.

In this section, we will consider settings where the state space is $S = \mathbb{R}^d$, and describe ways for solving such MDPs.

15.4.1 Discretization

Perhaps the simplest way to solve a continuous-state MDP is to discretize the state space, and then to use an algorithm like value iteration or policy iteration, as described previously.

For example, if we have 2d states (s_1, s_2), we can use a grid to discretize the state space:

[3]Technically, θ is an orientation and so the range of θ is better written $\theta \in [-\pi, \pi)$ than $\theta \in \mathbb{R}$; but for our purposes, this distinction is not important.

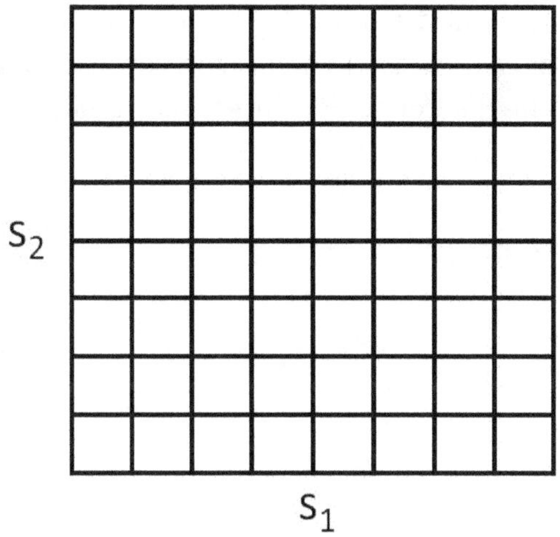

[t]

Here, each grid cell represents a separate discrete state $\bar{s}$. We can then approximate the continuous-state MDP via a discrete-state one $(\bar{S}, A, \{P_{\bar{s}a}\}, \gamma, R)$, where $\bar{S}$ is the set of discrete states, $\{P_{\bar{s}a}\}$ are our state transition probabilities over the discrete states, and so on. We can then use value iteration or policy iteration to solve for the $V^*(\bar{s})$ and $\pi^*(\bar{s})$ in the discrete state MDP $(\bar{S}, A, \{P_{\bar{s}a}\}, \gamma, R)$. When our actual system is in some continuous-valued state $s \in S$ and we need to pick an action to execute, we compute the corresponding discretized state $\bar{s}$, and execute action $\pi^*(\bar{s})$.

This discretization approach can work well for many problems. However, there are two downsides. First, it uses a fairly naive representation for V^* (and π^*). Specifically, it assumes that the value function is takes a constant value over each of the discretization intervals (i.e., that the value function is piecewise constant in each of the gridcells).

To better understand the limitations of such a representation, consider a *supervised learning* problem of fitting a function to this dataset:

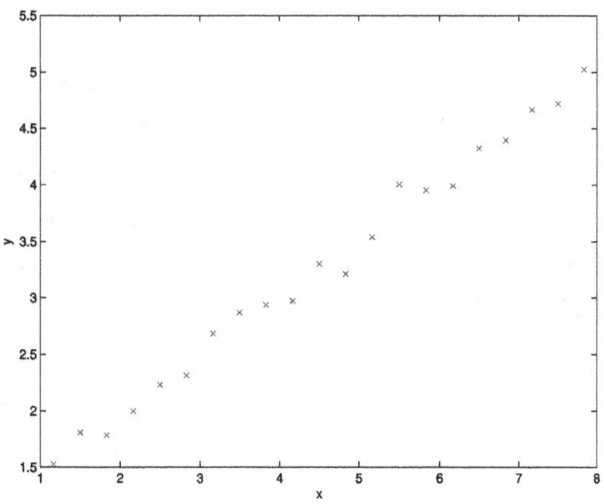

[t]

Clearly, linear regression would do fine on this problem. However, if we instead discretize the x-axis, and then use a representation that is piecewise constant in each of the discretization intervals, then our fit to the data would look like this:

[t] 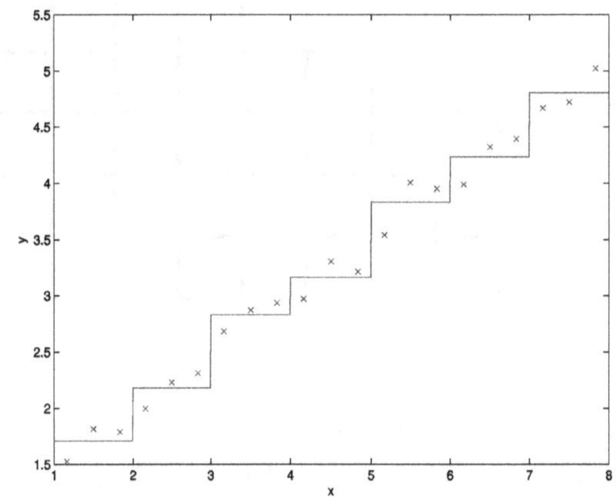

This piecewise constant representation just isn't a good representation for many smooth functions. It results in little smoothing over the inputs, and no generalization over the different grid cells. Using this sort of representation, we would also need a very fine discretization (very small grid cells) to get a good approximation.

A second downside of this representation is called the **curse of dimensionality**. Suppose $S = \mathbb{R}^d$, and we discretize each of the d dimensions of the state into k values. Then the total number of discrete states we have is k^d. This grows exponentially quickly in the dimension of the state space d, and thus does not scale well to large problems. For example, with a 10d state, if we discretize each state variable into 100 values, we would have $100^{10} = 10^{20}$ discrete states, which is far too many to represent even on a modern desktop computer.

As a rule of thumb, discretization usually works extremely well for 1d and 2d problems (and has the advantage of being simple and quick to implement). Perhaps with a little bit of cleverness and some care in choosing the discretization method, it often works well for problems with up to 4d states. If you're extremely clever, and somewhat lucky, you may even get it to work for some 6d problems. But it very rarely works for problems any higher dimensional than that.

15.4.2 Value function approximation

We now describe an alternative method for finding policies in continuous-state MDPs, in which we approximate V^* directly, without resorting to discretization. This approach, called value function approximation, has been successfully applied to many RL problems.

Using a model or simulator

To develop a value function approximation algorithm, we will assume that we have a **model**, or **simulator**, for the MDP. Informally, a simulator is a black-box that takes as input any (continuous-valued) state s_t and action a_t, and outputs a next-state s_{t+1} sampled according to the state transition probabilities $P_{s_t a_t}$:

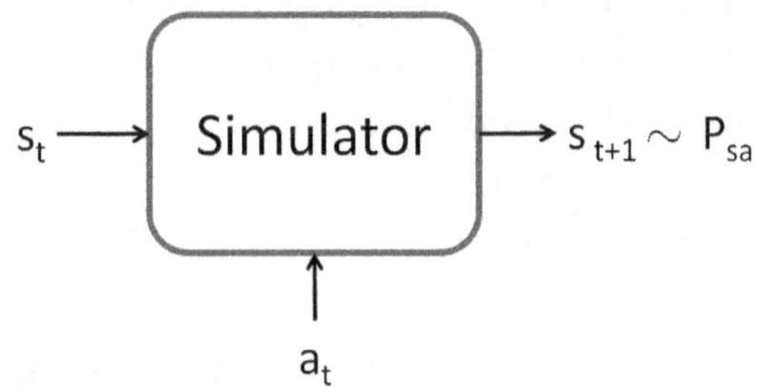

[t]

There are several ways that one can get such a model. One is to use physics simulation. For example, the simulator for the inverted pendulum in PS4 was obtained by using the laws of physics to calculate what position and orientation the cart/pole will be in at time $t+1$, given the current state at time t and the action a taken, assuming that we know all the parameters of the system such as the length of the pole, the mass of the pole, and so on. Alternatively, one can also use an off-the-shelf physics simulation software package which takes as input a complete physical description of a mechanical system, the current state s_t and action a_t, and computes the state s_{t+1} of the system a small fraction of a second into the future.[4]

An alternative way to get a model is to learn one from data collected in the MDP. For example, suppose we execute n **trials** in which we repeatedly take actions in an MDP, each trial for T timesteps. This can be done picking actions at random, executing some specific policy, or via some other way of

[4]Open Dynamics Engine (http://www.ode.com) is one example of a free/open-source physics simulator that can be used to simulate systems like the inverted pendulum, and that has been a reasonably popular choice among RL researchers.

choosing actions. We would then observe n state sequences like the following:

$$s_0^{(1)} \xrightarrow{a_0^{(1)}} s_1^{(1)} \xrightarrow{a_1^{(1)}} s_2^{(1)} \xrightarrow{a_2^{(1)}} \cdots \xrightarrow{a_{T-1}^{(1)}} s_T^{(1)}$$

$$s_0^{(2)} \xrightarrow{a_0^{(2)}} s_1^{(2)} \xrightarrow{a_1^{(2)}} s_2^{(2)} \xrightarrow{a_2^{(2)}} \cdots \xrightarrow{a_{T-1}^{(2)}} s_T^{(2)}$$

$$\cdots$$

$$s_0^{(n)} \xrightarrow{a_0^{(n)}} s_1^{(n)} \xrightarrow{a_1^{(n)}} s_2^{(n)} \xrightarrow{a_2^{(n)}} \cdots \xrightarrow{a_{T-1}^{(n)}} s_T^{(n)}$$

We can then apply a learning algorithm to predict s_{t+1} as a function of s_t and a_t.

For example, one may choose to learn a linear model of the form

$$s_{t+1} = As_t + Ba_t, \tag{15.6}$$

using an algorithm similar to linear regression. Here, the parameters of the model are the matrices A and B, and we can estimate them using the data collected from our n trials, by picking

$$\arg\min_{A,B} \sum_{i=1}^{n} \sum_{t=0}^{T-1} \left\| s_{t+1}^{(i)} - \left(As_t^{(i)} + Ba_t^{(i)} \right) \right\|_2^2 .$$

We could also potentially use other loss functions for learning the model. For example, it has been found in recent work Luo et al. [2018] that using $\|\cdot\|_2$ norm (without the square) may be helpful in certain cases.

Having learned A and B, one option is to build a **deterministic** model, in which given an input s_t and a_t, the output s_{t+1} is exactly determined. Specifically, we always compute s_{t+1} according to Equation (15.6). Alternatively, we may also build a **stochastic** model, in which s_{t+1} is a random function of the inputs, by modeling it as

$$s_{t+1} = As_t + Ba_t + \epsilon_t,$$

where here ϵ_t is a noise term, usually modeled as $\epsilon_t \sim \mathcal{N}(0, \Sigma)$. (The covariance matrix Σ can also be estimated from data in a straightforward way.)

Here, we've written the next-state s_{t+1} as a linear function of the current state and action; but of course, non-linear functions are also possible. Specifically, one can learn a model $s_{t+1} = A\phi_s(s_t) + B\phi_a(a_t)$, where ϕ_s and ϕ_a are some non-linear feature mappings of the states and actions. Alternatively, one can also use non-linear learning algorithms, such as locally weighted linear regression, to learn to estimate s_{t+1} as a function of s_t and a_t. These approaches can also be used to build either deterministic or stochastic simulators of an MDP.

Fitted value iteration

We now describe the **fitted value iteration** algorithm for approximating the value function of a continuous state MDP. In the sequel, we will assume that the problem has a continuous state space $S = \mathbb{R}^d$, but that the action space A is small and discrete.[5]

Recall that in value iteration, we would like to perform the update

$$\begin{aligned} V(s) &:= R(s) + \gamma \max_a \int_{s'} P_{sa}(s')V(s')ds' && (15.7) \\ &= R(s) + \gamma \max_a \mathrm{E}_{s'\sim P_{sa}}[V(s')] && (15.8) \end{aligned}$$

(In Section 15.2, we had written the value iteration update with a summation $V(s) := R(s) + \gamma \max_a \sum_{s'} P_{sa}(s')V(s')$ rather than an integral over states; the new notation reflects that we are now working in continuous states rather than discrete states.)

The main idea of fitted value iteration is that we are going to approximately carry out this step, over a finite sample of states $s^{(1)}, \ldots, s^{(n)}$. Specifically, we will use a supervised learning algorithm—linear regression in our description below—to approximate the value function as a linear or non-linear function of the states:

$$V(s) = \theta^T \phi(s).$$

Here, ϕ is some appropriate feature mapping of the states.

For each state s in our finite sample of n states, fitted value iteration will first compute a quantity $y^{(i)}$, which will be our approximation to $R(s) + \gamma \max_a \mathrm{E}_{s'\sim P_{sa}}[V(s')]$ (the right hand side of Equation 15.8). Then, it will apply a supervised learning algorithm to try to get $V(s)$ close to $R(s) + \gamma \max_a \mathrm{E}_{s'\sim P_{sa}}[V(s')]$ (or, in other words, to try to get $V(s)$ close to $y^{(i)}$).

In detail, the algorithm is as follows:

1. Randomly sample n states $s^{(1)}, s^{(2)}, \ldots s^{(n)} \in S$.

2. Initialize $\theta := 0$.

3. Repeat {

    For $i = 1, \ldots, n$ {

[5] In practice, most MDPs have much smaller action spaces than state spaces. E.g., a car has a 6d state space, and a 2d action space (steering and velocity controls); the inverted pendulum has a 4d state space, and a 1d action space; a helicopter has a 12d state space, and a 4d action space. So, discretizing this set of actions is usually less of a problem than discretizing the state space would have been.

For each action $a \in A$ {

Sample $s'_1, \dots, s'_k \sim P_{s^{(i)}a}$ (using a model of the MDP).

Set $q(a) = \frac{1}{k}\sum_{j=1}^{k} R(s^{(i)}) + \gamma V(s'_j)$

// Hence, $q(a)$ is an estimate of $R(s^{(i)}) + \gamma \mathrm{E}_{s' \sim P_{s^{(i)}a}}[V(s')]$.

}

Set $y^{(i)} = \max_a q(a)$.

// Hence, $y^{(i)}$ is an estimate of $R(s^{(i)}) + \gamma \max_a \mathrm{E}_{s' \sim P_{s^{(i)}a}}[V(s')]$.

}

// In the original value iteration algorithm (over discrete states)

// we updated the value function according to $V(s^{(i)}) := y^{(i)}$.

// In this algorithm, we want $V(s^{(i)}) \approx y^{(i)}$, which we'll achieve

// using supervised learning (linear regression).

Set $\theta := \arg\min_\theta \frac{1}{2}\sum_{i=1}^{n}\left(\theta^T\phi(s^{(i)}) - y^{(i)}\right)^2$

}

Above, we had written out fitted value iteration using linear regression as the algorithm to try to make $V(s^{(i)})$ close to $y^{(i)}$. That step of the algorithm is completely analogous to a standard supervised learning (regression) problem in which we have a training set $(x^{(1)}, y^{(1)}), (x^{(2)}, y^{(2)}), \dots, (x^{(n)}, y^{(n)})$, and want to learn a function mapping from x to y; the only difference is that here s plays the role of x. Even though our description above used linear regression, clearly other regression algorithms (such as locally weighted linear regression) can also be used.

Unlike value iteration over a discrete set of states, fitted value iteration cannot be proved to always to converge. However, in practice, it often does converge (or approximately converge), and works well for many problems. Note also that if we are using a deterministic simulator/model of the MDP, then fitted value iteration can be simplified by setting $k = 1$ in the algorithm. This is because the expectation in Equation (15.8) becomes an expectation over a deterministic distribution, and so a single example is sufficient to exactly compute that expectation. Otherwise, in the algorithm above, we had to draw k samples, and average to try to approximate that expectation (see the definition of $q(a)$, in the algorithm pseudo-code).

Finally, fitted value iteration outputs V, which is an approximation to V^*. This implicitly defines our policy. Specifically, when our system is in some state s, and we need to choose an action, we would like to choose the action

$$\arg\max_a \mathrm{E}_{s' \sim P_{sa}}[V(s')] \tag{15.9}$$

The process for computing/approximating this is similar to the inner-loop of fitted value iteration, where for each action, we sample $s'_1, \ldots, s'_k \sim P_{sa}$ to approximate the expectation. (And again, if the simulator is deterministic, we can set $k = 1$.)

In practice, there are often other ways to approximate this step as well. For example, one very common case is if the simulator is of the form $s_{t+1} = f(s_t, a_t) + \epsilon_t$, where f is some deterministic function of the states (such as $f(s_t, a_t) = As_t + Ba_t$), and ϵ is zero-mean Gaussian noise. In this case, we can pick the action given by

$$\arg\max_a V(f(s, a)).$$

In other words, here we are just setting $\epsilon_t = 0$ (i.e., ignoring the noise in the simulator), and setting $k = 1$. Equivalent, this can be derived from Equation (15.9) using the approximation

$$\begin{aligned} \mathrm{E}_{s'}[V(s')] &\approx V(\mathrm{E}_{s'}[s']) && (15.10) \\ &= V(f(s, a)), && (15.11) \end{aligned}$$

where here the expectation is over the random $s' \sim P_{sa}$. So long as the noise terms ϵ_t are small, this will usually be a reasonable approximation.

However, for problems that don't lend themselves to such approximations, having to sample $k|A|$ states using the model, in order to approximate the expectation above, can be computationally expensive.

15.5 Connections between Policy and Value Iteration (Optional)

In the policy iteration, line 3 of Algorithm 5, we typically use linear system solver to compute V^π. Alternatively, one can also the iterative Bellman updates, similarly to the value iteration, to evaluate V^π, as in the Procedure VE($\cdot$) in Line 1 of Algorithm 6 below. Here if we take option 1 in Line 2 of the Procedure VE, then the difference between the Procedure VE from the

Algorithm 6 Variant of Policy Iteration

procedure VE(π, k) ▷ To evaluate V^π

Option 1: initialize $V(s) := 0$; Option 2: Initialize from the current V in the main algorithm.

for $i = 0$ to $k - 1$ **do**

For every state s, update

$$V(s) := R(s) + \gamma \sum_{s'} P_{s\pi(s)}(s')V(s'). \tag{15.12}$$

return V

Require: hyperparameter k.

Initialize π randomly.

for until convergence **do**

Let $V = \text{VE}(\pi, k)$.

For each state s, let

$$\pi(s) := \arg\max_{a \in A} \sum_{s'} P_{sa}(s')V(s'). \tag{15.13}$$

value iteration (Algorithm 4) is that on line 4, the procedure is using the action from π instead of the greedy action.

Using the Procedure VE, we can build Algorithm 6, which is a variant of policy iteration that serves an intermediate algorithm that connects policy iteration and value iteration. Here we are going to use option 2 in VE to maximize the re-use of knowledge learned before. One can verify indeed that if we take $k = 1$ and use option 2 in Line 2 in Algorithm 6, then Algorithm 6 is semantically equivalent to value iteration (Algorithm 4). In other words, both Algorithm 6 and value iteration interleave the updates in (15.13) and (15.12). Algorithm 6 alternate between k steps of update (15.12) and one step of (15.13), whereas value iteration alternates between 1 steps of update (15.12) and one step of (15.13). Therefore generally Algorithm 6 should not be faster than value iteration, because assuming that update (15.12) and (15.13) are equally useful and time-consuming, then the optimal balance of the update frequencies could be just $k = 1$ or $k \approx 1$.

On the other hand, if k steps of update (15.12) can be done much faster than k times a single step of (15.12), then taking additional steps of equation (15.12) in group might be useful. This is what policy iteration is leveraging — the linear system solver can give us the result of Procedure VE with $k = \infty$ much faster than using the Procedure VE for a large k. On the flip side, when such a speeding-up effect no longer exists, e.g.,, when the state space is large and linear system solver is also not fast, then value iteration is more preferable.

Chapter 16

LQR, DDP and LQG

16.1 Finite-horizon MDPs

In Chapter 15, we defined Markov Decision Processes (MDPs) and covered Value Iteration / Policy Iteration in a simplified setting. More specifically we introduced the **optimal Bellman equation** that defines the optimal value function V^{π^*} of the optimal policy π^*.

$$V^{\pi^*}(s) = R(s) + \max_{a \in \mathcal{A}} \gamma \sum_{s' \in S} P_{sa}(s') V^{\pi^*}(s')$$

Recall that from the optimal value function, we were able to recover the optimal policy π^* with

$$\pi^*(s) = \operatorname{argmax}_{a \in \mathcal{A}} \sum_{s' \in S} P_{sa}(s') V^*(s')$$

In this chapter, we'll place ourselves in a more general setting:

1. We want to write equations that make sense for both the discrete and the continuous case. We'll therefore write

   $$\mathbb{E}_{s' \sim P_{sa}} \left[V^{\pi^*}(s') \right] \quad \text{instead of} \quad \sum_{s' \in S} P_{sa}(s') V^{\pi^*}(s')$$

   meaning that we take the expectation of the value function at the next state. In the finite case, we can rewrite the expectation as a sum over states. In the continuous case, we can rewrite the expectation as an integral. The notation $s' \sim P_{sa}$ means that the state s' is sampled from the distribution P_{sa}.

2. We'll assume that the rewards depend on **both states and actions**. In other words, $R : \mathcal{S} \times \mathcal{A} \to \mathbb{R}$. This implies that the previous mechanism for computing the optimal action is changed into

$$\pi^*(s) = \operatorname{argmax}_{a \in \mathcal{A}} R(s, a) + \gamma \mathbb{E}_{s' \sim P_{sa}} \left[V^{\pi^*}(s') \right]$$

3. Instead of considering an infinite horizon MDP, we'll assume that we have a **finite horizon MDP** that will be defined as a tuple

$$(\mathcal{S}, \mathcal{A}, P_{sa}, T, R)$$

with $T > 0$ the **time horizon** (for instance $T = 100$). In this setting, our definition of payoff is going to be (slightly) different:

$$R(s_0, a_0) + R(s_1, a_1) + \cdots + R(s_T, a_T)$$

instead of (infinite horizon case)

$$R(s_0, a_0) + \gamma R(s_1, a_1) + \gamma^2 R(s_2, a_2) + \ldots$$

$$\sum_{t=0}^{\infty} R(s_t, a_t) \gamma^t$$

What happened to the discount factor γ? Remember that the introduction of γ was (partly) justified by the necessity of making sure that the infinite sum would be finite and well-defined. If the rewards are bounded by a constant $\bar{R}$, the payoff is indeed bounded by

$$|\sum_{t=0}^{\infty} R(s_t) \gamma^t| \leq \bar{R} \sum_{t=0}^{\infty} \gamma^t$$

and we recognize a geometric sum! Here, as the payoff is a finite sum, the discount factor γ is not necessary anymore.

In this new setting, things behave quite differently. First, the optimal policy π^* might be non-stationary, meaning that **it changes over time**. In other words, now we have

$$\pi^{(t)} : \mathcal{S} \to \mathcal{A}$$

where the superscript (t) denotes the policy at time step t. The dynamics of the finite horizon MDP following policy $\pi^{(t)}$ proceeds as follows: we start in some state s_0, take some action $a_0 := \pi^{(0)}(s_0)$ according to our policy at time step 0. The MDP transitions to a successor s_1, drawn according to $P_{s_0 a_0}$. Then, we get to pick another action $a_1 := \pi^{(1)}(s_1)$ following our new policy at time step 1 and so on...

Why does the optimal policy happen to be non-stationary in the finite-horizon setting? Intuitively, as we have a finite numbers of actions to take, we might want to adopt different strategies depending on where we are in the environment and how much time we have left. Imagine a grid with 2 goals with rewards +1 and +10. At the beginning, we might want to take actions to aim for the +10 goal. But if after some steps, dynamics somehow pushed us closer to the +1 goal and we don't have enough steps left to be able to reach the +10 goal, then a better strategy would be to aim for the +1 goal...

4. This observation allows us to use **time dependent dynamics**

$$s_{t+1} \sim P^{(t)}_{s_t, a_t}$$

meaning that the transition's distribution $P^{(t)}_{s_t, a_t}$ changes over time. The same thing can be said about $R^{(t)}$. Note that this setting is a better model for real life. In a car, the gas tank empties, traffic changes, etc. Combining the previous remarks, we'll use the following general formulation for our finite horizon MDP

$$\left(\mathcal{S}, \mathcal{A}, P^{(t)}_{sa}, T, R^{(t)}\right)$$

Remark: notice that the above formulation would be equivalent to adding the time into the state.

The value function at time t for a policy π is then defined in the same way as before, as an expectation over trajectories generated following policy π starting in state s.

$$V_t(s) = \mathbb{E}\left[R^{(t)}(s_t, a_t) + \cdots + R^{(T)}(s_T, a_T) | s_t = s, \pi\right]$$

Now, the question is

In this finite-horizon setting, how do we find the optimal value function

$$V_t^*(s) = \max_{\pi} V_t^{\pi}(s)$$

It turns out that Bellman's equation for Value Iteration is made for **Dynamic Programming**. This may come as no surprise as Bellman is one of the fathers of dynamic programming and the Bellman equation is strongly related to the field. To understand how we can simplify the problem by adopting an iteration-based approach, we make the following observations:

1. Notice that at the end of the game (for time step T), the optimal value is obvious

$$\forall s \in \mathcal{S}: \quad V_T^*(s) := \max_{a \in \mathcal{A}} R^{(T)}(s, a) \tag{16.1}$$

2. For another time step $0 \leq t < T$, if we suppose that we know the optimal value function for the next time step V_{t+1}^*, then we have

$$\forall t < T, s \in \mathcal{S}: \quad V_t^*(s) := \max_{a \in \mathcal{A}} \left[R^{(t)}(s, a) + \mathbb{E}_{s' \sim P_{sa}^{(t)}} \left[V_{t+1}^*(s')\right]\right] \tag{16.2}$$

With these observations in mind, we can come up with a clever algorithm to solve for the optimal value function:

1. compute V_T^* using equation (16.1).
2. for $t = T - 1, \ldots, 0$:

   compute V_t^* using V_{t+1}^* using equation (16.2)

Side note We can interpret standard value iteration as a special case of this general case, but without keeping track of time. It turns out that in the standard setting, if we run value iteration for T steps, we get a γ^T approximation of the optimal value iteration (geometric convergence). See problem set 4 for a proof of the following result:

Theorem Let B denote the Bellman update and $||f(x)||_\infty := \sup_x |f(x)|$. If V_t denotes the value function at the t-th step, then

$$\begin{aligned} ||V_{t+1} - V^*||_\infty &= ||B(V_t) - V^*||_\infty \\ &\leq \gamma ||V_t - V^*||_\infty \\ &\leq \gamma^t ||V_1 - V^*||_\infty \end{aligned}$$

In other words, the Bellman operator B is a γ-contracting operator.

16.2 Linear Quadratic Regulation (LQR)

In this section, we'll cover a special case of the finite-horizon setting described in Section 16.1, for which the **exact solution** is (easily) tractable. This model is widely used in robotics, and a common technique in many problems is to reduce the formulation to this framework.

First, let's describe the model's assumptions. We place ourselves in the continuous setting, with

$$\mathcal{S} = \mathbb{R}^d, \quad \mathcal{A} = \mathbb{R}^d$$

and we'll assume **linear transitions** (with noise)

$$s_{t+1} = A_t s_t + B_t a_t + w_t$$

where $A_t \in R^{d \times d}, B_t \in R^{d \times d}$ are matrices and $w_t \sim \mathcal{N}(0, \Sigma_t)$ is some gaussian noise (with **zero** mean). As we'll show in the following paragraphs, it turns out that the noise, as long as it has zero mean, does not impact the optimal policy!

We'll also assume **quadratic rewards**

$$R^{(t)}(s_t, a_t) = -s_t^\top U_t s_t - a_t^\top W_t a_t$$

where $U_t \in R^{d\times n}, W_t \in R^{d\times d}$ are positive definite matrices (meaning that the reward is always **negative**).

Remark Note that the quadratic formulation of the reward is equivalent to saying that we want our state to be close to the origin (where the reward is higher). For example, if $U_t = I_d$ (the identity matrix) and $W_t = I_d$, then $R_t = -||s_t||^2 - ||a_t||^2$, meaning that we want to take smooth actions (small norm of a_t) to go back to the origin (small norm of s_t). This could model a car trying to stay in the middle of lane without making impulsive moves...

Now that we have defined the assumptions of our LQR model, let's cover the 2 steps of the LQR algorithm

step 1 suppose that we don't know the matrices A, B, Σ. To estimate them, we can follow the ideas outlined in the Value Approximation section of the RL notes. First, collect transitions from an arbitrary policy. Then, use linear regression to find $\text{argmin}_{A,B} \sum_{i=1}^{n} \sum_{t=0}^{T-1} \left\| s_{t+1}^{(i)} - \left(A s_t^{(i)} + B a_t^{(i)} \right) \right\|^2$. Finally, use a technique seen in Gaussian Discriminant Analysis to learn Σ.

step 2 assuming that the parameters of our model are known (given or estimated with step 1), we can derive the optimal policy using dynamic programming.

In other words, given

$$\begin{cases} s_{t+1} &= A_t s_t + B_t a_t + w_t \qquad A_t, B_t, U_t, W_t, \Sigma_t \text{ known} \\ R^{(t)}(s_t, a_t) &= -s_t^\top U_t s_t - a_t^\top W_t a_t \end{cases}$$

we want to compute V_t^*. If we go back to section 16.1, we can apply dynamic programming, which yields

1. **Initialization step**

   For the last time step T,

$$\begin{aligned} V_T^*(s_T) &= \max_{a_T \in \mathcal{A}} R_T(s_T, a_T) \\ &= \max_{a_T \in \mathcal{A}} -s_T^\top U_T s_T - a_T^\top W_t a_T \\ &= -s_T^\top U_t s_T \qquad \text{(maximized for } a_T = 0\text{)} \end{aligned}$$

2. **Recurrence step**

Let $t < T$. Suppose we know V_{t+1}^*.

Fact 1: It can be shown that if V_{t+1}^* is a quadratic function in s_t, then V_t^* is also a quadratic function. In other words, there exists some matrix Φ and some scalar Ψ such that

$$\begin{aligned} &\text{if } V_{t+1}^*(s_{t+1}) = s_{t+1}^\top \Phi_{t+1} s_{t+1} + \Psi_{t+1} \\ &\text{then } V_t^*(s_t) = s_t^\top \Phi_t s_t + \Psi_t \end{aligned}$$

For time step $t = T$, we had $\Phi_t = -U_T$ and $\Psi_T = 0$.

Fact 2: We can show that the optimal policy is just a linear function of the state.

Knowing V_{t+1}^* is equivalent to knowing Φ_{t+1} and Ψ_{t+1}, so we just need to explain how we compute Φ_t and Ψ_t from Φ_{t+1} and Ψ_{t+1} and the other parameters of the problem.

$$\begin{aligned} V_t^*(s_t) &= s_t^\top \Phi_t s_t + \Psi_t \\ &= \max_{a_t} \left[R^{(t)}(s_t, a_t) + \mathbb{E}_{s_{t+1} \sim P_{s_t,a_t}^{(t)}} [V_{t+1}^*(s_{t+1})] \right] \\ &= \max_{a_t} \left[-s_t^\top U_t s_t - a_t^\top V_t a_t + \mathbb{E}_{s_{t+1} \sim \mathcal{N}(A_t s_t + B_t a_t, \Sigma_t)} [s_{t+1}^\top \Phi_{t+1} s_{t+1} + \Psi_{t+1}] \right] \end{aligned}$$

where the second line is just the definition of the optimal value function and the third line is obtained by plugging in the dynamics of our model along with the quadratic assumption. Notice that the last expression is a quadratic function in a_t and can thus be (easily) optimized[1]. We get the optimal action a_t^*

$$\begin{aligned} a_t^* &= \left[(B_t^\top \Phi_{t+1} B_t - V_t)^{-1} B_t \Phi_{t+1} A_t \right] \cdot s_t \\ &= L_t \cdot s_t \end{aligned}$$

where

$$L_t := \left[(B_t^\top \Phi_{t+1} B_t - W_t)^{-1} B_t \Phi_{t+1} A_t \right]$$

[1]Use the identity $\mathbb{E}\left[w_t^\top \Phi_{t+1} w_t \right] = \mathrm{Tr}(\Sigma_t \Phi_{t+1})$ with $w_t \sim \mathcal{N}(0, \Sigma_t)$

which is an impressive result: our optimal policy is **linear in** s_t. Given a_t^* we can solve for Φ_t and Ψ_t. We finally get the **Discrete Ricatti equations**

$$\Phi_t = A_t^\top \left(\Phi_{t+1} - \Phi_{t+1}B_t \left(B_t^\top \Phi_{t+1}B_t - W_t\right)^{-1} B_t\Phi_{t+1}\right) A_t - U_t$$
$$\Psi_t = -\operatorname{tr}\left(\Sigma_t\Phi_{t+1}\right) + \Psi_{t+1}$$

Fact 3: we notice that Φ_t depends on neither Ψ nor the noise Σ_t! As L_t is a function of A_t, B_t and Φ_{t+1}, it implies that the optimal policy also **does not depend on the noise**! (But Ψ_t does depend on Σ_t, which implies that V_t^* depends on Σ_t.)

Then, to summarize, the LQR algorithm works as follows

1. (if necessary) estimate parameters A_t, B_t, Σ_t
2. initialize $\Phi_T := -U_T$ and $\Psi_T := 0$.
3. iterate from $t = T-1\ldots 0$ to update Φ_t and Ψ_t using Φ_{t+1} and Ψ_{t+1} using the discrete Ricatti equations. If there exists a policy that drives the state towards zero, then convergence is guaranteed!

Using Fact 3, we can be even more clever and make our algorithm run (slightly) faster! As the optimal policy does not depend on Ψ_t, and the update of Φ_t only depends on Φ_t, it is sufficient to update **only** Φ_t!

16.3 From non-linear dynamics to LQR

It turns out that a lot of problems can be reduced to LQR, even if dynamics are non-linear. While LQR is a nice formulation because we are able to come up with a nice exact solution, it is far from being general. Let's take for instance the case of the inverted pendulum. The transitions between states look like

$$\begin{pmatrix} x_{t+1} \\ \dot{x}_{t+1} \\ \theta_{t+1} \\ \dot{\theta}_{t+1} \end{pmatrix} = F\left(\begin{pmatrix} x_t \\ \dot{x}_t \\ \theta_t \\ \dot{\theta}_t \end{pmatrix}, a_t\right)$$

where the function F depends on the cos of the angle etc. Now, the question we may ask is

Can we linearize this system?

16.3.1 Linearization of dynamics

Let's suppose that at time t, the system spends most of its time in some state $\bar{s}_t$ and the actions we perform are around $\bar{a}_t$. For the inverted pendulum, if we reached some kind of optimal, this is true: our actions are small and we don't deviate much from the vertical.

We are going to use Taylor expansion to linearize the dynamics. In the simple case where the state is one-dimensional and the transition function F does not depend on the action, we would write something like

$$s_{t+1} = F(s_t) \approx F(\bar{s}_t) + F'(\bar{s}_t) \cdot (s_t - \bar{s}_t)$$

In the more general setting, the formula looks the same, with gradients instead of simple derivatives

$$s_{t+1} \approx F(\bar{s}_t, \bar{a}_t) + \nabla_s F(\bar{s}_t, \bar{a}_t) \cdot (s_t - \bar{s}_t) + \nabla_a F(\bar{s}_t, \bar{a}_t) \cdot (a_t - \bar{a}_t) \qquad (16.3)$$

and now, s_{t+1} is linear in s_t and a_t, because we can rewrite equation (16.3) as

$$s_{t+1} \approx As_t + Bs_t + \kappa$$

where κ is some constant and A, B are matrices. Now, this writing looks awfully similar to the assumptions made for LQR. We just have to get rid of the constant term κ! It turns out that the constant term can be absorbed into s_t by artificially increasing the dimension by one. This is the same trick that we used at the beginning of the class for linear regression...

16.3.2 Differential Dynamic Programming (DDP)

The previous method works well for cases where the goal is to stay around some state s^* (think about the inverted pendulum, or a car having to stay in the middle of a lane). However, in some cases, the goal can be more complicated.

We'll cover a method that applies when our system has to follow some trajectory (think about a rocket). This method is going to discretize the trajectory into discrete time steps, and create intermediary goals around which we will be able to use the previous technique! This method is called **Differential Dynamic Programming**. The main steps are

step 1 come up with a nominal trajectory using a naive controller, that approximate the trajectory we want to follow. In other words, our controller is able to approximate the gold trajectory with

$$s_0^*, a_0^* \rightarrow s_1^*, a_1^* \rightarrow \dots$$

step 2 linearize the dynamics around each trajectory point s_t^*, in other words

$$s_{t+1} \approx F(s_t^*, a_t^*) + \nabla_s F(s_t^*, a_t^*)(s_t - s_t^*) + \nabla_a F(s_t^*, a_t^*)(a_t - a_t^*)$$

where s_t, a_t would be our current state and action. Now that we have a linear approximation around each of these points, we can use the previous section and rewrite

$$s_{t+1} = A_t \cdot s_t + B_t \cdot a_t$$

(notice that in that case, we use the non-stationary dynamics setting that we mentioned at the beginning of these lecture notes)

Note We can apply a similar derivation for the reward $R^{(t)}$, with a second-order Taylor expansion.

$$\begin{aligned} R(s_t, a_t) \approx & R(s_t^*, a_t^*) + \nabla_s R(s_t^*, a_t^*)(s_t - s_t^*) + \nabla_a R(s_t^*, a_t^*)(a_t - a_t^*) \\ & + \frac{1}{2}(s_t - s_t^*)^\top H_{ss}(s_t - s_t^*) + (s_t - s_t^*)^\top H_{sa}(a_t - a_t^*) \\ & + \frac{1}{2}(a_t - a_t^*)^\top H_{aa}(a_t - a_t^*) \end{aligned}$$

where H_{xy} refers to the entry of the Hessian of R with respect to x and y evaluated in (s_t^*, a_t^*) (omitted for readability). This expression can be re-written as

$$R_t(s_t, a_t) = -s_t^\top U_t s_t - a_t^\top W_t a_t$$

for some matrices U_t, W_t, with the same trick of adding an extra dimension of ones. To convince yourself, notice that

$$\begin{pmatrix} 1 & x \end{pmatrix} \cdot \begin{pmatrix} a & b \\ b & c \end{pmatrix} \cdot \begin{pmatrix} 1 \\ x \end{pmatrix} = a + 2bx + cx^2$$

step 3 Now, you can convince yourself that our problem is **strictly** re-written in the LQR framework. Let's just use LQR to find the optimal policy π_t. As a result, our new controller will (hopefully) be better!

Note: Some problems might arise if the LQR trajectory deviates too much from the linearized approximation of the trajectory, but that can be fixed with reward-shaping...

step 4 Now that we get a new controller (our new policy π_t), we use it to produce a new trajectory

$$s_0^*, \pi_0(s_0^*) \to s_1^*, \pi_1(s_1^*) \to \ldots \to s_T^*$$

note that when we generate this new trajectory, we use the real F and not its linear approximation to compute transitions, meaning that

$$s_{t+1}^* = F(s_t^*, a_t^*)$$

then, go back to step 2 and repeat until some stopping criterion.

16.4 Linear Quadratic Gaussian (LQG)

Often, in the real word, we don't get to observe the full state s_t. For example, an autonomous car could receive an image from a camera, which is merely an **observation**, and not the full state of the world. So far, we assumed that the state was available. As this might not hold true for most of the real-world problems, we need a new tool to model this situation: **Partially Observable MDPs**.

A POMDP is an MDP with an extra observation layer. In other words, we introduce a new variable o_t, that follows some conditional distribution given the current state s_t

$$o_t|s_t \sim O(o|s)$$

Formally, a finite-horizon POMDP is given by a tuple

$$(\mathcal{S}, \mathcal{O}, \mathcal{A}, P_{sa}, T, R)$$

Within this framework, the general strategy is to maintain a **belief state** (distribution over states) based on the observation $o_1, \ldots, o_t$. Then, a policy in a POMDP maps this belief states to actions.

In this section, we'll present a extension of LQR to this new setting. Assume that we observe $y_t \in \mathbb{R}^n$ with $m < n$ such that

$$\begin{cases} y_t & = C \cdot s_t + v_t \\ s_{t+1} & = A \cdot s_t + B \cdot a_t + w_t \end{cases}$$

where $C \in R^{n \times d}$ is a compression matrix and v_t is the sensor noise (also gaussian, like w_t). Note that the reward function $R^{(t)}$ is left unchanged, as a function of the state (not the observation) and action. Also, as distributions are gaussian, the belief state is also going to be gaussian. In this new framework, let's give an overview of the strategy we are going to adopt to find the optimal policy:

step 1 first, compute the distribution on the possible states (the belief state), based on the observations we have. In other words, we want to compute the mean $s_{t|t}$ and the covariance $\Sigma_{t|t}$ of

$$s_t | y_1, \dots, y_t \sim \mathcal{N}\left(s_{t|t}, \Sigma_{t|t}\right)$$

to perform the computation efficiently over time, we'll use the **Kalman Filter** algorithm (used on-board Apollo Lunar Module!).

step 2 now that we have the distribution, we'll use the mean $s_{t|t}$ as the best approximation for s_t

step 3 then set the action $a_t := L_t s_{t|t}$ where L_t comes from the regular LQR algorithm.

Intuitively, to understand why this works, notice that $s_{t|t}$ is a noisy approximation of s_t (equivalent to adding more noise to LQR) but we proved that LQR is independent of the noise!

Step 1 needs to be explicated. We'll cover a simple case where there is no action dependence in our dynamics (but the general case follows the same idea). Suppose that

$$\begin{cases} s_{t+1} & = A \cdot s_t + w_t, \quad w_t \sim N(0, \Sigma_s) \\ y_t & = C \cdot s_t + v_t, \quad v_t \sim N(0, \Sigma_y) \end{cases}$$

As noises are Gaussians, we can easily prove that the joint distribution is also Gaussian

$$\begin{pmatrix} s_1 \\ \vdots \\ s_t \\ y_1 \\ \vdots \\ y_t \end{pmatrix} \sim \mathcal{N}(\mu, \Sigma) \qquad \text{for some } \mu, \Sigma$$

then, using the marginal formulas of gaussians (see Factor Analysis notes), we would get

$$s_t | y_1, \ldots, y_t \sim \mathcal{N}\left(s_{t|t}, \Sigma_{t|t}\right)$$

However, computing the marginal distribution parameters using these formulas would be computationally expensive! It would require manipulating matrices of shape $t \times t$. Recall that inverting a matrix can be done in $O(t^3)$, and it would then have to be repeated over the time steps, yielding a cost in $O(t^4)$!

The **Kalman filter** algorithm provides a much better way of computing the mean and variance, by updating them over time in **constant time in** t! The kalman filter is based on two basics steps. Assume that we know the distribution of $s_t | y_1, \ldots, y_t$:

predict step compute $s_{t+1} | y_1, \ldots, y_t$

update step compute $s_{t+1} | y_1, \ldots, y_{t+1}$

and iterate over time steps! The combination of the predict and update steps updates our belief states. In other words, the process looks like

$$(s_t | y_1, \ldots, y_t) \xrightarrow{\text{predict}} (s_{t+1} | y_1, \ldots, y_t) \xrightarrow{\text{update}} (s_{t+1} | y_1, \ldots, y_{t+1}) \xrightarrow{\text{predict}} \ldots$$

predict step Suppose that we know the distribution of

$$s_t | y_1, \ldots, y_t \sim \mathcal{N}\left(s_{t|t}, \Sigma_{t|t}\right)$$

then, the distribution over the next state is also a gaussian distribution

$$s_{t+1} | y_1, \ldots, y_t \sim \mathcal{N}\left(s_{t+1|t}, \Sigma_{t+1|t}\right)$$

where

$$\begin{cases} s_{t+1|t} & = A \cdot s_{t|t} \\ \Sigma_{t+1|t} & = A \cdot \Sigma_{t|t} \cdot A^\top + \Sigma_s \end{cases}$$

update step given $s_{t+1|t}$ and $\Sigma_{t+1|t}$ such that

$$s_{t+1}|y_1, \ldots, y_t \sim \mathcal{N}\left(s_{t+1|t}, \Sigma_{t+1|t}\right)$$

we can prove that

$$s_{t+1}|y_1, \ldots, y_{t+1} \sim \mathcal{N}\left(s_{t+1|t+1}, \Sigma_{t+1|t+1}\right)$$

where

$$\begin{cases} s_{t+1|t+1} & = s_{t+1|t} + K_t(y_{t+1} - Cs_{t+1|t}) \\ \Sigma_{t+1|t+1} & = \Sigma_{t+1|t} - K_t \cdot C \cdot \Sigma_{t+1|t} \end{cases}$$

with

$$K_t := \Sigma_{t+1|t}C^\top(C\Sigma_{t+1|t}C^\top + \Sigma_y)^{-1}$$

The matrix K_t is called the **Kalman gain**.

Now, if we have a closer look at the formulas, we notice that we don't need the observations prior to time step t! The update steps only depends on the previous distribution. Putting it all together, the algorithm first runs a forward pass to compute the K_t, $\Sigma_{t|t}$ and $s_{t|t}$ (sometimes referred to as $\hat{s}$ in the literature). Then, it runs a backward pass (the LQR updates) to compute the quantities Ψ_t, Ψ_t and L_t. Finally, we recover the optimal policy with $a_t^* = L_t s_{t|t}$.

Chapter 17

Policy Gradient (REINFORCE)

We will present a model-free algorithm called REINFORCE that does not require the notion of value functions and Q functions. It turns out to be more convenient to introduce REINFORCE in the finite horizon case, which will be assumed throughout this note: we use $\tau = (s_0, a_0, \ldots, s_{T-1}, a_{T-1}, s_T)$ to denote a trajectory, where $T < \infty$ is the length of the trajectory. Moreover, REINFORCE only applies to learning a **randomized policy**. We use $\pi_\theta(a|s)$ to denote the probability of the policy π_θ outputting the action a at state s. The other notations will be the same as in previous lecture notes.

The advantage of applying REINFORCE is that we only need to assume that we can sample from the transition probabilities $\{P_{sa}\}$ and can query the reward function $R(s, a)$ at state s and action a,[1] but we do not need to know the analytical form of the transition probabilities or the reward function. We do not explicitly learn the transition probabilities or the reward function either.

Let s_0 be sampled from some distribution μ. We consider optimizing the expected total payoff of the policy π_θ over the parameter θ defined as.

$$\eta(\theta) \triangleq \mathrm{E}\left[\sum_{t=0}^{T-1} \gamma^t R(s_t, a_t)\right] \tag{17.1}$$

Recall that $s_t \sim P_{s_{t-1}a_{t-1}}$ and $a_t \sim \pi_\theta(\cdot|s_t)$. Also note that $\eta(\theta) = \mathrm{E}_{s_0\sim P}\left[V^{\pi_\theta}(s_0)\right]$ if we ignore the difference between finite and infinite horizon.

[1]In this notes we will work with the general setting where the reward depends on both the state and the action.

We aim to use gradient ascent to maximize $\eta(\theta)$. The main challenge we face here is to compute (or estimate) the gradient of $\eta(\theta)$ without the knowledge of the form of the reward function and the transition probabilities.

Let $P_\theta(\tau)$ denote the distribution of τ (generated by the policy π_θ), and let $f(\tau) = \sum_{t=0}^{T-1} \gamma^t R(s_t, a_t)$. We can rewrite $\eta(\theta)$ as

$$\eta(\theta) = \mathrm{E}_{\tau \sim P_\theta}\left[f(\tau)\right] \tag{17.2}$$

We face a similar situations in the variational auto-encoder (VAE) setting covered in the previous lectures, where the we need to take the gradient w.r.t to a variable that shows up under the expectation — the distribution P_θ depends on θ. Recall that in VAE, we used the re-parametrization techniques to address this problem. However it does not apply here because we do know not how to compute the gradient of the function f. (We only have an efficient way to evaluate the function f by taking a weighted sum of the observed rewards, but we do not necessarily know the reward function itself to compute the gradient.)

The REINFORCE algorithm uses an another approach to estimate the gradient of $\eta(\theta)$. We start with the following derivation:

$$\begin{aligned}
\nabla_\theta \mathrm{E}_{\tau \sim P_\theta}\left[f(\tau)\right] &= \nabla_\theta \int P_\theta(\tau) f(\tau) d\tau \\
&= \int \nabla_\theta (P_\theta(\tau) f(\tau)) d\tau \quad \text{(swap integration with gradient)} \\
&= \int (\nabla_\theta P_\theta(\tau)) f(\tau) d\tau \quad \text{(becaue } f \text{ does not depend on } \theta) \\
&= \int P_\theta(\tau)(\nabla_\theta \log P_\theta(\tau)) f(\tau) d\tau \\
&\qquad\qquad \text{(because } \nabla \log P_\theta(\tau) = \tfrac{\nabla P_\theta(\tau)}{P_\theta(\tau)}) \\
&= \mathrm{E}_{\tau \sim P_\theta}\left[(\nabla_\theta \log P_\theta(\tau)) f(\tau)\right] \qquad (17.3)
\end{aligned}$$

Now we have a sample-based estimator for $\nabla_\theta \mathrm{E}_{\tau \sim P_\theta}\left[f(\tau)\right]$. Let $\tau^{(1)}, \ldots, \tau^{(n)}$ be n empirical samples from P_θ (which are obtained by running the policy π_θ for n times, with T steps for each run). We can estimate the gradient of $\eta(\theta)$ by

$$\begin{aligned}
\nabla_\theta \mathrm{E}_{\tau \sim P_\theta}\left[f(\tau)\right] &= \mathrm{E}_{\tau \sim P_\theta}\left[(\nabla_\theta \log P_\theta(\tau)) f(\tau)\right] && (17.4) \\
&\approx \frac{1}{n} \sum_{i=1}^{n} (\nabla_\theta \log P_\theta(\tau^{(i)})) f(\tau^{(i)}) && (17.5)
\end{aligned}$$

The next question is how to compute $\log P_\theta(\tau)$. We derive an analytical formula for $\log P_\theta(\tau)$ and compute its gradient w.r.t θ (using auto-differentiation). Using the definition of τ, we have

$$P_\theta(\tau) = \mu(s_0)\pi_\theta(a_0|s_0)P_{s_0a_0}(s_1)\pi_\theta(a_1|s_1)P_{s_1a_1}(s_2)\cdots P_{s_{T-1}a_{T-1}}(s_T) \quad (17.6)$$

Here recall that μ to used to denote the density of the distribution of s_0. It follows that

$$\begin{aligned}\log P_\theta(\tau) = \log\mu(s_0) + \log\pi_\theta(a_0|s_0) + \log P_{s_0a_0}(s_1) + \log\pi_\theta(a_1|s_1)\\ + \log P_{s_1a_1}(s_2) + \cdots + \log P_{s_{T-1}a_{T-1}}(s_T)\end{aligned} \quad (17.7)$$

Taking gradient w.r.t to θ, we obtain

$$\nabla_\theta \log P_\theta(\tau) = \nabla_\theta \log\pi_\theta(a_0|s_0) + \nabla_\theta \log\pi_\theta(a_1|s_1) + \cdots + \nabla_\theta \log\pi_\theta(a_{T-1}|s_{T-1})$$

Note that many of the terms disappear because they don't depend on θ and thus have zero gradients. (This is somewhat important — we don't know how to evaluate those terms such as $\log P_{s_0a_0}(s_1)$ because we don't have access to the transition probabilities, but luckily those terms have zero gradients!)

Plugging the equation above into equation (17.4), we conclude that

$$\begin{aligned}\nabla_\theta\eta(\theta) = \nabla_\theta \mathrm{E}_{\tau\sim P_\theta}[f(\tau)] &= \mathrm{E}_{\tau\sim P_\theta}\left[\left(\sum_{t=0}^{T-1}\nabla_\theta \log\pi_\theta(a_t|s_t)\right)\cdot f(\tau)\right]\\ &= \mathrm{E}_{\tau\sim P_\theta}\left[\left(\sum_{t=0}^{T-1}\nabla_\theta \log\pi_\theta(a_t|s_t)\right)\cdot\left(\sum_{t=0}^{T-1}\gamma^t R(s_t,a_t)\right)\right]\end{aligned} \quad (17.8)$$

We estimate the RHS of the equation above by empirical sample trajectories, and the estimate is unbiased. The vanilla REINFORCE algorithm iteratively updates the parameter by gradient ascent using the estimated gradients.

Interpretation of the policy gradient formula (17.8). The quantity $\nabla_\theta P_\theta(\tau) = \sum_{t=0}^{T-1}\nabla_\theta \log\pi_\theta(a_t|s_t)$ is intuitively the direction of the change of θ that will make the trajectory τ more likely to occur (or increase the probability of choosing action $a_0,\ldots,a_{t-1}$), and $f(\tau)$ is the total payoff of this trajectory. Thus, by taking a gradient step, intuitively we are trying to improve the likelihood of all the trajectories, but with a different emphasis or weight for each τ (or for each set of actions $a_0, a_1, \ldots, a_{t-1}$). If τ is very rewarding (that is, $f(\tau)$ is large), we try very hard to move in the direction that can increase the probability of the trajectory τ (or the direction that increases the probability of choosing $a_0, \ldots, a_{t-1}$), and if τ has low payoff, we try less hard with a smaller weight.

An interesting fact that follows from formula (17.3) is that

$$\mathrm{E}_{\tau \sim P_\theta}\left[\sum_{t=0}^{T-1} \nabla_\theta \log \pi_\theta(a_t|s_t)\right] = 0 \tag{17.9}$$

To see this, we take $f(\tau) = 1$ (that is, the reward is always a constant), then the LHS of (17.8) is zero because the payoff is always a fixed constant $\sum_{t=0}^{T} \gamma^t$. Thus the RHS of (17.8) is also zero, which implies (17.9).

In fact, one can verify that $\mathrm{E}_{a_t \sim \pi_\theta(\cdot|s_t)} \nabla_\theta \log \pi_\theta(a_t|s_t) = 0$ for any fixed t and s_t.[2] This fact has two consequences. First, we can simplify formula (17.8) to

$$\begin{aligned}
\nabla_\theta \eta(\theta) &= \sum_{t=0}^{T-1} \mathrm{E}_{\tau \sim P_\theta}\left[\nabla_\theta \log \pi_\theta(a_t|s_t) \cdot \left(\sum_{j=0}^{T-1} \gamma^j R(s_j, a_j)\right)\right] \\
&= \sum_{t=0}^{T-1} \mathrm{E}_{\tau \sim P_\theta}\left[\nabla_\theta \log \pi_\theta(a_t|s_t) \cdot \left(\sum_{j \ge t}^{T-1} \gamma^j R(s_j, a_j)\right)\right]
\end{aligned} \tag{17.10}$$

where the second equality follows from

$$\begin{aligned}
&\mathrm{E}_{\tau \sim P_\theta}\left[\nabla_\theta \log \pi_\theta(a_t|s_t) \cdot \left(\sum_{0 \le j < t} \gamma^j R(s_j, a_j)\right)\right] \\
&= \mathrm{E}\left[\mathrm{E}\left[\nabla_\theta \log \pi_\theta(a_t|s_t)|s_0, a_0, \ldots, s_{t-1}, a_{t-1}, s_t\right] \cdot \left(\sum_{0 \le j < t} \gamma^j R(s_j, a_j)\right)\right] \\
&= 0 \qquad \text{(because } \mathrm{E}\left[\nabla_\theta \log \pi_\theta(a_t|s_t)|s_0, a_0, \ldots, s_{t-1}, a_{t-1}, s_t\right] = 0\text{)}
\end{aligned}$$

Note that here we used the law of total expectation. The outer expectation in the second line above is over the randomness of $s_0, a_0, \ldots, a_{t-1}, s_t$, whereas the inner expectation is over the randomness of a_t (conditioned on $s_0, a_0, \ldots, a_{t-1}, s_t$.) We see that we've made the estimator slightly simpler. The second consequence of $\mathrm{E}_{a_t \sim \pi_\theta(\cdot|s_t)} \nabla_\theta \log \pi_\theta(a_t|s_t) = 0$ is the following: for any value $B(s_t)$ that only depends on s_t, it holds that

$$\begin{aligned}
&\mathrm{E}_{\tau \sim P_\theta}\left[\nabla_\theta \log \pi_\theta(a_t|s_t) \cdot B(s_t)\right] \\
&= \mathrm{E}\left[\mathrm{E}\left[\nabla_\theta \log \pi_\theta(a_t|s_t)|s_0, a_0, \ldots, s_{t-1}, a_{t-1}, s_t\right] B(s_t)\right] \\
&= 0 \qquad \text{(because } \mathrm{E}\left[\nabla_\theta \log \pi_\theta(a_t|s_t)|s_0, a_0, \ldots, s_{t-1}, a_{t-1}, s_t\right] = 0\text{)}
\end{aligned}$$

[2] In general, it's true that $\mathrm{E}_{x \sim p_\theta}[\nabla \log p_\theta(x)] = 0$.

Again here we used the law of total expectation. The outer expectation in the second line above is over the randomness of $s_0, a_0, \ldots, a_{t-1}, s_t$, whereas the inner expectation is over the randomness of a_t (conditioned on $s_0, a_0, \ldots, a_{t-1}, s_t$.) It follows from equation (17.10) and the equation above that

$$\begin{aligned}\nabla_\theta \eta(\theta) &= \sum_{t=0}^{T-1} \mathrm{E}_{\tau\sim P_\theta}\left[\nabla_\theta \log \pi_\theta(a_t|s_t) \cdot \left(\sum_{j\geq t}^{T-1} \gamma^j R(s_j, a_j) - \gamma^t B(s_t)\right)\right] \\ &= \sum_{t=0}^{T-1} \mathrm{E}_{\tau\sim P_\theta}\left[\nabla_\theta \log \pi_\theta(a_t|s_t) \cdot \gamma^t \left(\sum_{j\geq t}^{T-1} \gamma^{j-t} R(s_j, a_j) - B(s_t)\right)\right]\end{aligned} \tag{17.11}$$

Therefore, we will get a different estimator for estimating the $\nabla\eta(\theta)$ with a difference choice of $B(\cdot)$. The benefit of introducing a proper $B(\cdot)$ — which is often referred to as a **baseline** — is that it helps reduce the variance of the estimator.[3] It turns out that a near optimal estimator would be the expected future payoff $\mathrm{E}\left[\sum_{j\geq t}^{T-1} \gamma^{j-t} R(s_j, a_j)|s_t\right]$, which is pretty much the same as the value function $V^{\pi_\theta}(s_t)$ (if we ignore the difference between finite and infinite horizon.) Here one could estimate the value function $V^{\pi_\theta}(\cdot)$ in a crude way, because its precise value doesn't influence the mean of the estimator but only the variance. This leads to a policy gradient algorithm with baselines stated in Algorithm 7.[4]

[3]As a heuristic but illustrating example, suppose for a fixed t, the future reward $\sum_{j\geq t}^{T-1} \gamma^{j-t} R(s_j, a_j)$ randomly takes two values $1000 + 1$ and $1000 - 2$ with equal probability, and the corresponding values for $\nabla_\theta \log \pi_\theta(a_t|s_t)$ are vector z and $-z$. (Note that because $\mathrm{E}[\nabla_\theta \log \pi_\theta(a_t|s_t)] = 0$, if $\nabla_\theta \log \pi_\theta(a_t|s_t)$ can only take two values uniformly, then the two values have to two vectors in an opposite direction.) In this case, without subtracting the baseline, the estimators take two values $(1000 + 1)z$ and $-(1000 - 2)z$, whereas after subtracting a baseline of 1000, the estimator has two values z and $2z$. The latter estimator has much lower variance compared to the original estimator.

[4]We note that the estimator of the gradient in the algorithm does not exactly match the equation 17.11. If we multiply γ^t in the summand of equation (17.13), then they will exactly match. Removing such discount factors empirically works well because it gives a large update.

Algorithm 7 Vanilla policy gradient with baseline

for $i = 1, \cdots$ **do**

Collect a set of trajectories by executing the current policy. Use $R_{\geq t}$ as a shorthand for $\sum_{j \geq t}^{T-1} \gamma^{j-t} R(s_j, a_j)$

Fit the baseline by finding a function B that minimizes

$$\sum_{\tau} \sum_{t} (R_{\geq t} - B(s_t))^2 \tag{17.12}$$

Update the policy parameter θ with the gradient estimator

$$\sum_{\tau} \sum_{t} \nabla_\theta \log \pi_\theta(a_t|s_t) \cdot (R_{\geq t} - B(s_t)) \tag{17.13}$$

Index

C

Classification problems, 20, 24, 29, 34
Clustering, k-means algorithm, 145
Cost function (J), 9, 10, 15
Cross-entropy loss, 25–26
Cross-validation, model selection via, 139
Convex optimization, 12

www.ingramcontent.com/pod-product-compliance
Lightning Source LLC
LaVergne TN
LVHW060034210926
848481LV00013B/3860
* 9 7 9 8 3 4 9 3 4 2 8 3 7 *